# Mastering the Craft of Smoking Food

# Mastering the Craft of Smoking Food

## Warren R. Anderson

 **BURFORD BOOKS**

Printed in the United States of America.

10 9 8 7 6 5 4 3 2 1

Library of Congress Cataloging-in-Publication Data

Anderson, Warren R.
 Mastering the craft of smoking food / Warren R. Anderson.
    p. cm.
  ISBN 1-58080-135-8  3371  3073  5/06
 1. Smoked foods. 2. Cookery (Smoked foods) I. Title.

 TX609.A54 2006
 641.6'16—dc22

2005034438

# Contents

# Acknowledgments

I began food smoking about 20 years ago, and my first 15 years of food smoking were done in Japan. Because of that, many Japanese from various walks of life have contributed, in some way, to this book. As a way of saying thanks to all the Japanese who were so helpful, I would like to give a few examples:

The butcher in the grocery store next to my English school provided me with much of the raw material for my smoking. Since selling meat was his business, he was happy to make the sales. However, most of the time I did not want to buy the items he had in the display case; I wanted the meat cut in a special way, or I wanted something that is normally not sold in Japanese butcher shops such as pork liver or beef heart. In every case, he provided me with the items I needed at a reasonable price. In many cases, he had to make special arrangements with the slaughterhouse to have the item prepared. One unforgettable day, he loaned me a butcher's apron and a butcher's hat, and invited me to help him butcher a whole side of beef. In those few hours, he taught me a great deal about the different cuts of beef.

The fishmonger in the same grocery store gradually learned that when I came to buy seafood, I would invariably ask some esoteric questions about finfish and other ocean creatures—and he, invariably, was able to answer those questions. Few people in this world know more about seafood than a Japanese fishmonger.

At my request, the pharmacist down the street from my English school made a special order for a 500-gram jar of sodium nitrite for me to use in my curing formulas. However, because he sold it to me, he felt that he was personally responsible to make sure that I was using it correctly; he wanted to be absolutely sure that my products would be safe and wholesome. He borrowed copies of my basic curing formulations and spent over an hour by long-distance telephone (at his expense) talking to an expert in the Japanese government ministry in Tokyo that regulates food additives. To the great relief of the pharmacist, my formulations were pronounced safe and wholesome.

Because I taught English as a foreign language, I often taught English to university professors, scientists, researchers, and the like. Many of these men and women were specialists in areas related to animal husbandry, food, or food technology. I would teach English to them, and they would offer food-related information to me. Sometimes I felt more like a student than a teacher. These people, too, have made a contribution to this book, and I am indebted to them.

I have several American friends whom I met while teaching English in Japan, and most of them are still there: Bob Norris, Bill Cornet, Wes Injerd, and Richard Evanoff. Each of these men gave me great support and encouragement in the writing of this book. They instilled in me the determination to see the book through to completion. Two of them— Bob and Richard—are published authors.

My family, relatives, and friends here in the United States have also been very supportive and encouraging. Many of them have had to endure sampling the same smoked product over and over again until I was satisfied with the result. These people are too numerous to list by name, but I do want to mention my big sister, Patricia Brady. Patricia was the person who got me interested in food smoking; she brought some home-smoked steelhead with her when she came to visit us in Japan in 1985.

Warren R. Anderson
Aloha, Oregon
May 10, 2005

# CHAPTER 1

# Introduction

## A Brief History of Food Smoking

The smoking of meat must be one of the oldest forms of food preparation. It can be assumed that the first incidence of food smoking took place shortly after man learned how to start fires and control them. There is strong evidence that a hominid known as Peking Man used controlled fire about 500,000 years ago. So far, there is no evidence of man "discovering" fire earlier than that. Based on this, it appears that food smoking may have a history of about half a million years.

The first people to smoke food may have built a fire to keep themselves warm, to keep man-eating carnivores at bay, or to drive away annoying insects. While gnawing raw meat and enjoying the fire, someone may have thrown a bone very near it. It is not difficult to imagine that the people might have been attracted by the aroma of the scraps of meat roasting on the bone, and that one of them may have grabbed the bone and devoured those smoke-flavored scraps. This is only one possible scenario for the origin of smoked meat. We will never know the exact details regarding the first event, but it is obvious that man acquired a taste for cooked meat and the incidental smoke flavoring imparted by wood fires. The smoky flavor was appreciated to the extent that man eventually made a special effort to make sure that a strong smoky flavor would penetrate into the foods.

Along the way, probably about the 13th century BC, the ancestors of the modern Chinese began using salt to preserve food. In the Western world, the Greeks and the Romans were known to have used salt for curing meat as early as 200 BC. These peoples discovered that salt, often used together with drying and smoking, was a great help in preserving food. How wonderful it must have been to be able to preserve food for the lean times—salty though it was! Having this food enabled people to survive; not having it could mean death.

# Food Smoking in Modern Times

Preserving food by salting or drying, or both, has continued into the present. For ages, these methods were the most common ways to preserve food. If the food was meat or fish, it was often smoked in addition to drying and salting. In the old days, almost every farmstead in North America and Europe had a smokehouse. Then, in the 1800s, the technology of canning foods (originally developed in France) began to spread throughout much of the world. Furthermore, the old-fashioned icebox was coming into general use at about the same time. Later, the electric refrigerator and home freezer appeared. Constantly improving transportation systems throughout the United States and the world allowed the rapid transport of fresh meats. In the U.S., a well-to-do farmer with his Model T Ford often opted to sell his livestock to the meatpackers, and then drove into town to buy fresh meat as needed. This eliminated the chore of preserving and smoking the meat, and it allowed the farmer and his family to eat more fresh meat.

All of these developments caused a rapid decline in the number of people who did their own smoking. Commercial meat processors began to produce the most popular smoked items such as ham, bacon, and sausage, but the use of liquid smoke flavoring often replaced true smoking. The salting, smoking, and drying of meat, poultry, and fish by individuals was beginning to be more of a hobby than a necessary chore. Nevertheless, numerous people remained in love with the exquisite flavor of properly smoked bacon, ham, pastrami, salmon, sturgeon, poultry, sausage, and the like. These people kept food smoking alive.

After World War II, people in North America had more leisure time. Many people began to use some of this time to barbecue foods outdoors. They liked the slightly smoky flavor of barbecued foods, and some wanted an even smokier flavor. This led them to put a cover over the grill so it would function as a hot smoker. A number of people made their own equipment, and they called it a smoke cooker. These smoke cookers usually operated on charcoal and had tight-fitting lids. Food was placed inside, then exposed to heat from the charcoal and smoke from the hardwood that was placed on, or near, the charcoal.

In the 1970s, a few companies began to market portable smokers and smoke cookers. These small smokers (operating on electricity, propane, or charcoal) did much to popularize the smoking of food as a hobby. A rank amateur could buy one of these units and produce some delicious smoked food the same day. However, these ready-to-use units do have a few limitations. To overcome them, homemade smokers have been built in every design imaginable—and a few with designs unimaginable.

The smoking of foods has now become a recognized hobby rather than a necessity or some kind of curious endeavor. However, despite the long history of food smoking, the smoking of foods as a hobby is rather new: It became popular in the 1970s. Being a new hobby, innovation is not only possible—it is inevitable. As time passes, the useful elements of the food-smoking tradition will be combined with modern techniques developed by hobbyists such as you and me.

## About This Book

I grew up in Oregon, Washington, and Alaska. From time to time, my father would buy a small amount of smoked salmon for the family. (I am talking about hot-smoked salmon, or what some people call kippered salmon.) However, because it was expensive, we did not eat it frequently, and we never got our fill of it. Occasionally, it was a bit salty, but we always enjoyed it.

The opportunity to buy smoked salmon disappeared in 1980 when I moved to southern Japan with my wife and children. The hot-smoked salmon sold in the Pacific Northwest was not available there. However, a few years later, my sister, Patricia, who lives in Oregon, came to Japan for a visit. In her suitcase were some steelheads (large rainbow trout that migrate to the sea) that she had smoked for me. That smoked fish was excellent! Nevertheless, I did not question her about how she had smoked it—I thought (erroneously) that hickory was necessary for the smoking of all foods, and I was sure that hickory trees do not grow in Japan.

No more than two weeks after my sister had returned to the United States, some smoked trout were given to me by a Japanese acquaintance who enjoys camping and fishing. He had tried to smoke his catch of trout, and he wanted to know my opinion. He had obtained the directions, he explained, from a Japanese fishing magazine that he reads regularly. The trout were excellent, and I asked him where he had gotten the hickory to smoke them. He had never heard the word *hickory!* He had used a species of oak that is quite common in Japan. Mr. Nakamura, my acquaintance, was kind enough to explain how he had brined and smoked the fish. He showed me his smoker. It was a discarded kitchen cabinet with a pan of charcoal at the bottom; ventilation and heat control were accomplished by leaving the cabinet doors slightly ajar. He generated smoke by throwing chunks of wet oak on the charcoal.

Well, after seeing that, I was convinced that I, too, could learn how to smoke foods. I asked my brother in the United States to send me a copy of every book that he could find on food smoking. He was able to find only two books that contained information about the subject. Thus, about 20 years ago, I began this fascinating hobby.

The information contained in the books that I got from the United States (and in a few others that I was able to obtain several years later) was very helpful regarding the overall smoking process. I have learned many things from those books. Nevertheless, after hundreds of smoking sessions over the years, I found that a number of the techniques I had developed—especially for the curing of meat and fish—were not even mentioned in any of those books. These techniques allow me to make great products with a *consistently* excellent taste. They also allow me to make new products with a very high probability of complete satisfaction on the first try. I am sure that these easily mastered techniques will work for you, also. You can master smoking without being a culinary artist.

This book is based on the realization that amateur food smoking (with a few exceptions) is no longer done for the express purpose of food preservation. I assume, for example, that you have neither the need nor the desire for bacon that can be hung from the rafters for one year without spoiling. If my assumption is correct, then what you need is information on how to smoke things the modern way: how to impart just the right amount of smoke flavor, just the right amount of seasoning, and— *very importantly*—just the right amount of salt. Since you are probably not a culinary professional, you may require step-by-step instructions that tell you what to do, that tell you how to do it, and—in some cases— that tell you why you are doing it. It is likely that you have a limited amount of time to devote to this hobby, so a smoking session, normally, should not last more than a day. If this is a reasonably accurate description of your situation and requirements, I believe that the procedures contained in this manual will prove helpful.

Is the smoking of food an art, a science, or a skilled craft? *The smoking of food is a skilled craft.* A skilled craft employs a collection of special equipment and tools, a body of specialized knowledge, and numerous skills and techniques; usually the goal is to produce the same thing repeatedly, making improvements along the way. That is exactly what we are doing. Smoking food is indeed a skilled craft.

# CHAPTER 2

# Smokers and Smoker Temperatures

A smoker is a chamber in which food is exposed to smoke. Smoke passes through this chamber and imparts a smoky flavor to the food. The smoke may be generated inside the chamber or in a smoke generator outside the chamber. Additional heat, if required, is usually generated inside the chamber.

The chamber may be as small as a cigar box, or as large as a huge room or a multistoried building. If the smoke chamber is a building, it is usually called a smokehouse.

Unfortunately, some manufacturers of small, portable smokers refer to their equipment as smokehouses, and other manufacturers or writers may call them smoke ovens. One reason for this may be that using the word *smoker* to mean a comparatively small contraption for smoking food is a fairly new use of that word. The word has been traditionally used, of course, to refer to a person who consumes tobacco. The British use the word *kiln* to refer to a food smoker—but this word has the same problem as the term *smoke oven*; it implies equipment that produces much heat. A smoker used for cold smoking does not produce much heat, so the words *oven* and *kiln* are not always appropriate.

In this book, I will use the word *smoker* for the equipment that is used for either hot or cold smoking. The word *smokehouse* will be used for an independent building used for smoking foods. The terms *smoke oven* and *kiln* will be avoided.

Many amateurs use a small manufactured smoker. Such smokers are widely sold, and they are usually adequate for the average hobbyist. Several basic designs of manufactured smokers are available, and each has advantages and disadvantages. Each design will superbly smoke a variety of products, but none of the manufactured amateur smokers is perfect for every possible smoking project. For example, none of the inexpensive smokers will function well as a cold smoker, because the heat used to produce the smoke originates inside the unit.

A considerable number of people have built homemade smokers. A well-designed homemade smoker can overcome all the disadvantages of the inexpensive manufactured types. With a good homemade smoker, an advanced amateur can create products as good as or better than many professionals.

The kind of smoker you buy—or build—is an important decision: It will determine the products you can smoke and the ease with which you can smoke them. First, think about what you would like to smoke, and then determine the kind of smoker required. The descriptions of the various kinds of smokers given in this chapter should be helpful. If you already have a smoker—manufactured or homemade—these descriptions will help you decide how to modify it, how to build a new one, or which kind to buy as your second smoker.

Before smokers can be discussed, however, it is necessary to understand what is meant by the terms *cold smoking* and *hot smoking*.

## Cold Smoking and Hot Smoking

In the Western world, smoking temperature is divided into what is called cold smoking and hot smoking. Some cooking begins to take place when a product is heated to about 120º F (49º C). Smoking at this temperature, or higher, is called hot smoking. Cold smoking generally means smoking at temperatures below 85º F (29º C); fat liquefies above this temperature.

The temperature range between 85º and 120º F (29º and 49º C) is a useful range for some smoking operations, but this range, strangely, has no established name in English. The Japanese call this range *onkun*, and this word can be roughly translated as "warm smoking." I will use the term *warm smoking* to mean smoking in this temperature range.

This book will indicate the suggested smoking chamber temperatures in thermometer degrees, but the terms *hot smoke, warm smoke,* and *cold smoke* are also used. When these terms appear, please understand them to have the meanings indicated above.

### THE REASONS FOR COLD SMOKING

Cold smoking imparts smoke flavor, which is the main reason for smoking foods. Furthermore, because the temperature is low, it is possible to smoke some foods, such as cheese, that would be damaged by warm or hot temperatures. Some drying does take place during cold smoking because there is a steady flow of smoke-laden air. However, this drying is usually desirable or tolerable.

### THE REASONS FOR HOT SMOKING

It is often convenient, or desirable, to cook foods while smoking. Hot smoking can accomplish this. However, the steady flow of hot air will dry foods very fast. This can be a disadvantage for some products, but drying can be a goal for other products—jerky, for example. (Many products can be basted to reduce drying and shrinking, or a hot smoker with a water pan—a water smoker—can be used to retain succulence.)

### THE REASONS FOR WARM SMOKING

Sometimes the temperature range between cold smoking and hot smoking is ideal for the product being processed. Kippered salmon (called smoked salmon on the Pacific Coast) is a case in point. After cold smoking, this product needs to be dried slowly while the temperature is being raised, in steps, to the cooking temperature (a process called tempering). To do this, the salmon is warm smoked for about two hours at increasingly higher temperatures until the cooking temperature is reached. Tempering will not change the taste of the smoked salmon, but the appearance and texture will suffer if the fish is not tempered.

## Manufactured Smokers

Manufactured smokers are sold at prices that range from less than $100 for a small amateur model, to thousands of dollars for a large, fully automated, professional model. Descriptions of manufactured smokers will be limited to smokers that are designed for amateurs and have a modest price tag. The more elaborate and expensive smokers will have a built-in thermometer and automatic or manual devices to control such things as temperature, airflow, humidity, and the feeding of smoking fuel.

### PORTABLE ELECTRIC SMOKERS

Almost everyone can afford a portable electric smoker, and they are very easy to use. Although they employ electricity, there are no electrical controls to operate or adjust. They are lightweight and compact (some of them even have a knockdown design). Depending on the size, they are capable of holding from 20 to 100 pounds (9 to 45 kg) of product. These smokers are invariably designed to operate on the electrical power system used in all households in the United States and Canada. (Any appliance that specifies 110, 117, or 120 volts will work properly on this system.)

1. Front panel, removable.
2. Front flap—for removing and inserting the smoking chip pan.
3. Food racks.
4. Drip tray.
5. Smoking chip pan and heater.

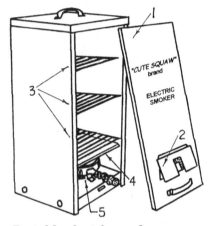

The electric heating element in the bottom will simultaneously provide heat to produce the smoke and heat to cook (or partially cook) the product. A small pan of hardwood chips is placed on this heating element to produce the smoke. Smoke-

**Portable electric smoker—front-loading type ("Cute Squaw" is a fictitious brand name).**

laden hot air rises to the top and escapes through vents. If the external (ambient) temperature is more than 70º F (21º C) and there is no strong wind, the internal temperature of the smoke chamber should reach at least 150º F (65º C).

The proliferation of these inexpensive manufactured smokers is the most important reason for the popularization of smoking as a hobby. These units are capable of producing a first-class smoked product, but they do have a few limitations and disadvantages:

♭ Because these aluminum smokers are not insulated, and because there is no easy way to provide supplementary heat, the maximum temperature produced (if the smoker is used according to the manufacturer's instructions) depends on the outside temperature and the strength of the wind blowing on the smoker. The resulting temperature may not be hot enough to cook the product thoroughly. To compensate for this, some people apply some kind of insulating material to the outside of the smoker.

◗ There is no easy way to lower the internal temperature, except by partially opening the door, by opening the flap near the bottom, or by using an electric fan directed toward the smoker.

◗ In the portable electric smoker, a water pan cannot be used to create steam. Consequently, a long exposure to a draft of hot air can cause the product to dry excessively. To prevent excessive drying, you may be obliged to limit the time that the food is in the smoker. After the food is removed from the smoker, it may require more cooking in the kitchen oven or in a water smoker.

◗ These smokers are truly portable, but they can't be used just anywhere. Electricity is required, so precautions must be taken, and conditions must be met. The unit should be operated outside in the open air, and it should be placed on a dry, noncombustible surface (a concrete slab, for example). Furthermore, if there is a possibility of precipitation, the smoker should be under a protective roof. If an extension cord is used, it should be short (about 6 to 12 feet—2 to 4 meters), and it should be rated to carry the electric current required by the smoker. The electric cord plug has three prongs (the round prong is the ground connection), and it requires a grounded electrical outlet to help protect against electrical shock, or fire, that might result from a short circuit.

## SMOKE COOKERS

There are two types of smoke cookers. One type has a water pan. The type that does not have a water pan is actually a barbecue grill with a cover on it; some of the better ones have an offset firebox. The type that has a water pan directly above the heat source has an interesting history that began in China.

### Water Smokers

Since ancient times, the Chinese have used steam cookers. These cookers have a pan of water that is placed between the food and the heat source. This results in slow and moist cooking, because heating the water to 212° F (100° C) causes the water to boil and generate steam. Indeed, this is a simple but ingenious way to reduce moisture loss while cooking foods. Properly used, this cooking method produces food of unsurpassed succulence with minimal shrinkage. A minor negative point is that the lower cooking temperature results in a cooking time about twice as long (or longer) as cooking in a kitchen oven. This Chinese method of cooking stood the test of time, and it eventually found its way to such a distant place as North America.

The southern states of the United States, particularly, had a number of devotees of this style of cooking. Some of these Americans made a habit of putting hardwood chunks on the charcoal fire. The entire system was put in a single enclosure to ensure that the food was exposed to steam from the water pan and smoke from the hardwood. By doing this, water smoking was invented!

If you desire succulent hot-smoked products, the water smoker will do the job. It will do an excellent job of hot smoking fowl, meat, and fish. If water is not used, it will efficiently dry foods while it smokes them.

1. Heat gauge.
2. Smoke vent.
3. Temperature control (regulates the flow of propane).
4. Igniter (for propane).
5. Upper food rack.
6. Lower food rack.
7. Water pan.
8. Propane burner.

**Water smoker—propane type.**

A typical water smoker will hold a maximum of about 50 pounds (22 kg) of food. They come in various shapes, but they are often round and have a dome-shaped lid; the height is about twice the diameter. In addition to the traditional charcoal-burning units, some manufacturers offer the easier-to-use propane and electric models. The propane models have a control knob to control the heat by regulating the flow of propane. Most water smokers have either a built-in heat gauge or an optional thermometer for measuring the internal temperature. No matter whether charcoal, propane, or electricity is used, the product will taste the same if it is seasoned and processed in the same way. Many of these water smokers can be used as barbecue grills if the water pan is not used.

Heat is produced in the bottom of the unit directly under the water pan. There are chrome- or nickel-plated cooking racks above the water pan. Wire-mesh baskets can be purchased separately for processing small items such as shrimp.

For the charcoal burners, putting water-soaked chunks of hardwood near the charcoal produces smoke. The propane and electric models require that the water-soaked wood be put on a special tray or in another designated place. In some cases, the instructions will suggest wrapping the chunks of smoking fuel in aluminum foil to promote smoldering and to contain the ashes.

Hot water is put into the water pan, and the chamber is preheated. When the heat gauge or thermometer indicates that the correct temperature has been reached, the seasoned or cured food is put on the racks and smoked. You need to check the heat gauge and the water pan from time to time to make sure everything is progressing properly. Make sure that the water pan is always filled with hot water, and make sure it never goes dry. If the water pan goes dry and the residue in the bottom begins to scorch, the food will be tainted by that odor. Avoid raising the lid frequently to peek; this will cause excessive heat loss. Every peek will add about 10 minutes to the cooking time.

Despite all the wonderful characteristics of manufactured water smokers, there are a few negative features:

ᨀ If the water smoker is electric, the same precautions as for the portable electric smokers must be taken.

ᨀ Because the units are not insulated, wind, precipitation, and external temperatures can affect the cooking time.

ᨀ Too much heat is produced for smoke cookers, such as water smokers, to be used as cold smokers. For example, there is no way that they can be used to cold smoke either cheese or Scotch-style smoked salmon. These quality products require cold smoke.

⚑ It is difficult to maintain a steady flow of smoke because the heat that is produced to maintain the correct cooking temperature may not be optimal to smolder the smoking fuel slowly. The wood will fail to produce any smoke if it is not heated enough, and it will burst into flames if it is heated too much. (However, maintaining a steady flow of smoke is not critical.)

⚑ Most water smokers have a built-in heat gauge, but these heat gauges are not very accurate and not very consistent. The heat gauge may indicate such ranges as WARM, IDEAL, and HOT, but sometimes the IDEAL range is not ideal. The ideal temperature to cook meat and poultry in the water smoker is between 225° and 275° F (107° and 135° C). Fish should not be water smoked at more than 225° F (107° C). However, the internal temperature in some water smokers may be 280° to 300° F (138° to 149° C) when the needle of the heat gauge is in the middle of the IDEAL range. Consequently, it is best to use a real thermometer to measure the smoker's internal temperature. Try a common liquid-in-glass thermometer, or try a dial thermometer with a stem. Wrap a small cloth around the stem, and plug it into one of the vent holes. Better yet, get a rubber plug of the proper size from a large hardware store, and drill a hole in it for the thermometer. Recently, for my water smoker, I drilled a small hole just above the heat gauge, and then I inserted a short-stemmed dial thermometer that measures up to 500° F (260° C). It was purchased at a barbecue equipment shop.

⚑ Smoking food in a water smoker produces a less intense smoke flavor than smoking it in other kinds of smokers. One reason for this is that the steam absorbs the smoke aroma that would otherwise be imparted to the food. But the main reason is that the steam condenses on the food; a dry surface is required for the smoke flavor to penetrate deeply. However, this is a minor disadvantage because any degree of smoke flavor desired can be imparted if the product is smoked in a cold smoker before it is water smoked.

I mentioned above that the IDEAL range of many water smokers is often too hot to get the best results. If the temperature is too high, the corners and the edges of the product may blacken and take on a charred appearance. Another possible problem is that high heat may cause small dark spots to appear on the surface of the food. Unfortunately, turning down the heat to the temperature range suggested above might cause another problem: The water could stop boiling, and that might lower the humidity. To prevent this problem, you may wish to alter your smoker so that more heat will hit the water pan directly. If your water smoker uses lava rock to spread the heat, you need to move all the lava stones away from the center, and pile them around the edge. This will allow more heat to strike the water pan directly. If your smoker has a metal heat deflector, you may be able to remove it or have some large holes punched in it. If it can be done easily, try to move the water pan closer to the heat source. However, before any changes are made, it is best to get to know your water smoker well. Try to avoid making irreversible changes.

### Barbecue-Type Smoke Cooker

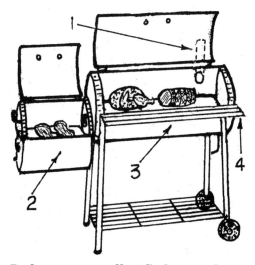

1. Chimney.
2. Offset firebox.
3. Smoking chamber.
4. Wooden shelf.

New Braunfels Smoker Company, and several other manufacturers, sell various models of smoke cookers. In most models, **Barbecue type—offset-firebox smoker.** the firebox (combustion compartment) is offset to the right or left. Depending on the model, the food racks may be contained either in an offset vertical chamber (the chamber is above the firebox, but offset to the right or the left) or in an offset chamber that is essentially horizontal to the combustion chamber (as indicated in the drawing). Some of these units were designed for use with a water pan, but others were not. If a water pan is not used, they are designed so that it is easy to baste the foods. These smokers are constructed of heavy-gauge steel. One smoker may weigh as much as 250 pounds (115 kg).

# Homemade Smokers

A homemade smoker can be built to perform exactly the same as either a portable electric smoker or a smoke cooker. Alternatively, a homemade smoker can be built so that the disadvantages of those types of smokers are eliminated or minimized. A homemade smoker can:

𖣓 Hot smoke at high temperatures (with or without a water pan).

𖣓 Hot smoke at moderately high temperatures (like the portable electric smokers).

𖣓 Warm smoke.

𖣓 Cold smoke.

Moreover, greater temperature stability and control are possible with a homemade smoker. These are the reasons why some people build a smoker.

The drum-can smoker is one of the easiest to make. It will do a good job on some products, but it does have obvious disadvantages. Nevertheless, I will start by describing this simple smoker, and then add modifications and refinements that will result in an excellent homemade smoker.

## A BASIC (DRUM-CAN) HOT SMOKER

**A basic (drum-can) hot smoker.**

1. Earth fill.
2. A new or very clean 55-gallon drum can. Food racks can be installed. Instead of using a drum can, you can use a chamber made of wood or even a cardboard box.
3. Wooden lid.
4. Broom handles or narrow boards about 1 inch (2.5 cm) thick. These will provide a means to hang meat, and these boards will raise the lid to allow necessary smoke exhaust.

**5.** Pit. This may be a hole in the ground, or you can bury something like a large pot or steel can in the ground. Another option is to form the hole with something more permanent—concrete or brick, for example.

If you have access to the proper tools, and if you know how to use them, it is not difficult to build an excellent smoker—a smoker much better than this basic drum-can type. The tools and skills required depend on the kind of smoker you want to build and the materials you want to use. Planning is important; make drawings, and list the materials you will need. Do you have the tools and skills to do the job with the materials you want to use? If not, reconsider the plans and materials, or get a little help from a talented friend.

If 10 knowledgeable people were asked to build a food smoker of their own design, and if each of these people was provided with whatever materials and tools were needed, 10 unique smokers would be built. There are many ways to build a good smoker, and many kinds of materials can be used. Consequently, I will not attempt to provide a blueprint and a bill of materials. Instead, the features of the various elements of good smokers will be explained. Certain materials are proposed, but these are nothing more than suggestions.

## SMOKE CHAMBER AND SMOKE SPREADER

The smoke chamber is the heart of any smoker. It can be any size or shape, but the capacity should be great enough to hold the maximum quantity of product you will smoke at one time—without crowding.

If the smoker is going to be used exclusively for cold smoking, the only other size consideration is that there should be a little space near the bottom to insert a smoke spreader.

The smoke spreader is located a short distance above the smoke source and, if used, the auxiliary heat source. The spreader encourages an even distribution of smoke and heat. The material used to make the spreader must be fireproof if the chamber will have an auxiliary heat source in the bottom. Some experts argue that a spreader is not required because the path of smoke and heat is not predictable. However, if a spreader is not used, the heat and smoke might establish the most direct route to the chimney without being uniformly distributed.

If a drip pan is used, it will function as a smoke spreader. However, if the smoker will be used for hot smoking, a smoke spreader below the

drip pan will help to prevent the scorching of oils
and juices in the pan. The
foul odor of scorched drippings can taint the food
that is being smoked.

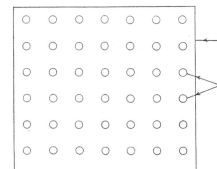

If a water pan will
always be used, a smoke
spreader may not be necessary if the pan will spread
the heat and smoke.

**Smoke spreader.**

1. Steel plate about 5/32
   inch (4 mm) thick, cut by a blacksmith. Durock brand cement board
   is another material that you might consider. Durock can be cut easily with a box cutter: Score the cutting line several times until the
   blade cuts through the thin layer of cement and netting. The Durock
   will now break easily where the material has been scored. Use a
   coarse file to smooth the edges.

2. Holes about 1 inch (2.5 cm) in diameter with centers about 4 inches
   (10 cm) apart, cut by a blacksmith. If Durock is used, a carbide-tip
   drill bit can be employed to drill many small holes around the 1-inch
   circles. After the small holes have been drilled, the 1-inch-diameter
   hole can be tapped out with a hammer. The holes in either the steel
   plate or the cement board are optional if there is space for the smoke
   to pass around the edges of the spreader—front and back, or right
   and left. Obviously, allowing space for the smoke to pass around the
   edges of the spreader is easier than cutting many holes.

Chambers have been fashioned from such things as cleaned 55-gal-
lon oil drums, packing crates, or cabinets. An old refrigerator can be
used for cold smoking (the materials used in refrigerators will not withstand hot smoking). Chambers can be built of plywood.

It is desirable for the smoke chamber to be insulated. In any smoking operation, insulation helps to stabilize the temperature. For hot
smoking, insulation helps to hold the heat inside, and it helps to reduce
the chilling effect of wind. When cold smoking is taking place, insulation
will reduce the warming effect of sunlight hitting the smoker.

A smoke chamber made from an old refrigerator needs no additional insulation. A steel drum is difficult to insulate. Thick plywood

provides considerable insulation, so no other insulation may be required. If the chamber is made of thin plywood, nailing strips about 1 inch thick and 1½ inches wide (2.5 x 3.75 cm) can be attached to the outside edges. Insulation can be laid into the area between these strips. Plywood veneer or some other sheeting or siding material can then be nailed on the outside (on top of the nailing strips) to cover the insulation. If the chamber is going to be used for hot smoking, make sure that the insulation will withstand about 250° F (121° C).

The chamber must, of course, have a door or a removable top cover to enable loading and unloading of the product. Most people favor the convenience of a door, but a removable lid is easier to build than a hinged door. A chamber with a door is called a *front-loading smoker*; one with a removable lid is called a *top-loading smoker*. My first home-made smoker was a top-loading type, but my new homemade smoker is a front-loading type.

If a door is used, it should seal tightly when closed. A well-stocked hardware store will usually have *stove gasket*—a rope-like woven fiber-glass tubing that is used to seal stove and oven doors. This material provides a good seal for a door, but it is not required if the door closes snugly.

### SMOKER RACK ASSEMBLY

When food is put into the smoker, it is hung from rods or placed on smoking racks. In most cases, the rods are made of steel. The smoking racks are usually barbecue racks that are made of coarse wire mesh or small-diameter metal bars. It is desirable to hang some kinds of products, but others are best laid on racks. For this reason, it is convenient if either rods or racks can be used optionally. Below is a drawing of how this can be accomplished easily. The illustrated assembly is suitable for either a front-loading or a top-loading smoker.

1. Steel rods for hanging food or for supporting food racks. A good material to use for these rods is 3/8-inch-diameter (12 mm) concrete-reinforcing rod (called *rebar* by professionals). This rod material is easily cut with a hacksaw.

2. Wire-mesh or metal-bar food rack. The wire-mesh or metal-bar racks used for barbecuing will work perfectly. Metal-bar racks are popular in the United States. These barbecuing racks can be purchased at hardware stores and home centers. Beware of using racks

from appliances such as old refrigerators, because they may be plated with cadmium, a poisonous metal. If the plating metal is pale blue, it may be cadmium. Zinc plating is not poisonous, but it is also pale blue.

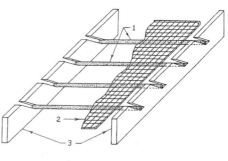

**Smoker rack assembly.**

*Important hint:* Before designing your smoker, go to hardware stores or home centers to determine the sizes of barbecue racks available: It is best to design the internal dimensions of your smoker to accommodate off-the-shelf barbecue racks. Retailers display the best selection of racks during spring and early summer—the beginning of the barbecue season.

3. Rod supports. Plywood at least 3/8 inch (12 mm) thick is an excellent material, but boards having a similar thickness can be used. These rod supports are attached to the inside walls of the smoker. The slots for the rods may be cut either diagonally or straight down.

Four rods are indicated in the illustration, but the actual number of rods that can be installed depends on the size of the smoker. There should be about 6 inches (15 cm) between each rod.

Several of these rack-and-rod assemblies can be mounted, one above the other, in the smoker. If, for example, a second assembly is mounted below this one, the second assembly should have only three rods. Each of these three rods should be located midway between the rods above it. If rods are staggered in this way, they are less likely to interfere with food that is hanging from the tier above.

## CHIMNEY AND DAMPER

There should be an exhaust chimney on (or very near) the top. A homemade smoker about the size of a refrigerator should have a chimney with a diameter of about 3 to 4 inches (7.5 to 10 cm). If a butterfly damper is built into the chimney, it is very easy to modify the draft. Alternatively, the chimney draft can be dampened by partially obstructing the smoke exiting the chimney; use a metal or wood plate to cover part of the top of the chimney. The draft is dampened when it is desirable to reduce the drying effect of the warm or hot air.

*Important:* The damper should never obstruct the flow of smoke completely because stale smoke trapped in the chamber will make the food taste rancid.

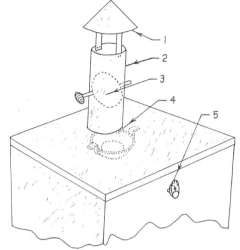

If a chimney is mounted on the top of the smoker, there should be a small tar catcher located directly under the chimney. This will protect your products from a tar-like substance that drips from the chimney under certain conditions.

**Smoker top with hooded chimney, damper, and tar catcher.**

1. Hood. The hood prevents precipitation from entering the chimney. It is not required if the smoker will be used under a roof.
2. Exhaust chimney. Three- to 4-inch-diameter (7.5 to 10 cm) stovepipe or vent pipe—galvanized or stainless steel pipe is preferred.
3. Damper.
4. Tar catcher. The small pan will prevent chimney tar from dripping on the product.
5. Thermometer. Either a dial-type thermometer or a liquid-in-glass type can be used.

## VENT HOLES

Rather than a chimney and damper, smoke-vent holes can be employed.

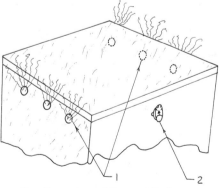

1. Vent holes for smoke. The total open area should be about the same as what would be provided by the chimney described above.

**Smoker top with vent holes.**

Some of these holes can be plugged to dampen the draft.
2. Thermometer.

## SMOKER CHAMBER—UPPER SECTION

**1.** Insulation.

**2.** Top. This smoker could be made with a removable top (a top-loading smoker). If that is the case, the front should be closed permanently by using the same material that was employed for the back and the sides. The unit could be made into a front-loading smoker by permanently attaching the top and putting a door on the front.

**3.** Smoker rack assemblies. See the Smoker Rack Assembly drawing that appeared earlier in this chapter.

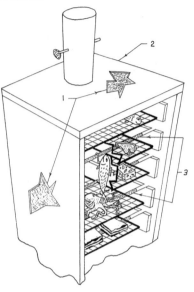

**Smoker chamber with racks— upper section.**

## SMOKE CHAMBER—LOWER SECTION

**1.** Drip tray. It is best if the drip tray sets on some kind of supports so that it is raised slightly above the smoke spreader. This will allow the free flow of smoke through the holes in the smoke spreader. Furthermore, if the drip tray is not in contact with the smoke spreader, the drippings in the tray are less apt to char and taint the product with a bad odor. For easy cleanup, use heavy-duty aluminum foil on the tray.

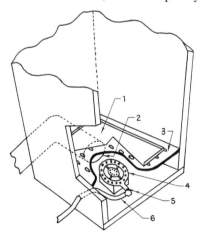

**Smoke chamber—lower section.**

**2.** Smoke flue. The smoke flue may enter the smoke chamber through the bottom, the back wall, or either side. It need not be centered. Of course, a smoke flue is not used if a wood chip pan will be used to generate smoke within the chamber.

3. Smoke spreader. (See the Smoke Spreader drawing earlier in this chapter.)

4. Propane burner (or electric heating element). A propane burner is pictured in this illustration, but an adjustable electric heating element may be used instead.

5. Propane burner adjustment cock. If the neck of the propane burner protrudes through one of the walls, the heat output of the burner can be conveniently adjusted from the outside of the chamber. (See The Author's First Smoker—Lower Section drawing, page 39.) Alternatively, an in-line adjustment cock in the hose line that is outside of the smoke chamber can be employed.

6. Propane hose. Propane hose is normally covered with rubber. However, for safety reasons, the portion of the hose located inside the smoke chamber should be made of flexible metal tube. The use of a metal tube can be avoided if the neck of the burner is long and if that neck protrudes through a hole in the wall of the chamber.

## EXTERNAL SMOKE GENERATOR AND FLUE

If smoke is generated outside the chamber, the place where the smoke is produced is called a *smoke generator*, or sometimes an *external smoke generator*. An external smoke generator is essential for a good cold smoker, and the smoke produced by it should pass through a long flue so that it is sufficiently cooled for cold smoking. An external smoke generator can also be used to provide smoke for hot smoking, but supplementary heat inside the chamber is required.

*External smoke generator* is a very fancy term considering that it may be nothing more than a covered hole in the ground with some wood burning in it. The flue may be simply a covered trench that slopes slightly upward toward the bottom of the chamber.

## BASIC COLD SMOKER

Two examples of basic cold smokers are shown below. One of them employs a pit in the earth as the smoke generator. The other uses a drum can that is set downslope from the smoke chamber.

### Smoke Pit and Drum-Can Smoker

1. Pit. This may be a hole in the ground, or it could be constructed more substantially.

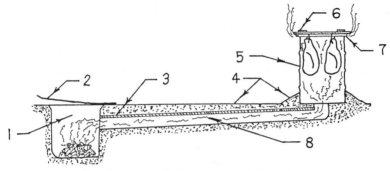

**Smoke pit and drum-can cold smoker.**

**2.** Lid for pit. Thin sheet metal will suffice.

**3.** Boards or other material to cover trench. If boards are used, metal, stone, or other fireproof material should be used near the pit because a wood cover might be scorched or ignited.

**4.** Earth fill.

**5.** A 55-gallon metal drum. The drum should be new or very clean. A chamber made of wood, or even a cardboard box, could be used instead of a drum can.

**6.** Wooden lid.

**7.** Broom handles or narrow boards about 1 inch (2.5 cm) thick. Either will provide a means to hang meat and allow necessary smoke ventilation.

**8.** Smoke flue. This may be a narrow trench, drainpipe material, or stovepipe material.

## Drum-Can Smoke Generator and Cold Smoker

It is not necessary for the smoke generator to be below ground, but the smoke exit port must be at least slightly below the level of where the flue enters the chamber; this is required in order to create a natural draft. If this requirement is met, it is acceptable for the flue to be horizontal for most of the length.

**1.** Large drum can. The drum-can smoke generator should have a door cut in the lower section so that the hardwood fire can be tended easily, or so that smoking fuel and charcoal can be added easily.

**2.** Metal lid.

**3.** Smoke flue. Preferably galvanized-steel or stainless-steel vent pipe.

**4.** Plywood smoking chamber. The smoking chamber, too, could be made of a metal drum.

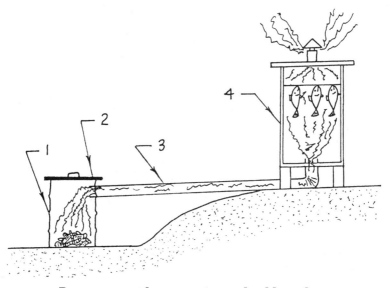

**Drum-can smoke generator and cold smoker.**

If smoking is done on a regular basis, a permanent and sophisticated smoke generator is desirable. If it is below ground, concrete is the best material to use.

### PROPANE BURNERS

Propane burners in various configurations are frequently used in smokers. A propane dealer, or a dealer in barbecue equipment, will usually have burners that can be used in a smoker. The styles of cast-iron burners in the photograph are my favorites, but they must be ordered from a dealer of cast-iron cookware. Professional cooks commonly use such long-neck burners all

**Propane burners.**

over Asia and in some parts of Europe, but they are rare in the United States. (Each of the burners in the photograph is setting in a bowl-shaped windbreaker made of cast iron. The windbreakers are not essential.)

The smallest burner in the photograph is suitable for a small hot smoker or for the smoke generator of a cold smoker. It is about 9,000 BTU (British thermal units). The large burner in the photograph is my favorite for use inside a hot smoker (or for auxiliary heat in a cold smoker). It has two independent control cocks; one operates the center gas ring, and the other operates the outer ring. Either ring can be used, or both can be used at the same time. It is about 18,500 BTU. (If you are interested in purchasing cast-iron burners, see appendix 5.)

# The Author's First Homemade Smoker

Examples of simple smokers have been shown. Also, the principles of smoker construction have been shown and explained. On the following pages are photographs and drawings of how one person—me—applied these principles to build his homemade smokers. The units described below, I believe, represent good designs for use by an amateur food smoker. However, I do not suggest that either of these designs be copied slavishly. First, consider such things as the price and availability of materials, the space available, the size of smoker required, and your skills. If you are skilled at bricklaying, for example, you could make a first-class smoker and smoke generator by using bricks as the main material.

**The author's first smoker when not in use.**

The first smoker described below is the one I built in my backyard in rural Japan. It will be referred to as "the author's first smoker." The second smoker described will be called "the author's new smoker"; it was built in Aloha, Oregon, a suburb of Portland.

### THE FIRST SMOKER—WHEN NOT IN USE

My first smoker, when it is not being used, is shown in the photograph and drawing. The smoke flues have been disconnected, and they are hung from the rafters with rope loops, as is the bamboo-mat windbreaker. A cover is placed over the underground smoke generator, and another over the lower half of the smoke chamber. Both of these covers help to protect the equipment from windblown rain.

The roof that covers both the smoker and smoke generator was built about a year after the main equipment was built. A roof over the smoker, I have found, makes smoking during a rainstorm much more pleasant.

1. Lid to cover the underground smoke generator when the smoker is not being used. This lid was made of plywood that was nailed onto a wooden frame. Next, it was covered with thin galvanized sheet steel. Galvanized corner material was tacked to the edges. Finally, it was painted with enamel.

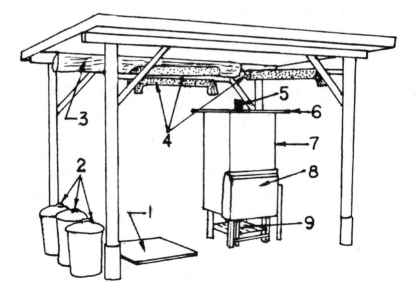

**2.** Containers for hardwood smoking fuel or for equipment and tools.

**3.** Windbreaker (a woven bamboo mat, rolled up for storage). This mat is unrolled and stood upright (against the corner posts that support the roof) whenever the wind is strong. This helps to keep the temperature of the smoke chamber stable, and it provides comfort for the person tending the smoker.

**4.** Smoke flue sections made of stainless steel. They are stored by hanging from the underside of the roof when not in use. (Galvanized smoke flue is acceptable, cheaper, and easier to buy in the United States.)

**5.** Chimney for the smoke chamber. This chimney does not have a butterfly damper. Instead, when necessary, a steel plate is set on top of the chimney to partially obstruct and dampen the flow of the smoke. A tar catcher (similar to the one shown earlier in this chapter in the Smoker Top with Hooded Chimney, Damper, and Tar Catcher drawing) is mounted on the underside of the smoke chamber lid directly below the chimney.

**6.** Smoke chamber lid. This lid is completely removed when the smoke chamber is loaded or unloaded.

**7.** Smoke chamber. There are four smoker rack assemblies inside the smoke chamber, and they are exactly the same design as shown in the Smoker Rack Assembly drawing earlier in this chapter.

**8.** Removable cover for the lower access door. This cover is attached only when the smoker is not being used.

**9.** Shelf for tools and equipment.

## SETUP FOR USE

This smoker employs a smoke flue that is exposed to the air. The smoke flue could have been routed underground, but I believe that exposing the smoke flue to air is a better option. Both air and earth are heat insulators, but if air around the smoke flue moves, the heat will be carried away more effectively than if it were surrounded by earth. There have been several occasions when cold smoking cheese, for example, that I have been able to reduce the temperature of the smoke to an acceptable level by directing a powerful electric fan toward the smoke flue. This technique would not be possible if the smoke flue were underground.

**1.** Rubber propane hose. The hose leads to the auxiliary propane burner in the lower section of the smoke chamber.

**2.** Propane tank. The high-quality propane hose used in the United States is expensive. Consequently it would be more economical to use two propane tanks instead of using long hoses from a single tank.

**3.** Smoke generator lid (steel plate).

**The author's first smoker set up for use.**

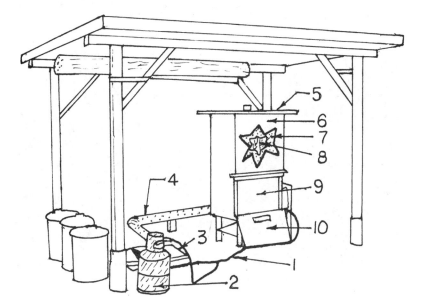

4. Smoke flue. This flue goes from the top of the underground smoke generator to the bottom of the smoke chamber.
5. Removable smoke chamber lid. This lid is removed when the chamber is loaded or unloaded.
6. Smoke chamber siding. This is house siding material made of galvanized sheet steel with a baked-enamel finish. Plywood or other sheeting material can be used.
7. Fiberglass insulation.
8. Smoke chamber box: The box is made of ⅜-inch (12 mm) plywood.
9. Lower portion of the smoke chamber. This contains the auxiliary propane burner, the exhaust end of the smoke flue, and the smoke spreader.
10. Hinged door in the open position. The door is opened for access to the lower portion of the smoke chamber.

## REAR VIEW

This view shows the U-shaped routing of the smoke flue. The U-shaped routing was used so that the smoke generator could be located near the smoke chamber. It also allows the generator and the smoke chamber to be covered easily with one roof.

1. Support block for smoke flue.
2. Smoke flue.
3. Smoke chamber—rear view.

**The author's first smoker—rear view.**

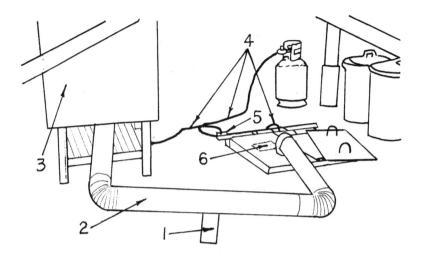

**4.** Rubber propane hose.

**5.** T connector for rubber propane hoses. In the United States, such connectors have a Y configuration, and they are called Y connectors.

**6.** Cover plate for the hole in the lid where the smoke flue is now inserted. This cover plate is placed over that hole when the smoke flue is removed and stored.

## LOWER SECTION OF THE SMOKE CHAMBER

Of course, the door shown below is closed while smoking. If the auxiliary burner is used, the door needs to be opened to light the burner. If the smoker is being used for water smoking, the door will be opened from time to time to add water to a pan. This water pan would be placed on the burner.

**1.** Bolt latches that are used to secure the door in the closed position.

**2.** Sheet metal (optional). The bottom, the inside of the door, and all walls in the lower portion of the chamber are covered with sheet metal (copper). This helps to distribute the heat evenly. The sheet metal may be either copper or galvanized sheet steel. Copper is easier to work with, but more expensive. The copper sheet, by the way, is the same material used for the roofing of some churches, public buildings, and the like (exposed to the weather, the copper roofing soon takes on a dull green color). As you will see later, I did not use sheet metal in my new smoker.

3. Cement board or some other kind of rigid, fireproof material. Such material should be placed on all wooden surfaces near the burner. This material will prevent the wooden smoke chamber from catching fire or scorching if the unit is used for hot smoking.

4. Plywood smoke chamber wall.

5. Smoke spreader. (See the Smoke Spreader drawing that appeared earlier in this chapter.) This rests on four L brackets, and it will slide out for easy cleaning.

6. Porthole to the outside of the smoke chamber. This hole permits the neck of the burner to extend to the outside of the smoke chamber, which allows the heat-sensitive propane hose to be connected outside of the chamber. Another advantage is that the burner controls at the end of the neck can be operated from outside the chamber.

7. Wind buffer assembly. The strong winds that were often present in my backyard would sometimes enter the porthole and extinguish the auxiliary propane burner. To prevent that problem, I constructed a wind buffer that was nothing more than a box with legs on it that covered the porthole mentioned in item 6. One side of the box and one end of the box are open. The open side of the box rests against the smoker. The open end of this box is covered with a cloth curtain that buffers the gusts of wind. The propane burner is adjusted by reaching behind the curtain.

**The author's first smoker—lower section.**

**8.** Wind buffer curtain (see item 7).

**9.** Rubber propane hose.

**10.** Sliding metal doors for air intake. This smoker was originally built to be used as a hot smoker, and charcoal was used to produce heat. If charcoal is used (not recommended), these adjustable air doors are required. They may be omitted if electricity or propane is being used. (If propane is being used for the auxiliary burner, there is enough oxygen to support combustion. The required oxygen comes through the porthole. Furthermore, there is considerable oxygen mixed with the cold smoke.)

**11.** Door hinges.

**12.** Steel plate with a hole for the smoke flue. This steel plate is movable in any direction, and it covers a square hole that is significantly larger than the diameter of the smoke flue. The result is that the smoke flue need not be positioned precisely when the unit is being set up for a smoking session; the steel plate can be moved to match the position of the smoke flue.

**13.** Smoke flue.

**14.** Auxiliary propane burner.

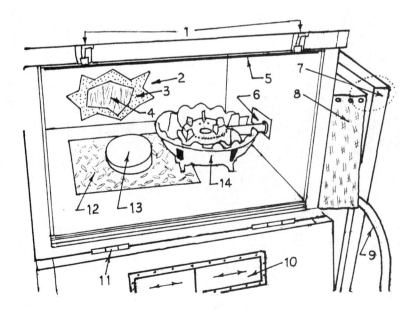

## SMOKE GENERATOR FOR THE AUTHOR'S FIRST SMOKER—OUTSIDE DETAILS

During a smoking session, the half of the lid with handles attached will have to be moved (as shown in the photograph) in order to add hardwood smoking fuel.

1. Smoke flue.
2. Half of the smoke generator lid. It is made of steel plate about $5/32$ inch (4 mm) thick.
3. Cover plate for hole in the lid (where the smoke flue is now inserted).
4. Smoke fuel pan, made from a discarded aluminum frying pan. The plastic handle was replaced with a handle made of steel water pipe. A long bolt inserted into the pipe attaches it to the frying pan.
5. Spacer bricks. Used to space the concrete slab (item 12) away from the concrete smoke generator enclosure. These spacer bricks, together with the concrete slab, serve to form the air intake holes (See item 9.)
6. Rubber propane hose leading to the smoke chamber.
7. T connector for the rubber propane hoses.
8. Rubber propane hose coming from the propane tank.
9. Air intake holes. Air to support burner combustion is drawn down

**Smoke generator for first smoker—outside details.**

these holes and into the smoke generator. (See Smoke Generator Box, page 42.)

**10.** Cutoff valve for the propane burner inside the smoke generator.

**11.** Rubber propane hose leading to a flexible metal hose. The metal hose connects to the propane burner.

**12.** Concrete slab. This slab, together with the spacer bricks (item 5), is used to create the air intake holes (item 9).

**13.** Sliding covers for the air intake holes (optional). These covers are made of steel plate, and they are used to cover the holes when the smoke generator is not being used.

**14.** Concrete smoke generator enclosure. This off-the-shelf, preformed concrete "box" (open at the top and the bottom) measures about 24 inches by 24 inches (61 x 61 cm), and it is about 15 inches (38 cm) tall. The walls are about 2 inches (5 cm) thick. First, a hole was dug, and a "stepped" concrete slab was poured with the step-down located toward the front. (See Smoke Generator Box, page 42.) The depth of the poured concrete slab (the distance below ground level) was calculated so that the "box" would protrude about 3 inches (8 cm) above the earth when it is placed on the slab. In addition, the front edge of the "box" was placed over the edge of the step-down so that air could flow down, through the air intake holes, under the

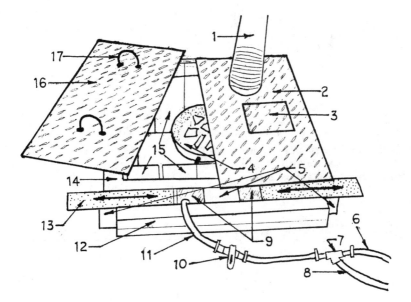

overhanging edge of the box, and enter the open bottom of the smoke generator. The rubber propane hose connects to a flexible metal hose, and then the metal hose connects to the propane burner (using the same route as the airflow to that burner).

**15.** Firebricks. Firebricks were used to cover the floor and the inside walls of the smoke generator in order to protect the concrete from heat (which could cause the concrete to crack). The heat generated, however, was not as much as I had expected. Consequently, I believe that either common bricks or cement board panels, which are much cheaper than firebricks, would have been adequate.

**16.** Lid half. Made of steel plate about $5/32$ inch (4 mm) thick. Instead of using steel, the lid could be made of plywood with a cement board bolted on the inside to protect the wood from heat.

**17.** U bolts used as handles. If this lid is turned upside down when it is not being used, the handles will not interfere with the placement of a cover.

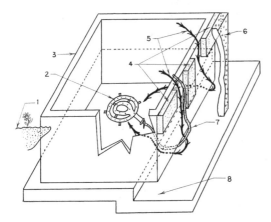

**Smoke generator box—airflow and propane hose routing (belowground spacer bricks are not shown).**

**1.** Ground level.
**2.** Propane burner.
**3.** Precast concrete box.
**4.** Spacer bricks (some spacer bricks are not shown in this drawing).
**5.** Intake draft (intake airflow).
**6.** Precast concrete slab.
**7.** Propane hose—flexible metal type.
**8.** Poured concrete—stepped slab.

## SMOKE GENERATOR FOR FIRST SMOKER—INSIDE DETAILS

**1.** Flue to carry smoke to the smoke chamber.
**2.** Steel plate to cover the flue hole when the generator is not in use.
**3.** Aluminum pan for smoking fuel. A cast-iron frying pan would also work well.

**4.** One of the two steel plates (optional) that slide to cover, or open, the two draft intake holes.

**5.** Rubber propane hose going to the smoke chamber.

**6.** Rubber propane hose going to the propane tank.

**7.** Draft intake holes. The intake draft (to support combustion of the propane) takes the same route as the propane hose.

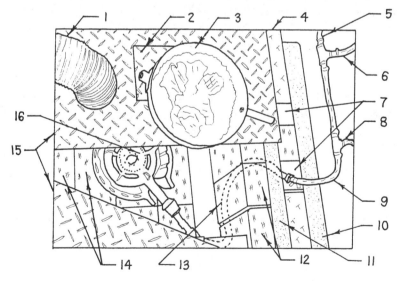

**Smoke generator for first smoker—inside details.**

8. In-line valve to shut off propane to the propane burner in the smoke generator.
9. Rubber propane hose that is connected to a metal hose that goes to the burner in the smoke generator.
10. Concrete slab (precast). The top edge is visible—the slab extends about 12 inches (30 cm) into the ground.
11. Concrete wall of the precast smoke generator box.
12. Bricks. To insulate the concrete from the heat produced by the burner.
13. Heavy-duty propane tube made of metal. Flexible type.
14. Bricks. Used to insulate the concrete floor from heat.
15. Smoke generator lids: Made of 4 mm—about 5/32 -inch—steel plate.
16. Small propane burner. The control valve was permanently set so that the flames of the burner are about ¼ inch (7 mm) high. This flame height, I found, is ideal to carbonize the smoking fuel and produce smoke without causing the smoking fuel to catch fire and burn.

# The Author's New Smoker

Portability may be an important consideration for you when contemplating a new homemade smoker. It was important for me after I moved into my house in Oregon. I needed a *portable* smoke generator and a *portable* smoke chamber because I wanted to store them in my garage. Moreover, I wanted to be able to open the garage door, roll my smoker and smoke generator to the front of the garage, and do the food smoking there.

In order for these goals to be realized, I had to have casters on the equipment. Also, I had to design a smoke generator that would emit smoke from the bottom rather than the top. This was necessary in order to create an upward-sloping draft to the bottom of the smoke chamber.

I had never seen or heard of a smoke generator that emitted smoke from the bottom. However, I thought it might be possible if the top lid of the generator was tight fitting and if the main air intake hole was located in the bottom panel of the generator. I also theorized that the air intake hole should be on the opposite side of the generator from the smoke exit port. I designed such a smoke generator, built it, and then tested it. It worked! I completed the project by building the smoke chamber. Whenever I want to smoke some food, I open the garage door, roll the chamber and generator to the front of the garage, connect the propane, connect the smoke flue to the generator, and begin smoking!

The photographs of this new smoking system were taken soon after the system was built and tested. I have used it many times since then. The equipment works very well, but there is one minor problem: The smoke generator lid must be opened and closed *very slowly*, because a sudden change of air pressure will blow out the burner flame. If this simple precaution is taken, the smoker system works perfectly. (I have also discovered that the flame is less likely to be blown out if the generator is preheated for about 20 minutes before the lid is completely closed.) The modification explained at the end of this chapter makes it easy to confirm that the flame was not blown out when the lid was closed.

My first smoker system and the new smoker system are basically the same; they are both natural draft smokers of about the same size, and both have a long smoke flue that is exposed to the air. However, there are many construction differences. These differences are outlined below and indicated in the photographs. It is impossible to say that one design is better than the other. They are simply two designs. Certain features of each might be useful if you decide to build your own smoker. The new smoker, however, was easier and cheaper to build—and it is more suitable for use in a suburban neighborhood. The construction of the new smoker required only basic woodworking skills and elementary sheet-metal skills.

## PHOTOGRAPHS AND DETAILS OF THE NEW SMOKER

🕯 The internal dimensions of the chamber are: 4 feet 7 inches (140 cm) high, 2 feet (60 cm) wide, and 22 inches (55 cm) from front to back. The height from the floor to the top of the flue pipe storage rack is 5 feet 9 inches (175 cm).

🕯 The smoking chamber of the new smoker sets on legs, and the legs are attached to a platform that is equipped with casters.

🕯 The smoke generator for the new smoker has a separate platform dolly that is available when I need to move it.

🕯 The new chamber and the smoke generator are made of ¾-inch-thick (2 cm) plywood that was salvaged from a very large packing crate. The first smoker chamber was made of plywood about half that thickness, but it was insulated and covered with house siding. Consequently, the new chamber is not as well insulated, but the insulation provided by the thick plywood seems to be adequate.

Below are photographs of the new smoker. The photographs and notes will clarify other differences. The photographs, by the way, were taken in the street in front of my house because the lighting in the garage was not suitable for photography.

♭ The smoking chamber is a front-loading type. The door of the smoke chamber is facing the camera.

♭ When the new smoker is set up in the garage, the garage floor supports the entire U-shaped smoke flue. The back of the smoker will face the driveway that leads to the garage.

♭ Note that the smoke flue is connected to the *bottom* of the smoke generator, and the smoke flue rises gradually and enters the bottom of the smoke chamber. This gradual rise is enough to create a natural draft.

♭ The chimney pipe and the smoke flue pipes are stored on top of the smoke chamber when the smoker is not being used (see page 47).

♭ A lever has been inserted under the smoker platform. This lever is pushed down to raise the corner of the smoker so that one of the

**The author with his new smoker and smoke generator.**

wheel blocks (in the foreground of the photo) can be inserted under the caster wheel.

🔥 A dial thermometer is inserted into a hole in the top center of the door. That thermometer is used to measure the chamber's internal temperature.

🔥 On the top left part of the door is an electronic meat thermometer that is magnetically attached to a steel L bracket. The cable for that thermometer is inserted into a hole on the left side of the chamber. The black rubber plug hanging on a chain is used to plug that hole when the thermometer is not being used.

🔥 Visible hardware on the right side: side handle; two door latches.

🔥 Visible hardware on the front: door handle; a dial thermometer to measure the chamber temperature; a steel L bracket to magnetically attach an electronic meat thermometer.

🔥 The propane hose is connected to the neck of the propane burner that is protruding from the lower right side of the chamber.

🔥 A small door is hanging above the right-side handle. When the smoker is not being used,

**New smoke chamber before being set up for use.**

**Front and right-side view of smoke chamber.**

this door is used to cover the hole where the neck of the propane burner is now protruding. To cover the hole, the door is inserted into the channels at the sides of the hole and pushed down. (See the Sliding Door and Door Channels drawing.)

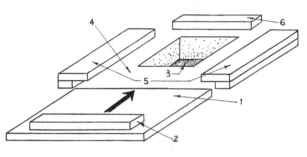

**Sliding door and door channels.**

**1.** Sliding door.

**2.** Sliding door handle.

**3.** Hole in smoke chamber or smoke generator.

**4.** Outside surface of smoke chamber or smoke generator.

**5.** Door channels.

**6.** Door bumper.

Various holes in the chamber and generator are covered with the sliding door and door channels assembly. Covering these holes discourages nest building by various critters, varmints, and crawly things.

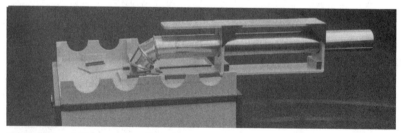

**Top view of the smoke chamber.**

🔥 Chimney assembly. The chimney elbow is inserted into the hole in the top center of the smoke chamber, and then the chimney support rack is slid over the end of the chimney and into the support channels on the top of the chamber. The channels are similar to those in the Sliding Door and Door Channels drawing. The chimney protrudes quite far from the rear of the smoker. The smoke will exit about 2 feet (60 cm) beyond the open garage door.

🔥 A small door (visible on the top of the chamber in the left, far corner) is used to cover the hole for the chimney when the smoker is not being used.

༢ On top of the chamber, there are two upright boards with four half-circle cuts in each board. These boards comprise the flue pipe storage rack.

༢ Four food racks are visible in the photo below. These are manufactured barbecue racks. They are porcelain coated, and very easy to clean.

**Smoke chamber with the door open.**

༢ A board that extends from the right side to the left side of the chamber walls, in front of the third rack from the top. This board functions as a spacer and a stabilizer; it prevents the walls from bowing inward or outward.

༢ Steel-rod (rebar) racks are visible. These bars are for hanging food that is suspended by metal hooks or twine. The ends of each rod are inserted in slots.

༢ A full-length piano hinge attaches the door to the smoke chamber.

༢ The tar catcher assembly is barely visible inside of the chamber (on the underside of the top). There is a close-up photo of this assembly later in this chapter.

༢ The drip tray is setting on a smoke-and-heat baffle (smoke spreader) made of Durock cement board. I could not find a factory-made tray of the proper size, so I handmade the drip tray of galvanized sheet metal and aluminum L-channel material (corner material). Assembly of the drip tray required 70 small bolts. This tray is always lined with heavy-duty aluminum foil to facilitate easy cleaning. Smoke and heat pass upward, in front of and behind the baffle. There are no holes in the baffle.

🔥 Durock cement board protects the lower part of the door from the heat produced by the auxiliary propane burner. This panel of cement board was attached to the inside of the door with four bolts.

**Lower section of the smoke chamber.**

🔥 The entire lower section is lined with Durock cement board. Each cement board panel was attached with four bolts.

🔥 The smoke flue can be seen protruding into the smoke chamber from the bottom. The square hole in the Durock board was made as follows: First, I drilled many holes on the cut line with a small-diameter carbide-tip drill bit; next, I tapped out the square with a hammer. A round hole could have been made in the same way.

🔥 Each ring of the two-ring propane burner is controlled independently by its own cock on the outside—at the end of the burner neck. (The cocks are not visible in this photo.)

🔥 Near the end of the neck of the propane burner, there is a small piece of Durock board that has a rectangular notch at the bottom. The notch is just large enough to fit around the neck. This Durock board acts to block the gusts of wind that would otherwise enter though the large hole in the side of the chamber where the neck of the burner protrudes to the outside. To secure the cement board, a long bolt with a wing nut passes through the top of this board and through the chamber wall. (The bolt is not visible in the photo.)

🔥 The tar catcher assembly can be seen mounted on the underside of the top of the smoke chamber, directly under the chimney.

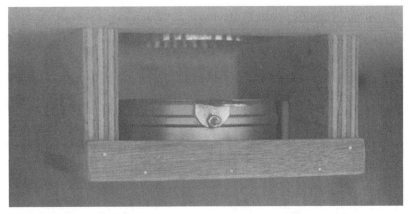

**Tar catcher assembly.**

🔥 The tar catcher pan was made from the lid of a candy tin. An L bracket was bolted onto the tin to make the handle. It looks like a miniature frying pan.

🔥 Several photographs have shown a dial thermometer inserted through the top of the chamber door. The photo at right shows the stem of that same dial thermometer protruding inside the door. A homemade leaf spring (made of galvanized sheet steel) prevents vibration from causing rotation of the thermometer in the hole.

🔥 The U-shaped guard protects you from being impaled on the pointed stem. It also helps to protect the stem from damage

**Leaf spring and guard assembly for the thermometer stem.**

caused by unintentional bumps. The guard, too, was made of galvanized sheet steel.

🔥 There are three darkly painted smoke flue supports shown in the photo on page 52. Note that the height of the support block in the notch of each support is increasingly taller. The increasing height helps to create the draft from the generator to the bottom of the smoke chamber.

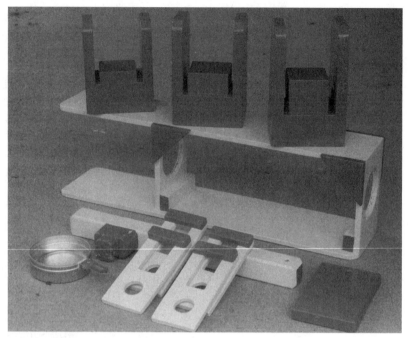

**Smoke chamber accessories.**

💧 Directly under the flue supports is the chimney support rack. (When the rack is slid over the chimney and mounted on the top of the chamber, the lower tongue of the rack is inserted into channels that are similar to those previously shown in the Sliding Door and Door Channels drawing.)

💧 In front of the chimney support rack is the previously mentioned lever used to raise each corner of the caster platform.

💧 Inclined on the lever handle are four wheel blocks, which are used to prevent the chamber casters from moving. (Putting a caster wheel in the round hole in a wheel block will prevent the caster from rolling.)

💧 The tar catcher pan is pictured on the left.

💧 On the right, near the bottom of the photo, is a darkly painted rectangular board. This board is placed on the caster platform that is under the chamber. The elbow of the smoke flue will rest on this board as it enters the bottom of the smoke chamber. The purpose of this board is to boost the elbow upward, into the chamber, and to prevent that elbow from falling out of the hole.

The propane burners for my first smoker—shown on page 31, earlier in this chapter—are almost identical to the burners used in my new smoker. The only significant difference is that the burners for this second smoker do not set inside cast-iron windbreaks. Both of the burners in my new smoker were made in China, but were purchased from an Internet retailer in the United States. The hose connectors had to be replaced with U.S.-standard hose connectors. A barbecue equipment dealer easily installed the new brass connector fittings.

A single-ring burner like the one at the top of the photo on page 31 is used in the smoke generator. The two-ring burner like the one on the left is used in the smoke chamber. (A medium sized burner like the one at the bottom of the photo is not used in my new smoker.) There are two cocks visible on the large burner. Each cock is dedicated to the control of one of the rings. The single-ring burner is about 9,000 BTU, and the double-ring burner is about 18,500 BTU.

**Smoke generator with top closed.**

♭ The top lid of the smoke generator is in place.

♭ Leaning against the smoke generator is the platform dolly used to move the generator.

♭ The propane hose is connected to the neck of the propane burner protruding through the hole in the side. The small door hanging to the right of the handle is used to cover this hole when the generator has been stored away. This door slides into the darkly painted channels on the right and the left sides of the hole.

◊ Smoke exits from the generator into the galvanized pipe at the bottom right side.

**Smoke generator, top view, open.**

◊ The top lid is leaning against the left side of the generator.

◊ The round hole in the wall near the edge of the frying pan is the smoke exit port.

◊ The dark slot inside the smoke generator near the bottom of the photograph is the fresh air intake slot. It was cut into the *bottom* of the generator so that the fresh air intake would be slightly lower than the smoke exit port. (Also, note that the slot is located near the front of the generator, and the smoke exit port is at the back of the generator.) The generator is raised ¾ inch (2 cm) off the garage floor with "feet" made of 2-inch (5-cm) squares of plywood that are attached to the bottom. (The feet are not visible in the photo.)

◊ All interior sides, the interior bottom, and the interior top have Durock cement board attached with four bolts each (except for the bottom—the bottom Durock board simply lies in place). The cement board provides adequate insulation and protection for the plywood, even though the heat that is produced by the propane burner is considerable. (The Durock on the inside of this smoke generator has gradually become jet black since the photo was taken—the result of many smoking sessions.)

◊ The aluminum frying pan normally sits directly on top of the burner. The original plastic handle of the frying pan was replaced with a metal handle made of steel water pipe. A disk of applewood can be seen inside the frying pan. At the sides of the applewood disk are split hazelnut tree branches.

Since this photo was taken, there has been one minor modification: I drilled a peekhole into one wall of the smoke generator. This peekhole makes it easy to confirm that the burner flame was not extinguished by closing the lid too quickly. The hole is located about 3 inches (12 cm) above the air intake slot (see the drawing). The diameter is 1½ inches (3 cm), and it aims directly at the burner flame. A short section of copper pipe was friction-fitted into this hole. A hardwood plug is normally inserted into the copper pipe. After the generator lid is closed, I remove the hardwood plug from the pipe and hold a pocket mirror at a 45-degree angle to peek inside and confirm that the burner is still lit.

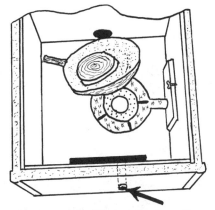

**The arrow indicates the location of the peekhole.**

# CHAPTER 3

# Wood for Smoke and Fuels for Heat

## Wood for the Production of Smoke

Those who have had no experience in smoking food often believe that the kind of wood used to make the smoke is the most important factor in making good smoked foods. Many Americans are convinced that hickory must be used to get the best result. Oak, however, is the traditional smoking fuel in Great Britain. Laplanders—the nomadic reindeer herders in northern Finland and Sweden—use birch. Most Japanese have never heard of hickory, and they tend to believe that the best products are always smoked with cherry wood.

### THE BEST KIND OF WOODS FOR PRODUCING SMOKE

As long as it comes from some kind of suitable hardwood tree, the kind of wood used to generate smoke is one of the *least* important factors in the production of high-quality smoked foods. Very few people in this world can taste a product and identify the kind of wood used to smoke it. To be sure, the composition and aroma of the smoke will differ somewhat from one kind of hardwood to another, but the imparted smoke flavor is only one part of the total flavor complex. The smoky flavor of the product is often competing with an array of seasonings and spices, plus the natural flavor of the raw material itself (the meat, fish, or poultry, for example). Under these conditions, an extremely sensitive palate would be required to identify the kind of wood used to make the smoke.

Woods from all the fruit trees in the following list make excellent smoke:

- apple
- apricot
- cherry
- grapefruit
- lemon
- nectarine
- orange
- peach
- pear
- persimmon
- plum
- tangerine

The woods from the trees in the list below are also excellent. The list is probably not complete, but all of these woods are used for smoking and barbecuing:

- alder
- almond
- ash
- beech
- birch (barked)
- butternut
- chestnut
- cottonwood
- elm
- gum
- hazelnut
- hickory
- maple
- mesquite
- mulberry
- oak
- olive
- pecan
- walnut
- willow

In other words, the woods from many species of deciduous (hardwood) trees will produce very flavorful smoked foods. Softwood trees (conifers) are not recommended because they will impart a bitter, pitchy, and sooty flavor. Softwood will also cause excessively dark coloration of whatever you smoke. Furthermore, a resinous coating on the inside of your smoker will result from using conifers.

Many writers of barbecue and smoking books, and distributors of smoking chips, have worked very hard to explain the characteristics of the various woods mentioned above. One writer might make a list of the woods suitable for fish and a list of the woods suitable for poultry, for example. The smoky flavor produced by one species of wood will be described as "sweet"—or "strong"—or "hearty." Another writer might draw different conclusions about the same species of wood.

As long as the wood is one of the hardwoods mentioned in the two lists above, you will get good results with it. The kind of wood will make little difference.

On the other hand, it is not wise to use an exotic or an unknown hardwood for smoking fuel unless you know for sure that the tree has no poisonous properties. For example, mango fruit and cashew nuts are safe to eat, but the smoke produced by burning the wood from either of these trees contains toxic fumes that can cause serious irritation of the eyes and lungs. Both trees are in the poison sumac family.

There was an ugly hardwood tree in my backyard in Japan that I intended to cut down someday. I could not identify the tree, but I thought that I might use the wood for smoking fuel. One hot and humid summer day, I spent several hours drinking iced tea while sitting in the shade under that tree. The next day I developed a severe rash over most of my body. The tree, I found out later, was a Japanese lacquer tree (it is also called a Japanese wax tree). It is in the poison ivy family, and it adversely affects some people during certain times of the year. What would have happened if I had used the wood from this tree as smoking fuel? I do not know, but my research on this wood revealed that ". . . the smoke contains highly irritating particles."

Below is some additional information about smoking fuel that may be of interest. Obviously, some of these statements should be considered to be opinions or beliefs rather than a facts.

🔥 Horse chestnut smoke is reported to be toxic.

🔥 Although pine is usually considered unsuitable for smoking, Polish researchers report that it is the best smoke fuel for lightly smoking sardines.

🔥 Juniper is an evergreen tree, but many salmon smokers mix a few twigs of juniper with hardwood smoking fuel.

🔥 Some people claim that dried corncobs make a better smoking fuel than any kind of hardwood.

🔥 Californians say that grapevines make good smoking fuel.

🔥 Many people believe that wood from fruit trees produces a milder smoke flavor than the wood from many other trees, especially nut trees. (I have never noticed this. However, even if this is true, smoking a little longer with fruitwood will likely produce the same smoke flavor intensity.)

In the beginning, if you can find an adequate supply, you may decide to stick with one species of hardwood that is definitely good for smoking.

Then, after you have mastered the many other flavoring and processing techniques, you could try some other kind of hardwood. If you try
new wood for smoking products that you have perfected and made
many times, you will be able to determine if the smoke from your new
wood makes any difference.

I have used Japanese wild cherry, pie cherry, Japanese oak,
mesquite, hazelnut, Oriental pear, common pear, European birch,
hickory, plum, apple, alder, and Japanese wild apricot. All make excellent smoking fuels. I have no strong preference. However, I do avoid
oak because it is a very hard wood; oak is difficult to cut and split.

## SAWDUST, CHIPS, CHUNKS, AND LOGS

The physical form of the wood is not critical. However, depending on
your smoking equipment, you may need to use sawdust, chips,
chunks, or even small logs. In other words, the design of your smoker
or smoke generator may dictate the best physical form of the smoking fuel. For example, manufacturers of easy-to-use electric smokers
recommend that chips or very small chunks be used in the little pan
that holds the smoking fuel. The commercially produced smoke
cookers that are fired with charcoal will work well with 2- to 3-inch (5
to 8 cm) chunks of wood. Such units have no pan for smoking fuel, so
these chunks must be put directly on, or near, the burning charcoal.
If sawdust or chips are put directly on the charcoal, they will burn up
right away and produce very little smoke. Some homemade smokers
and large barbecue smokers burn logs that have been cut to short
lengths, and these logs function as both the heat source and the
smoke source.

The physical form of the smoking fuel you use may be influenced
by economic considerations as well. For example, packaged hardwood
chips for smoking food are very expensive in Japan, but I could easily
obtain and cut hardwood logs at essentially no cost. I could use disks,
chunks, chips, or sawdust in my smoke generator; it made no difference, so I used whatever I could cut with my chain saw. My new smoker, as well, will accept any form of smoking fuel.

Some knowledgeable people say that sawdust or small chips produce "uniform" smoke. This may be true, but I don't think that I will
ever meet a person who can taste a product and tell me the physical
form of the wood that was used for the smoking.

## WET WOOD OR DRY WOOD

Wet wood or green wood makes more smoke than dry wood, but that does not mean it should always be used. For example, if you are smoking salmon (either cold smoking or kippering), the necessary drying of the fish will be more difficult to accomplish if wet or green wood is used. On the other hand, if you are hot smoking some kind of meat with a charcoal smoker and putting the smoking fuel directly on the charcoal, you should soak the chunks in water or use green wood. If dry wood is used, the wood will burn quickly, and the smoke will be short-lived. In summary, the product you are smoking and the equipment you are using will determine whether dry wood or wet wood is best.

It is my personal opinion that smoking fuel should not be wet unless there is some compelling reason to wet it. Using dry, seasoned wood whenever possible results in almost the same quality of smoke every time, and that means that there are fewer variables to cause concern.

Another point that should be kept in mind is that mold and other parasitic growths can develop on damp or wet wood; these can give a musty taint to the foods you are smoking. It is best to stockpile wood under dry and airy conditions that will retard parasitic growths.

## HEAVY SMOKE AND LIGHT SMOKE

It seems logical to assume that heavy smoke will produce a smokier product than light smoke. In fact, many experts on smoking and barbecuing believe this to be true. However, my experience leads me to believe that the degree of smoky flavor imparted into the food has little or no relation to the density of the smoke. Many other experienced food smokers agree.

When smoking fuel is burned or carbonized, many kinds of aromatic gases are driven from the wood, and a great many of these gases are invisible. The visible components that are driven from the wood are collectively referred to as smoke. Both the visible and invisible components impart the smoky flavor. Even a small amount of smoke is enough to indicate that the desired aromatic components are being driven from the wood.

In my opinion, the total time that the product is exposed to smoke is the most significant factor influencing the smokiness of the product. I believe that the time the product is exposed to smoke is more important than the density of the visible smoke.

Regardless of the smoke density, foods that are smoked in a water smoker or a barbecue-type hot smoker will have a mild and pleasant smoky taste even if they are consumed soon after processing. However, if a product has been cold smoked, it will usually have a harsh taste if it is eaten immediately. If cold-smoked products are stored in a refrigerator overnight, the harsh taste will be transformed into a mellow and pleasant smoky flavor.

## SOURCES OF SMOKING FUEL

Chips and chunks can be purchased in some supermarkets, hardware stores, and the like. They can be ordered on the Internet as well. However, if you do a lot of smoking, a more economical source might be desirable.

Alder is abundant in the Pacific Northwest, so it can be obtained here cheaply or even at no cost. The same thing can be said for mesquite in the Southwest. Industries in your area that use hardwood might be willing to sell cutoffs or sawdust at a reasonable price, but you need to make sure that the hardwood is not mixed with softwood, and you need to be certain that it has not been treated with chemicals. Fruit or nut orchards in your area might supply you with branch cuttings during the pruning season, or they might even give you a whole tree that they wish to cull. When I first started smoking many years ago, I used branch cuttings that I obtained from a nearby Oriental pear orchard.

Another good idea is to look in the yellow pages under tree services. You will likely find many listings for arborists that specialize in tree removal. If you make a few telephone calls, you will probably find a tree service company that will deliver suitable hardwood logs and large branches to your home for a reasonable price. If you haul it yourself, it might be cheaper.

Wild cherry is a common tree in southern Japan, and I was able to obtain a whole tree at no charge when the electric power company felled one that was interfering with the power lines. Although I do a lot of smoking, this single wild cherry tree provided me with a 10-year supply of high-quality smoking fuel.

## CUTTING SMOKING FUEL

If the wood is not too hard, you can use an ax, a plane, a wood-splitting wedge, or a handsaw to cut it into something usable. However, if you are cutting up logs, bulky slabs, or very hard wood such as oak, it is easier to use an electric chain saw. (An electric chain saw is recommended because it is much cheaper than an engine-powered saw. It is easier to start, too: Just plug it in and pull the trigger.)

Of course, if you use a chain saw for cutting smoking fuel, chain oil should not be used to lubricate the chain. If chain oil is used, the wood you are cutting will absorb that oil, which may impart a petroleum taste to whatever you smoke. If the logs were previously cut with a chain saw that used chain oil, it is best to cut off, and discard, a thin slice of the wood where that cut was made. The oil might not be visible, but you must assume that some chain oil has permeated the surface of the cut.

Because there will be no oil in the oil reservoir of the electric chain saw, the blade will not receive lubrication, and it will become quite hot after a few cuts. When this happens, let the saw cool for about 15 minutes, and do something else in the meantime. If you give the saw a chance to cool from time to time, you need not worry about heat damage to the unlubricated saw blade and chain. It is a common practice in Scandinavian countries to use an unlubricated saw to cut smoking fuel, and I know a man in Japan who has used the same unlubricated saw for 10 years to sculpt logs into yard furniture.

**Cutting disks of wild cherry.**

I cut through logs or large branches to make smoking fuel disks that are about an inch (2.5 cm) thick, but you should cut the wood to suit your needs and preference. In only one day, enough wood can be cut for about six months of weekly smoking sessions. Be sure to catch the sawdust with a large plastic or canvas sheet placed under the log. If you require chunks of wood rather than disks, the large disks that you cut off can be broken into chunks easily. To make chunks, incline the disks on something hard, such as a brick, and give them a good solid whack with a hammer. Obviously, thin disks break more easily than thick ones.

**Cutting chips (note that the saw blade is near the end of the log).**

If you must have chips and sawdust rather than chunks, make all the cuts just a little thicker than the width of the chain on the saw blade. This is a bit more tedious, but the result will be chips and sawdust.

Using a chain saw—or any kind of a power tool—can be dangerous, so be sure to read the manufacturer's instructions carefully. Never try to force a power tool to do something it hesitates to do. Always remember that a chain saw cannot distinguish between the limb of a tree and the limb of a human being.

## TO BARK OR NOT TO BARK

Some people believe that the bark on smoking fuel gives a bitter taste to smoked foods, so they remove all the bark from logs before the wood is cut. Others believe that bark gives a good flavor to the food, so they use all they can get their hands on. Who is right? Taste is such a personal thing that it is not at all strange for one person to describe a food as being bitter and another person to describe the same food as flavorful. The personal tolerance for bitterness is probably much like the tolerance for salt. Such tolerance can differ greatly among individuals, and the tolerance for bitterness is probably the same. Do what you think is best. I remove the bark if it is easy to remove, but I leave it on if removal is difficult. I can't tell the difference, but I remove as much bark as possible because it might make a difference to someone who eats my product.

A drawknife is most effective for barking, but a hatchet can be used as well. A large chisel and wooden mallet work well for some bark.

Birch, by the way, *must* be barked because birch bark gives off a copious amount of sticky, resinous soot when it burns. However, if the logs are green, birch bark is very easy to remove with the large chisel and mallet mentioned above; it peels off in sheets.

**Barking a wild cherry log.**

# Fuels for Heating

No matter what kind of smoker you use, and no matter what kind of smoking you do, at least one source of heat is required: *heat to generate smoke*. This heat for smoke generation could be provided by electricity, charcoal, a gas such as propane or natural gas—or even by burning hardwood. (Technically speaking, electricity is not a fuel because it does not burn, but please permit me to consider it to be a fuel for the moment.)

In some cases, an additional heat source is required or desirable. For example, if you have a homemade smoker with an external smoke generator, you will need another source of heat inside the smoke chamber unless you do nothing but the simplest cold smoking.

For factory-made, portable electric smokers, smoke is produced in the bottom of the smoking chamber. Some homemade smokers operate in the same way. The heat used to produce the smoke passes upward, through the smoking chamber. This makes hot smoking possible with only one heat source.

Smoke cookers are basically cookers, so the main function of the fuel is to produce heat for cooking. Nevertheless, this heat can also be used to heat smoking fuel for smoke production. The result is that one source of heat has a dual purpose: It heats the cooking chamber, and it heats the hardwood to produce smoke.

The most common types of smokers are mentioned above: the homemade smokers, the portable electric smokers, and the smoke cookers. Heating fuels (for smoke production or for cooking) used in these smokers have one thing in common—they produce *clean* heat that has no offensive odors. (An exception to the clean heat requirement is a smoker in which smoking fuel is burned to produce smoke and heat simultaneously. Heat that contains hardwood smoke is not clean, but such heat is acceptable because hardwood smoke is desirable.)

Many materials can be burned to produce heat, but fuels that will burn cleanly with no offensive odors or toxic properties are limited. When it is also required that the fuels be economical and easy to obtain, the list of good fuels is shortened further. What we have left on the list are those fuels mentioned above: charcoal, gases such as natural gas or propane, hardwood, and—the fuel that is not really a fuel—electricity. Some of the obvious and not-so-obvious good and bad points of each are noted below.

## ELECTRICITY

Electricity is excellent for the production of smoke and the production of supplementary heat.

### Advantages

♭ The heat from electricity is pure heat. There are no by-products of combustion as there are with true fuels.

♭ If electricity is reasonably priced where you live, it may be affordable, and it may be the most readily available source of heat.

♭ It is convenient: Turn the switch on (or plug it in).

♭ The heat output of electricity is easy to control if there are numerous step switches, as there are on the common kitchen ranges or on quality electric hot plates.

### Disadvantages

♭ Electricity is dangerous. The smoker (and external smoke generator—if one is used) must be protected from rain and water to prevent short circuits that could cause a fire or an electric shock. For related reasons, placement of the smoker on a concrete slab or concrete platform is advisable. (Concrete is fireproof and, if dry, will not conduct electricity.)

♭ The smoker should be close to the electric outlet. A long extension cord will cause a voltage drop, and it will also result in lower heat output. Extension cords of inadequate current-carrying capability will do the same thing, regardless of the length, and they will create a fire hazard as well.

♭ Installation of electric heating elements and controls in a homemade smoker requires a sophisticated knowledge of electricity. Technical assistance may be required.

## PROPANE

Propane, too, is excellent for the production of both smoke and supplementary heat. (Propane is also known *as liquid petroleum gas* or *LP gas*).

## Advantages

◊ If combustion is complete, the only by-products of burning propane are carbon dioxide (the same gas that plants need to live) and water vapor. Consequently, propane produces very clean heat. Water vapor is not always desirable, but the amount of water vapor in the heated air is not enough to prevent the necessary drying of certain meat and fish products.

◊ Propane is an odorless gas. It is scented with a mildly offensive odor to make leaks more detectable, but this scent is destroyed when the propane burns.

◊ Propane in a small tank is very portable. Your smoker can be a considerable distance from your house, or it can even be in a remote and undeveloped location.

◊ Propane is widely available, and it is usually economical.

◊ Adjustment cocks on the burners offer excellent control of heat.

## Disadvantages

Explosions are rare, but they are a possibility. The hoses can leak if not attached properly, but that risk has been minimized with the new safety valves, quality hoses, and quality fittings that are required in the United States. Even if the burner is inside a smoker or smoke generator, strong winds can extinguish the flames. However, because propane is used outdoors, it is unlikely for a dangerous explosion to occur under these conditions. Nevertheless, it is prudent to locate the smoker some distance away from anything that could be adversely affected.

### NATURAL GAS

For smoking purposes, there is no difference between using propane gas and using natural gas. However, compared with propane, there are a few advantages and disadvantages. For example, natural gas is likely to be cheaper than propane, and it has another advantage: There are no tanks to be filled, because natural gas is piped in. On the negative side, the use of natural gas for smoking will most likely require hiring a licensed professional to install the pipe. If you want to change the location of your smoker because the smoke is offending a neighbor, this might become a big and expensive job.

Burners used for propane gas are not the same as those used for natural gas. Burners are designed to be used specifically with propane or specifically with natural gas because the physical properties of the two gases differ.

## CHARCOAL

High-quality charcoal is over 85 percent pure carbon. For that reason, it burns very cleanly, and it can produce intense heat if given enough oxygen. For some manufactured smokers, charcoal is the required fuel.

### Advantages

๒ Charcoal is a simple fuel. A steel container in which to burn the charcoal is needed, as is some way to regulate the oxygen flow—and that's all. Give it more oxygen, and it will produce more heat. If it is burned outdoors, the only hazard is fire—but all smokers present a fire hazard no matter what fuel is used. (Burning charcoal indoors is dangerous because of the danger of carbon monoxide poisoning.)

๒ A smoker or smoke generator using charcoal is self-contained. It does not require an electric cord, pipes, hoses, or tanks.

### Disadvantages

๒ Depending on where you live and how much smoking you do, charcoal can be very expensive.

๒ Controlling the oxygen flow will effectively control the heat produced by a charcoal fire, but frequent monitoring is required to maintain a reasonably constant temperature. If it is left untended for 20 minutes or so, the temperature can drop quite low or shoot up quite high—high enough to ruin a delicate smoking operation such as the smoking of fish.

๒ Charcoal fires can produce intense heat. When you are smoking with an external smoke generator but want to boost the smoke chamber temperature just a few degrees, a charcoal fire inside the chamber is not suitable—the heat is difficult to control.

๒ Charcoal fires are time consuming to light, and they require time to stabilize. Petroleum-based charcoal lighting fluid can taint the food you are smoking.

## HARDWOOD

Obviously, burning smoking fuel (hardwood) will produce both smoke and heat. No other heat source is needed to make smoke, and it is possible to use the heat to do hot smoking.

Hardwood is usually burned in an external smoke generator or on the floor of a smokehouse. Some large barbecue smokers, however, burn hardwood in the chamber. It is rarely burned inside a small smoker because the heat output is difficult to control. If you can get a plentiful supply of hardwood at a low price, and you intend to use it in a smokehouse, in a large barbecue-type smoker, or in an external smoke generator, burning hardwood might be worthy of consideration.

Burning hardwood to produce smoke and heat requires frequent attention to ensure that it neither burns too intensely nor goes out. Control of heat output and smoke output is difficult. To avoid excessive water vapor in the smoke, the fire should be dampened with sand rather than water.

# Fuels for Heating—Summary and Conclusion

If you are using a factory-made smoker or smoke cooker, use the fuel for which it was designed. If you intend to build a homemade smoker, I suggest you consider electricity or propane for the heat source(s)—both are excellent. Either electricity or propane gas is likely to be an affordable heat source, and one of the two is likely to meet your overall requirements. Both are easy to control. If heat sources are easy to control, it is easier to make quality products consistently, and it is less likely that you will ruin batches of food with excessively high heat. If you need two heat sources—one for smoldering the smoking fuel and one for supplementary heat—keep in mind that the two heat sources need not be the same. For example, one heat source can be electricity, and the other can be gas or some other kind of suitable fuel.

# CHAPTER 4

# Additional Equipment

Some of the equipment described here can be found in your kitchen or elsewhere around the house. In a few cases, you may wish to buy something that you already have, and keep it together with your smoking equipment so that it will be nearby when you need it. Appendix 5 may assist you in locating hard-to-find items. (If equipment is unique to a certain chapter and described there, it might not be mentioned below.)

## Cutting Board

It is difficult and awkward to prepare food for smoking without using a cutting board. If you don't have one, consider buying the modern plastic type. Wooden cutting boards are porous and difficult to clean, so they are good breeding grounds for germs and bacteria. A big board is better than a small one—you may have to trim and cut large objects such as pork bellies (for bacon), beef plate (for pastrami), and some large fish. A stiff scrub brush used with dish detergent and hot water is very effective for cleaning your plastic cutting board. Use a bleach-and-water solution to remove most stains and sterilize the board.

## Weight Scales

To the extent possible, measurements have been specified in terms of volume rather than weight. That is, whenever possible, the amount of an ingredient is indicated in teaspoons, tablespoons, American cups, American quarts, or American gallons (together with the metric equivalent).

Obviously, the quantity of meats, poultry, and fish must be expressed in units of weight. However, if you buy these raw ingredients at a market, the weight will usually be indicated on the wrapping, so it may not be necessary to weigh them. If you must trim the material, you can usually estimate the weight of the trimmings, and subtract that from the weight written on the wrapping. Furthermore, if you are brine curing or simply sprinkling seasoning on the item to be smoked, the weight is not an important factor. In other words, you will be able to process many products without using a scale at all.

The *classical* dry cure method used to preserve meat requires knowledge of the approximate weight of the meat. The *modern* dry cure method most certainly requires that the weight of the meat or fish be known if you want the best possible results every time.

A scale is sometimes used to weigh the product during the smoking process. For example, when kippering (hot smoking) fish, the percentage of weight loss is a guide to doneness.

For record-keeping purposes, you may wish to know the weight of a product before and after smoking.

If you think you will need a scale, you might consider an inexpensive kitchen scale that will weigh up to about 5 pounds (about 2 or 3 kg). Such scales have sufficient accuracy if used properly. If the raw material is cut into pieces that do not exceed the weight limit of the scale, you will be able to process an unlimited amount of product at one time.

**A 2 kg (4.4 pound) weight scale.**

# Refrigerator

A refrigerator is basic equipment. If you always smoke your food right away (without using a lengthy curing process)—and then eat it soon after it is smoked—you may never need one. Such cases are the exception, though, so it is more realistic to say that a refrigerator is essential for processing smoked food.

If you already have at least one refrigerator, and if the quantities of product you intend to smoke are modest, this presents no major problem. The main thing is to make sure that the required refrigeration space is available when you need it.

Until you have some experience in smoking, it is a little difficult to judge how much space you will need. However, a surprisingly large amount of product can be processed with as little as 1 cubic foot (30 x 30 x 30 cm) of refrigerator space. The processing in this book is designed to make the best use of limited refrigeration space without sacrificing quality.

The internal temperature of a refrigerator is very important. The refrigeration compartment should be kept within a range of 36° to 40° F (2.2° to 4.4° C). This temperature range is high enough to allow meat, fowl, and fish to cure properly, but low enough to retard spoilage effectively.

There is a temperature adjustment dial in your refrigerator. The easiest way to measure the temperature is to use a refrigerator thermometer or to use the type of electronic meat thermometer that appears in a photo later in this chapter. (See Electronic Cooking Thermometer with a Cable Probe and Timer.)

To get an accurate reading of the temperature using a common thermometer (such as a liquid-in-glass or dial thermometer), first place the thermometer in a large container of water (either a 1-liter soft drink bottle or a quart jar works very nicely). Next, place this container of water in the refrigerator near the spot that you will most likely place your product. Wait two days, and then read the thermometer. If adjustment is necessary, turn the refrigerator adjustment dial a little in the proper direction. Wait for two more days, and then measure the temperature again. Make another adjustment if necessary. Repeat these steps until the proper temperature range is reached. Whenever you read the thermometer, make sure that its tip is submerged in the water. The temperature of this water will accurately reflect the internal temperature of the refrigerator.

After your refrigerator is adjusted, it will be ready to use whenever you need it. It is a good idea to mark the proper setting on the adjustment dial. The temperature should be rechecked every few months.

# Freezer

A freezer is useful for storing raw material before you begin processing and smoking. You may want to buy raw material in advance, especially if it is on sale, and then freeze it until you need it. Sometimes you might obtain raw material and then find that, for some reason or another, you can't process it right away. In most cases, freezer storage will keep it in good condition. Furthermore, smoked foods keep very well in a freezer for about two months, so you can smoke a little more than what you need for immediate use, and then freeze the remainder.

# Hot Water Cooker and Chinese Steamer

The use of these utensils is suggested for cooking cold-smoked food and cured sausages. Photographs of the utensils and instructions on how to use them are in chapter 8.

# Oven Mitts

You may have a pair of oven mitts in the kitchen, but it is desirable to have a second pair near your smoker. They are very useful for handling things such as hot smoker racks and hot smoking fuel pans. Having mitts near the smoker when you need them is a good reason to have an extra set. If you need another reason, consider that the ones used for smoking food are likely to get a little too stained and ugly to use in your kitchen. Mitts that are designed for barbecue use will work very well.

# Rubber Gloves

If you have a normal threshold for pain, a pair of rubber gloves will be useful. Preparing foods for smoking often involves the use of salt, and your hands may be in contact with it for a long time. The salt will make you painfully aware of even the smallest cut or scrape on either hand. Rubber gloves will prevent this.

When you take meat out of a 38° F (3° C) refrigerator to be overhauled, your hands may be in contact with the cold meat for several minutes. Pain caused by touching cold meat with bare hands for an extended time is considerable. Rubber gloves will insulate your hands from the cold very well, even if the rubber is thin.

Rubber gloves of the type used to wash dishes and do light household cleaning are effective, easy to use, inexpensive, and obtainable almost anywhere.

# Thermometers

There are very few cases when you can complete a smoking session without using a thermometer; thermometers are essential—or at least desirable—for all types of smoking. Additionally, they are often needed for processing foods before or after smoking. The kind of thermometer required will depend on what you want to accomplish. Those described below will meet all of your needs adequately, and all are affordable.

**Baby-dial thermometer, ovenproof meat thermometer, and two liquid-in-glass thermometers (one in a stainless steel case).**

### LIQUID-IN-GLASS THERMOMETER

The liquid-in-glass thermometer is a sealed glass rod with a very small hole running down the center. It has a glass bulb at the base that contains either mercury or another type of liquid. If mercury is not used, then alcohol that has been dyed red, blue, or green is normally used. The mercury thermometers are more accurate, especially at higher temperatures, but they are a hazard to the environment, and they are in the process of being banned. Fortunately, for our applications, alcohol thermometer accuracy is quite adequate, and it has the advantage of being cheaper.

A common and very useful length for a liquid-in-glass thermometer is about 1 foot (30 cm). A temperature scale ranging from somewhere below 32° F (0° C) to about 225° F (107° C) is very useful. Such a thermometer can be used to set the temperature of a refrigerator, control the temperature of water in a hot water cooker, and monitor the temperature of a smoke chamber. A higher temperature range is required to measure the chamber temperature for very hot smoking.

A glass thermometer is not recommended to check the internal temperature of meats. Also, do not try to use the liquid-in-glass thermometer in the kitchen oven; its length makes it very awkward, and it may crack due to temperature variations along the body. This kind of thermometer does have one bad point: It is fragile, and it may break at the worst possible time, so always keep a spare handy.

Some people do not like glass thermometers because they find them difficult to read.

Although the liquid-in-glass thermometers are widely used, dial thermometers and digital thermometers are becoming more common on the store shelves.

## OVENPROOF MEAT THERMOMETER

You may already have an ovenproof meat thermometer in your home. This type of thermometer is useful when the final cooking of meat is done in a common kitchen oven or hot smoker. Many people say that this thermometer is essential for cooking all thick pieces of meat that cannot be inspected internally for doneness.

An ovenproof meat thermometer can also be used to measure the temperature of a moderately hot smoke chamber. The configuration is quite suitable for this purpose since the stem can be inserted through a hole in the smoker, but it is not calibrated low enough to measure the temperature for all smoking operations—cold smoking or drying, for example.

## DIAL AND BABY-DIAL THERMOMETERS

The baby-dial thermometer is very useful to check the internal temperature of cooked sausage. When it is used in this way, you might say that it is a kind of a miniature meat thermometer. It has a temperature dial about the size of the face of a round wristwatch. The nail-like stem is more slender than that of the ovenproof meat thermometer, and there are other significant differences. The stem of the baby-dial thermometer will withstand very high temperatures, but the dial itself is delicate, and it cannot withstand the hot temperatures present inside a kitchen oven or hot smoke chamber. *Important:* Using this thermometer in such a hot environment will likely destroy or damage it.

On the positive side, the slender stem of the baby-dial does not leave a large hole in the meat. Additionally, the dial has a wider range than the ovenproof type, and it is calibrated in greater detail. This wider range allows you to observe the internal temperature of meat as it climbs from a very low temperature. If you use the special method of hot water cooking that is suggested in chapter 8, you will find the baby-dial thermometer very useful. This thermometer can also be used to check the internal temperature of meat being cooked in an oven or in a hot smoker; however, the meat must be removed from the oven or smoker before using the thermometer. The dial will show the internal temperature just a few seconds after it is inserted.

If the stem is inserted into a hole in the wall of the smoke chamber, the baby-dial can be used to monitor the internal chamber temperature for cold smoking and moderately hot smoking. However, for this purpose, it does not offer significant advantages over the liquid-in-glass thermometer.

The calibration of the baby-dial thermometer is from about $0°$ F (-$18°$ C) to $220°$ F ($104°$ C). You should be able to obtain a baby-dial from a mail-order establishment that deals in sausage-making equipment and supplies, a hardware store, or a store that sells culinary items.

A larger type of dial thermometer is calibrated in the same way as the baby-dial thermometer, and it can be used in its place for all applications. It has a longer and thicker stem, and it will probably cost over twice as much as a baby-dial. The dial of this thermometer is just as delicate as the dial of the baby-dial thermometer; it cannot be used inside an oven or in a hot smoke chamber.

As time passes, there are more and more varieties of dial thermometers on the market. With a little searching, a dial thermometer for almost any purpose can be found.

## DIGITAL STEM THERMOMETERS

Improving technology has made it possible to manufacture digital stem thermometers and sell them at a price that is competitive with dial thermometers. They do cost more than dial thermometers and require a battery, but many people do not hesitate to spend a little extra money for high-tech equipment.

## OVEN THERMOMETER

The temperature of a modern kitchen oven is usually controlled very well with the built-in oven thermostat. If you have doubts about the accuracy of your thermostat, check it with an oven thermometer. Oven thermometers are set on, or are attached to, an oven rack. If your oven has a glass door, position the thermometer so that it is visible through the glass. It may be easier to read with a flashlight.

## OTHER THERMOMETERS

Companies that offer sausage-making or food-smoking supplies will offer electronic or thermocouple-type thermometers at prices ranging from about $30 to $150. These thermometers are variously designed to measure such things as the smoke chamber temperature or the internal temperature of meats.

The inexpensive electronic thermometers with a probe and a cable that are used to measure the internal temperature of meat (shown in the photograph) are almost essential for water smoking and hot smoking. The type of retailers mentioned above offer these thermometers. However, because they are also useful in a kitchen, you will find them wherever kitchen equipment and supplies are sold. The advantage of using these electronic thermometers for water smoking and hot smoking is that the smoke chamber need not be opened to check the internal temperature of the meat. Heat is lost every time the chamber is opened, so the total cooking time will increase with every peek.

The probe is inserted into the meat that is cooking in the smoker, in the steamer, or in the oven. The cable connected to that probe plugs

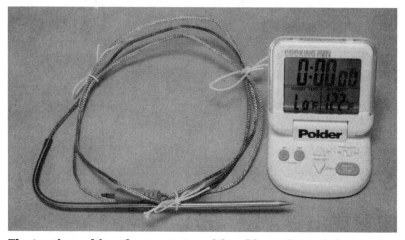

**Electronic cooking thermometer with cable-probe and timer.**

into a digital display unit placed on the outside of the smoker, steamer, or oven.

If you try your hand at making sausage, you will probably conclude that you do not want to be without this type of thermometer.

As mentioned previously, this electronic thermometer with a cable and a probe is very useful to measure the temperature of your refrigerator. It could also be used to monitor the smoke chamber temperature, but leaving it on continuously would require the batteries to be replaced more often.

# S Hooks

Products to be smoked can usually be laid on the racks in the smoke chamber, but some fare better if they are suspended from rods with butcher's twine. For example, beef tongue and whole chicken legs are two products that will be more attractive if they are hung in the smoker while being processed. S hooks are not essential for this, but they are convenient.

Hardware stores sell various sizes of S hooks. A homemade S hook that is sharpened to a point on one end is shown in chapter 8, page 137. A stainless-steel rod was used to make this hook. If the hooks are pointed, a piece of meat or a small whole fish can be hung directly on them.

# Meat Piercing Tool

Before starting to cure meat, it is best to pierce it *if:*

- The meat is covered with fat or marbled with fat.

- The meat is covered with membrane.

- It is covered by skin (poultry or tongue, for example).

- It is thick.

Piercing the meat allows the cure to penetrate more easily. The prongs of the piercing tool will make capillary-like

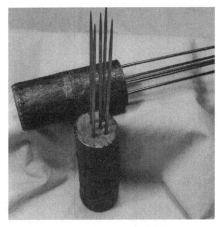

**Two homemade meat piercers.**

channels in the meat. The cure or marinade can penetrate faster by capillary action than by osmosis.

There are multipronged meat piercing tools called tenderizers. These tools work well in some applications, but the prongs are too short and too thick for others. Sausage prickers are available, but the tines are too short for thick pieces of meat. You may have to improvise or make one yourself. A strong fork with long, sturdy, and sharp tines is commonly used. A better tool would be such a fork with a comfortable handle attached to it. An ice pick or an awl makes a good piercing tool, but piercing takes more time because of the single point. The best option, I believe, is to make a meat piercing tool. It is not difficult.

## HOW TO MAKE A MEAT PIERCING TOOL

*Note:* While reading this description of how to make a meat piercing tool, you may wish to glance at the photograph from time to time. The two meat piercing tools pictured in the photo were made according to the following directions:

Get a piece of tree branch (or rounded wood) about 4 inches (10 cm) long and about 1¼ inches (3.5 cm) in diameter. Hardwood is preferred. Buy five round stainless-steel skewers, and use a hacksaw to cut them to 6 inches (15 cm) long. (Stainless-steel rods cut to the same length could be used, but they would have to be sharpened to a point with a grinder or a file.)

Cut the piece of branch in half so that there are two pieces about 2 inches (5 cm) long. Before you cut it, put a light pencil mark along the length. (You will use this pencil mark to align the two pieces later on when you glue them back together.)

Select an electric drill bit that is slightly smaller than the diameter of the skewers. Drill five holes through the wood on an end where it was cut in half. Insert the points of the skewers in the holes (again, on the end where it was cut in half), and tap them down, flush with the wood. Use a nail set, or a nail, and tap the rods down about ⅟₃₂ inch (1 mm) below the surface of the wood.

Use yellow carpenter's glue (Titebond II is a good brand) and two C clamps to join the two halves back together at the same place where the branch was cut in half. (Be sure to align the pencil marks.) Wait a day or so, remove the clamps, and then varnish the handle several times with polyurethane varnish, or paint it with enamel paint; this will waterproof the handle and make it attractive, durable, and easy to clean. After painting or varnishing, the handle may be washed in hot water, but it should not be soaked in water or washed in a dishwasher.

# Fish-Bone Tweezers

For fish lovers, there are few things more satisfying than well-prepared fish with few bones—or none. If fish are filleted, it is possible to reduce further the number of bones in each fillet. The size and species of fish determine the ease with which the bones can be located and extracted.

Fish-bone tweezers are very helpful to remove the row of thin bones that lie just above the centerline of the fillets of many species of fish. Run your fingers over the surface of the fillet while pressing down slightly. When you feel the sharp end of one of these bones, pull it out with the bone tweezers. The rib bones in the belly flaps of the fillets are usually sliced out with a knife. However, in some cases, the rib bones, too, can be pulled out with the tweezers.

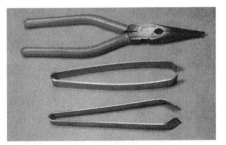

**Tools for removing fish bones: long-nose pliers and two styles of bone tweezers.**

Fish-bone tweezers are made of sturdy stainless steel. The bone gripping ends are bevel-sharpened, and they are about ½ inch (13 mm) wide. Sometimes the ends are angled, sometimes squared. Either style works well. You should be able to find these tweezers at a culinary supply store. Long-nose pliers, such as those shown in the photo, will do the job just as well. On some fillets, the pliers seem to work better because they grip the bone tightly without cutting through or breaking the bone.

# Volume-Measuring Equipment

You will need a set of American-standard (or metric-standard) measuring cups and spoons. Fluid ounce units are never used in this book. The British measuring system is never used.

Some kind of a bottle or jar with a mark on it to measure 1 quart (or 1 liter) will come in handy to measure water for brine solutions. A 1-liter soft drink bottle works well for this. A 1-gallon milk jug, or a 4-liter wine jug, is useful to measure water when you make a large quantity of brine.

All volume measurements are intended to be *level* measurements. One teaspoon of salt, for example, means 1 *level* teaspoon of salt.

# Salinometers

**A homemade salinometer (top) and a manufactured salinometer (bottom).**

A manufactured salinometer is a long glass tube with a weight in the bottom and a percentage scale inside the top of the transparent stem. Its purpose is to measure the amount of salt dissolved in water. A zero reading indicates that the water contains no salt. A 100 percent reading indicates that the water is saturated with salt, and no more salt can be dissolved. The manufactured salinometer is not recommended because it is very fragile and awkward to use. (In most cases, you would have to transfer some of the brine to a tall, small-diameter vessel so that the brine will be deep enough to float the instrument.)

### HOW TO MAKE A SALINOMETER

Nothing could be easier than making a salinometer. The homemade type is easier to use, is much less fragile, and can be made at no cost. You will need the following two materials: some dry sand and a small jar or bottle with a plastic screw-on lid. A small medicine jar or vitamin jar can be used. A fingernail polish bottle, especially one with a stem-like handle on the cap, is also excellent. The volume of the jar is not important. It may be glass or hard plastic; it may be transparent or opaque. The height of the jar should be about 2 inches (5 cm).

- Consult the brine tables in appendix 3, and make a small batch of 50 percent brine.

- Pour some dry sand in the jar, screw on the lid, and put it in the brine. Add or remove sand until the jar floats just enough for the lid to break the surface of the water. If you like, you can seal the lid permanently with a small amount of 100 percent silicon sealer. Finished!

You now have a salinometer calibrated to measure 50 percent brine strength, and you can now make 50 percent brine without having to measure either the water or the salt. If you discover that you need a little more brine than you had anticipated, it is easy to add a little more water, and then add salt until the salinometer rises to the surface again. Without this homemade salinometer, calculation and measuring would be required to increase the volume of the brine.

You can also use a homemade salinometer to replenish the salt in brine that was previously used; see page 123.

The most commonly used brine strength is about 50 percent, but you can use the same procedure to make another salinometer for stronger or weaker brine. They are very easy and inexpensive to make, so several can be made—one for each brine strength you will use. It is wise to use a permanent marker to indicate the brine strength that your salinometer was designed to measure.

## Knives

Knives are very important tools. They should be the proper shape and length to do the job at hand. If they are always kept sharp and used properly, your work will proceed efficiently and safely. At the most, four knives will do everything you have to do; you can probably get by with

**Knives (top to bottom)—boning knife (extra slender); stepped-blade knife; slicing knife; fish-filleting knife; and, at bottom, a Japanese fish-filleting knife for right-handed people.**

only two. They need not be expensive. Almost all of my knives were bought very cheaply at garage sales or Salvation Army–type stores. These used knives were high quality and in good condition. They had been discarded simply because they were dull.

Knives with plain edges are better than those with serrated cutting edges. Serrated edges tend to saw food rather than cut it cleanly. Furthermore, serrated blades are difficult or impossible to sharpen.

If the shank of a knife is at least 75 percent the length of the handle, it is one indication of a high-quality knife. If the knife has the typical riveted-wood handle, another indication of quality is three rivets in the handle rather than only two.

Knives should never be washed in a dishwasher, especially those that have wooden handles. The very hot water used for washing in a dishwasher, and the high heat used for drying, will gradually damage the wood by removing the natural oils. The loss of natural oils and the resultant cracking of the wood will cause the handle rivets to loosen.

If you are going to buy a knife, you may wish to consider the various materials used to make a knife blade.

## KNIFE BLADE MATERIAL

๑ **Carbon steel** is the choice of many because it holds its edge fairly well and is quite easy to sharpen. One disadvantage is that the blade will rust and tarnish—but if you use it often, it will not get a chance to rust, and most of the tarnish can be removed with steel wool. Another minor negative point is that a carbon-steel blade may impart a metallic taste and odor to acidic foods such as tomatoes, onions, and citrus fruits.

๑ **Stainless steel** that is used to make high-quality knives is not the same kind used to make your mixing bowls or rustproof mailbox. *Stainless steel* is a general term for many different alloys. Your mixing bowls are probably made with 18 percent chromium and 8 percent nickel. An alloy used to make high-quality stainless-steel knives might contain small amounts of molybdenum, vanadium, manganese, and carbon besides the chromium and nickel. In other words, *stainless steel* is not an exact term, but a high-quality stainless-steel knife will be made of an alloy that will hold its edge for a long time. This is good, of course. The other side of the coin is that a knife that holds its edge well, such as one made of high-quality stainless steel, will be difficult to sharpen once the edge is dull.

ᕔ **High-carbon stainless-steel** knives are among the most expensive. The steel used in these knives has the rust- and stain-resistant properties of ordinary stainless-steel knives, but they sharpen as easily as the carbon-steel knives. Of course, because they are easy to sharpen, they do not hold their edge as well as the common stainless-steel knives.

ᕔ **Ceramic** knives represent the leading edge of knife technology. Kyocera of Japan is a well-known manufacturer. The ceramic material used is very hard, and the cutting edges are very tough. Such knives are expensive, however. The price tag for a paring knife is about $50, while a chef's knife can cost over $150.

## BONING KNIFE

The term *boning knife* may be a slight misnomer. With its slender blade and length of 6 inches (15 cm) or less, it is a very handy knife for boning meat, but it is used more often to trim meat. For example, the first step in making bacon is to trim a slab of pork belly. Cutting out the gristle where the rib bones used to be is not difficult if a boning knife is used. The boning knife is one of the essential knives.

## SLICING KNIFE

It is difficult to do a good job of slicing meat such as ham, bacon, or pastrami unless you use a straight knife with a blade at least 12 inches (30 cm) long—longer is better. This, too, is an essential knife. With this knife and the boning knife described above, you can do everything that needs to be done.

## GENERAL-PURPOSE KNIFE

A knife with a blade about 8 inches (20 cm) long is good to have around for general use. A chef's knife, or some other kind of knife with a stepped blade, is a good choice. (A knife with a stepped blade is one whose cutting edge is considerably lower than its handle.) The stepped blade keeps your knuckles from banging on the cutting board or countertop. Such a knife is especially useful when you are cutting cubes of meat in preparation for grinding raw material for sausage.

### FILLETING KNIFE

A fish can be filleted with any of the knives described above, but what is the best knife for filleting? Most North Americans would say that a very sharp knife with a long, slender, and flexible blade is ideal. Many other people all over the world would agree, but not everyone.

The British, I understand, prefer a medium-length broad knife with a stiff blade. The Japanese use a short and broad stepped knife with the blade sharpened like a chisel (it is most certainly a strange-looking knife—see the photo earlier in this chapter, page 83). Japanese filleting knives for right-handed people are beveled on one side, and those for left-handed people are beveled on the other. If you often fillet large fish and prefer to cut through the rib bones, a knife with a thick blade will prove useful; thick blades will withstand the cutting of fish bones better than thin blades.

## Whetstone and Butcher's Steel

You will need a whetstone to keep your knives sharp. A Carborundum whetstone is inexpensive, and it is easily found at a culinary supply or hardware store. I suggest you buy one at least 8 inches (20 cm) long and 2 inches (5 cm) wide. A laminated stone that is coarse on one side and fine on the other is convenient. There are instructions for sharpening knives on page 145.

A butcher's steel (also called knife steel or sharpening steel) looks something like a long rat-tail file. Most sharpening steels will not remove metal from the knife blade, but they will straighten the edge curl that develops when a knife is used. The frequent use of a butcher's steel will prolong the sharpness of the blade. The longer the butcher's steel, the easier it is to use—especially for long knives. Ceramic rod is also used to make this knife-honing tool. Ceramic works equally well.

## Wire-Mesh Smoking Basket

One or more wire-mesh smoking baskets are very useful for smoking small items such as shrimp, scallops, oysters, nuts, and the like. They also work well for jerky. The Brinkmann Corporation offers wire-mesh smoking baskets as accessory equipment for its water smokers (see Italian shrimp on page 231). The baskets have a diameter of about 15½ inches (39 cm), and they are 2 inches (5 cm) deep. They are constructed of nickel-plated wire mesh with holes measuring about ¼ inch (7 mm). If you can't find them at a barbecue equipment shop, see appendix 5.

# Shaker—for Seasonings and Cures

A shaker—something like a common salt-shaker but with much larger holes—is very handy for applying seasoning to fresh meat or fish before smoking. It is also handy for applying *modern dry cure*. Just put in the proper amount of curing mixture and sprinkle it on the meat or fish. A homemade shaker (as shown in the photo) can be made easily, or one can be purchased at a culinary supply store. Some containers for grated Parmesan cheese make excellent shakers.

**Shaker—for seasonings and cures.**

# Basting Brushes

Basting brushes are useful when hot smoking and when cooking in a kitchen oven. When kippering salmon and some other kinds of fish, a yellowish white curd composed of water-soluble protein will appear on the surface of the flesh. This curd is ugly, but it is harmless, nutritious, and quite tasty. Nevertheless, it can be removed with a basting brush and a paper towel if you want to improve the appearance of the fish.

The best basting brushes are made of bleached natural bristle, and they look exactly like a paintbrush. Brushes with nylon bristles are a poor choice. Nylon will absorb moisture and become limp. The basting of hot meat will cause nylon bristles to curl permanently.

# Bagging Tape Machine

A bagging tape machine looks a little like a large dispenser for cellophane tape. However, its sole function is to put a piece of tape around the neck of a plastic bag that has been twisted closed.

The tape is installed in the machine upside down (the adhesive side of the tape is up). A plastic bag is twisted closed, and then it is

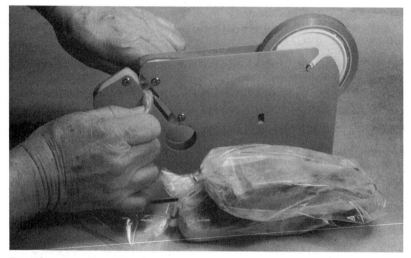

**Bagging tape machine.**

pressed down through a slot near the front of the machine. The tape automatically wraps around the twisted bag, and it is automatically cut off at the proper length; the bag is taped closed with just one downward movement.

The result looks professional, and it is very fast. If your smoking sessions frequently produce numerous pieces of product that must be individually bagged, this machine might be a wise investment. Vacuum-bagging equipment, ziplock bags, or bags closed with wire ties are alternative ideas.

# Curing Containers

If you are going to do either wet or dry curing, you will need some curing containers. It is probably best to gather these containers one at a time, because it is difficult for most people to foresee all their needs. The largest container you will need must be able to hold the largest object that you will smoke—a whole turkey, for example.

You may want to use the modern dry cure method to cure a moderate quantity of small items—25 pounds (11 kg) of pork hunks or salmon hunks, for example—in which case you could use one large container or several smaller ones. The brine curing of many small items can be done in one large container or in a smaller container using the same brine several times (after restrengthening the brine each time).

Containers for curing should be made of food-grade plastic, glass, enameled steel, stainless steel, or pottery. If pottery is used, it is best to use glazed pottery because it is easier to keep clean, and it will not absorb odors. Metal containers, other than a good grade of stainless steel, may impart a metallic taste to your product. Wooden containers were often used in the old days, but they are unsanitary and, like unglazed pottery, will absorb various odors that might be transmitted to your products. You may have containers around the house that will do very nicely for curing.

If you intend to buy containers, consider ones made of food-grade plastic that have tight-fitting lids. Another very important consideration is that the containers should fit into your refrigerator easily. Rectangular containers with flat tops make the best use of refrigerator space. Large food containers can be found in restaurant supply shops.

## Mortar and Pestle

Chemists, primarily, use the mortar and pestle. A pharmacist might use them occasionally, but not as much as he or she would have in the old days.

They come in handy for a person who smokes food, a sausage maker, or even a gourmet cook who

**Mortar and pestle.**

is fond of kitchen gadgets. Use the mortar and pestle to powder spices that are to be used in either wet or dry cures. Powdering a spice will cause more flavor to be released. Powdered spices are also good for making sausage because they are less visible and more uniformly distributed.

The mortar and pestle can be obtained from a laboratory supply company or chemical supply company. A pharmacist may be able to order a set for you. Often they are available at large culinary supply stores.

## Butane Lighter

A butane lighter with a long nose is almost a necessity for lighting propane burners. It is very convenient for lighting charcoal and wood. Such lighters can be purchased in hardware stores, or wherever barbecue or fireplace equipment is sold.

# CHAPTER 5

# Supplies

You will need a number of consumable items. Your exact needs will depend on what you are going to smoke, the curing and other techniques you will employ, and the seasonings you wish to use.

## Salt

One of the best kinds of salt to use for all curing purposes is the kind known as *pickling salt* or *canning salt*. This salt is over 99 percent pure, and it contains no iodine or other additives. Equally acceptable is *non-iodized table salt* (also known as *plain salt*); only a free-flow agent (usually calcium silicate or magnesium carbonate) is added. This salt, too, is also over 99 percent pure. When used for curing, the impurities or additives in salt, depending on the kind and amount, can cause discoloration and bitterness in fish and, to a lesser extent, in meats. The free-flow agent will cause no problems.

A 5-pound (2.27 kg) box of pickling salt can be obtained in most grocery stores for about $1.50. A 25-pound (11.35 kg) bag of table salt (containing the acceptable free-flow agent) can be purchased at a wholesale grocery store for about $3.50. There are few reasons to use anything other than one of these two varieties for curing. Iodized salt and sea salt contain minerals that are good for you, but they are not the best salts for curing fish and meat.

Pickling salt and table salt are fine-grain salts. Fine-grain salts are best for the following reasons:

🔥 Fine-grain crystals dissolve faster than large crystals.

🔥 Fine-grain salt can be measured accurately by volume.

◊ Fine-grain salt is necessary for the modern dry cure method of curing.

◊ Fine-grain salt is required for sausage making.

Meat-curing formulas dating back 100 years, or even earlier, are still being printed in today's books. To maintain authenticity, rock salt is specified if rock salt was called for in the original formula—and it probably was. In days past, rock salt was commonly used because it was the purest form of salt available, and the purity of the distinctly cubic-shaped crystals could be judged by eye. If the tug of nostalgia tempts you to try some of these recipes, just remember that you will get the same result by using fine-grain salt. There is nothing magic about rock salt.

Kosher salt, especially flaked kosher salt, is quite acceptable for curing because it is a pure salt with no additives. The only negative point is that it will not dissolve as quickly as the fine-grain salt mentioned above. However, if you need to use it for religious reasons, or if you want to use it because you believe that it has a better flavor, you can rest assured that it will do an excellent job of curing. (Numerous gourmands believe that kosher salt tastes better than either plain or iodized salt.)

Store salt in a tightly sealed plastic bag to protect it from humidity. Pure salt may become lumpy even if it is stored in a plastic bag, but its quality will not be diminished. Storage time does not lessen the quality, either, so don't hesitate to buy a large quantity if that is most economical.

If it becomes lumpy, break the lumps and use it. The best way to deal with lumpy salt, sugar, or spices is to put the seasoning into a strainer or a flour sifter, and then break the lumps. If the seasoning passes through the wire mesh, it is fine enough to use. This technique also works well for curing blends that have been premixed in bulk. Such cures often become lumpy when stored.

## Sweeteners

Some kind of sweetener is a basic ingredient in all good cures and in many seasoning blends. Sweeteners help to tenderize meat; they counteract the toughening caused by salt. Sweeteners also mellow the harsh taste of salt. Although a sweetener is a basic ingredient for a cure, the kind of sweetener used is a matter of preference and availability. If a certain kind of sweetener is called for in a formula, feel free to substitute another kind.

## WHITE SUGAR

Whenever the word *sugar* is used in this book, understand it to mean the common granulated white sugar made from either sugarcane or sugar beets. In some countries—but not the United States—nongranulated white sugar is more common than the granulated type. If the nongranulated type is used, and if you measure by volume, pack it in the measuring cup or measuring spoon. Use about 10 percent more to achieve the same degree of sweetness.

## BROWN SUGAR

Dark brown sugar has a stronger taste than light brown sugar because of the addition of molasses. Using one of these sugars can impart a slightly different flavor nuance to your product. Brown sugar is usually not granulated. Nongranulated brown sugar should be packed firmly in the measuring spoon so that the measurements will be consistent from batch to batch.

## HONEY

If you have ever tasted honey-cured ham or bacon, you already know the special flavor that only honey can impart. Use honey as a sweetener in any curing or seasoning operation if you think it will help to achieve your flavor goal. Keep in mind, however, that honey is the sweetest of the sweeteners; a one-to-one substitution for another sweetener might make your product a little too sweet. If honey is substituted for granulated sugar, reduce the amount by 20 percent.

If honey has crystallized, liquefy it by putting the jar in a pan of hot water for a few hours. If you need to liquefy it faster than that, use a microwave oven at full power, and zap it 15 seconds at a time until the honey is clear. Of course, if the honey jar is not made of glass, you will need to use a microwave-proof dish.

## CORN SYRUP

In this book, corn syrup is used as a sweetener and a binder in sausage making. You will find more information about corn syrup in chapter 12.

## MAPLE SYRUP

I truly enjoy ham and bacon when it is cured with honey, but I think I like it just a little better cured with maple syrup. In my opinion, the maple syrup can be either the real stuff or imitation. The syrup you can concoct yourself (using imitation maple flavor, brown sugar, water, and corn syrup) is also excellent for curing. I can certainly distinguish between real maple syrup and the imitation type when I eat it on pancakes or waffles, but not when it is used as a meat-curing ingredient.

To retard mold formation on either natural maple syrup or homemade maple syrup, store it in the refrigerator or freezer. If it crystallizes, liquefy it as you would liquefy honey (see above).

### IMITATION MAPLE FLAVOR

When making maple-syrup-cured bacon or ham, the addition of about ½ teaspoon (2.5 ml) of imitation maple flavor per pound (450 g) of meat will enhance the maple aroma of these products. Add this imitation flavor to the modern dry cure blend at the same time as the maple syrup. This flavoring can be found in almost any grocery store where spices and flavorings are displayed.

### MOLASSES

Light, unsulfured molasses is preferred. The next best is mild-flavored unsulfured molasses; this is more common, and it is easier to buy. Full-flavored or dark molasses has a stronger taste—unsulfured is best. Blackstrap molasses has a very strong flavor that many people find disagreeable, particularly if it is sulfured.

## Spices and Herbs

For most of us, there is no clear distinction between the word *spice* and the word *herb*, especially when the subject is seasoning for food. Even the experts do not always agree. If I were to try to distinguish between the two words, the most likely result would be that your eyelids would begin to droop, and I would be in need of a tranquilizer. It is more fun to talk about food smoking than about semantics, so let's use the word *spices* to mean "spices and herbs."

Certain smoked foods can't be made unless many kinds of spices are used; pastrami is one example. On the other hand, all meats, poultry, and fish can be seasoned exquisitely without using a speck of spice. The kinds of spices you will need depends on your taste, your smoking objectives, and your desire for culinary adventure. Appendix 1 contains a list of spices commonly used in smoking and sausage making.

The curing, seasoning, and marinating formulas in this book will suggest certain spices. If you have experience with the suggested spices, and if you can imagine the resulting taste, you should make changes to match your preferences. If you can't imagine the taste of the finished product, but you want to try the suggested seasonings, you should make a small batch of the product. In fact, it is wise to make a small batch anytime you make a product for the first time.

Some people believe that the only spice they need is nothing more than good ol' black pepper. Other people believe that nothing less than a treasure chest of spices will do. For most of us, the variety of spices we need lies somewhere between these two extremes. In any case, the dried spices should be of good quality.

As far as quality is concerned, we have little choice but to trust the reputation of the brand. Very few of us are qualified to judge the quality of a spice by peering through the glass or plastic container.

The freshness of dried spices is, to some extent, under our control. Often, there is an expiration date on the spice container. If you have some spices sitting around the house and the dates have passed, or if you have no idea how old they are, the best thing to do is to throw them out.

The company that processes and packs the spice decides the expiration date. The expertise of specialists in the company is used to determine the shelf life of the particular spice. They assume that the spice will be tightly sealed, struck by an average amount of light, and exposed to room temperature. If the actual storage conditions are worse than expected, the spice will go bad faster. If the actual storage conditions are better than they expected, the particular spice may be usable well past the expiration date.

In summary, the freshness and shelf life of the spices you use can be greatly extended by following these suggestions:

↳ Buy your spices at retail outlets that have a rapid turnover of goods. Dried spices sold at such stores are likely to be fresher than those sold at mom-and-pop-type retailers.

↳ Buy spices in quantities that will be consumed in a reasonable time so that the length of storage time before consumption is minimized.

↳ Buy a brand name you trust, or get your spices from a distributor you trust.

◊ Check the expiration date. The expiration dates on the containers sitting on the same shelf of the grocery store may vary considerably, even if it is the same spice with the same brand name. The spices toward the back of the display may be fresher than those toward the front. The expiration date is sometimes stamped on the bottom of the container.

◊ Keep the spice in a container with a tight-fitting lid, preferably a screw-on lid, even if this necessitates transferring the spice to a different container. This will help to protect the spices from humidity, and it will help to retard the evaporation and deterioration of aromatic oils.

◊ If there is space available, store spices in the refrigerator or freezer. This will help to protect them from the other two enemies of spices: heat and light.

# Paper Towels

The use of paper towels is mentioned in countless places in this book. They are very useful and convenient. They are labor saving because they are disposable. Nevertheless, paper towels are not essential. If there are instructions to blot or wrap meat with paper towels, the same thing can be accomplished with a clean cloth.

If cloth is used, use 100 percent cotton cloth—either white or unbleached. Avoid using dyed cloth. Lightweight dishtowel material or lightweight muslin works well. New material may have been treated with fabric conditioners, so it should be laundered before using.

These blotting cloths or wrapping cloths can be washed and used repeatedly. Drying them well in sunlight or in a hot dryer will sterilize them, but you may want to boil them for a few minutes before drying them.

# Newspaper

There are many uses for newspaper, so it is wise to keep a good supply on hand. When processing meat, fowl, and fish, the raw material is often wrapped with paper towels and newspaper to absorb the excess moisture. You will also find newspaper useful when you want to put a greasy smoker rack or a greasy smoker basket on a table. Several layers of newspaper under a cutting board will absorb any blood or juices that dribble off the board.

# Twine

Cotton twine of the type used to tie rolled roasts is known as butcher's twine. You will find it useful for the following purposes:

❧ To truss poultry legs and wings (when processing a whole bird).

❧ To hang meat in the smoke chamber.

❧ To net-tie large pieces of meat and large sausages.

❧ To seal plastic bags and tie thermometers (when using the hot water cooker).

The diameter of the twine need not be large; I use 1 mm (0.04 inch—between $\frac{1}{32}$ and $\frac{1}{16}$ inch) twine for everything. You can get this at a culinary supply shop, but you might discover that a large spool of twine is cheaper at a hardware store.

## Sodium Nitrite

If you intend to use the curing method known as *brine curing* (also called *wet curing* or *sweet pickle curing*), you may wish to use sodium nitrite ($NaNO_2$), as specified in some of the brine cure formulations. The two main functions of this additive are to fix the red or pink color of the meat and to protect against botulism. Food-grade (or USP grade—United States Pure grade) sodium nitrite should be used. You may be able to order it at a pharmacy, but you will likely find it easier to obtain from a chemical supply firm such as Nurnberg Scientific. Check the yellow pages or go to www.nurnberg.com on the Internet to find the closest location. *Important:* Make sure that you don't order sodium nitrate ($NaNO_3$) by mistake.

Making homemade curing powder (homemade Prague Powder #1) is another use for sodium nitrite. To do this, see the following two sections. Also, for additional information on nitrites and nitrates, turn to chapter 6.

## Curing Powder (Prague Powder #1)

The following is a bit technical, but a basic understanding of curing powders is necessary for those who use them.

Curing powders, also known as *cures*, normally contain either sodium nitrite ($NaNO_2$) or a combination of sodium nitrite and sodium nitr*ate* ($NaNO_3$). These preparations are widely used by commercial meat processors, amateur smokers, and sausage makers. Some curing formulations in this book will specify a curing powder for products cured by a method known as *modern dry cure*. Also, some sausage formulas presented in this book require a curing powder.

The nitrites or nitrates in the curing powders are largely responsible for the pink color of ham, bacon, luncheon meats, and some types of sausages. The red color of corned beef, and the reddish color of most commercially produced jerky, is also caused by sodium nitrite. Without these chemicals, all of the fully cooked meats mentioned above would be brownish or grayish like ordinary cooked meat. The lean part of bacon, for example, would turn brown while cooking; luncheon meats would not be pink—they would be brownish. (Correctly speaking, chemicals that occur naturally in smoke and certain seasonings will provide some color fixing. Consequently, smoked products may be slightly pink or red, especially near the surface, even if nitrites and nitrates are not used.)

Meats cured with nitrites or nitrates also have a distinctive flavor that many people like. (The flavor difference can be readily understood by comparing the taste of cured ham with that of roast pork.) Furthermore, rancidity is inhibited, shelf life is extended, and positive protection against botulism is provided with the proper use of these additives.

Despite all the benefits provided by these curing chemicals, they are harmful if used in *large* quantities. Fortunately, it takes only a very small amount to obtain the desired result, and the amount of these chemicals specified in this book is considered safe. Nevertheless, if you never eat commercially processed meats because of the additives they contain, then you may not want to use a curing powder in your products. If you make that decision, however, you should forgo making *smoked* sausage, because *smoked* sausage without the addition of nitrites or nitrates presents a considerable risk of botulism poisoning. It could prove fatal.

I mentioned above that nitrites and nitrates are used in very small amounts. In fact, the amount required to cure 2½ pounds (1.135 kg) of ground meat is so small (approximately ¹⁄₃₂ teaspoon) that it can only be weighed accurately with scales found in a scientific laboratory or in a pharmacy. This is obviously impractical for either the amateur smoker or a small commercial processor, and it is not possible to accurately measure such a small amount with a measuring spoon.

To overcome this obstacle, several companies have mixed 16 parts (by weight) of salt with 1 part (by weight) of sodium nitrite ($NaNO_2$) to make a product containing 6.25 percent sodium nitrite. Such a blend that uses salt as a carrier can be measured with reasonable accuracy by using measuring spoons commonly found in the household kitchen. Only ½ teaspoon (2.5 ml) of this curing powder blend will cure 2½ pounds (1.135 kg) of ground meat. *Prague Powder #1, Modern Cure,* and *Insta Cure #1* are three brands of curing powder that contain 6.25 percent sodium nitrite. These curing powders often have pink food color added so that they will not be confused with salt. Consequently, curing powder is sometimes called *pink powder*.

Whenever Prague Powder #1 is specified in this book, you may use any brand of curing powder that contains 6.25 percent sodium nitrite. These commercial curing powders are available by mail order from establishments that offer sausage-making or smoking equipment (see appendix 5). Butcher supply firms often sell curing powder; check out *butcher supplies* in the yellow pages. You may also be able to obtain it from sausage-making establishments. You will not find these products in a common grocery store.

Some curing products that contain a very low percentage of sodium nitrite (about 0.5 percent) in the salt carrier are available in grocery stores. However, such products are not recommended because (if used as directed by the manufacturer) they allow very little control of the salt content in your products. Your products will probably be too salty.

Prague Powder #2 and Insta Cure #2 contain sodium nitrate in addition to sodium nitrite. These special curing powders are mainly used for fermented sausages. Fermented sausages are not covered in this book, so these curing powders will not be used.

# Homemade Curing Powder

I recommend that you buy a commercially prepared curing powder even if you live in a country where it is not available locally, and you have to obtain it by international mail. However, it is possible to make curing powder. The only ingredients you will need are pure, fine-grain, noniodized salt and food-grade sodium nitrite ($NaNO_2$). You need to go to a pharmacy or chemical supply firm in your country and place an order for that chemical. When the sodium nitrite arrives, take the non-iodized salt with you, and ask a pharmacist to weigh 16 parts of salt per

1 part of sodium nitrite: 16 ounces of salt and 1 ounce of sodium nitrite, for example, or 480 g of salt and 30 g of sodium nitrite. The scales used in a pharmacy in all countries measure grams, so it is best to use the metric system when requesting help from a pharmacist.

Take these measured ingredients home, and blend them in a large mixing bowl. Make sure that the mixture is free of lumps. Stir it very well until you are sure it is *perfectly uniform.* Use a wire whisk or use an electric mixer at low speed.

In Japan, I used this homemade curing powder for several years until I finally found a Canadian supplier for Prague Powder #1 that was willing to ship overseas. Nowadays, the Internet makes it much easier to locate a supplier that is willing to ship to anywhere in the world.

When curing powders are commercially produced, a special process is used to bond the proper ratio of salt and sodium nitrite into each crystal so that the blend will always remain uniform. This is the main advantage of using the commercially prepared curing powders, and why I recommend them. A perfectly uniform curing powder helps to ensure that the correct amount of nitrite is added to the product. (For additional information, see chapter 6.)

# Vitamin C and Related Chemicals

Ascorbic acid (vitamin C) and two chemicals related to this acid are permitted by the U.S. Department of Agriculture for use in meat processing. All of these substances function to *accelerate color development.* They also *stabilize the color* during storage. These two effects can be very important for commercial processors. Rapid color development may lead to reduced processing time. Greater color stability can result in a product remaining attractive even after days of storage in refrigerated display cases that are struck with artificial light. Without the use of one of these chemicals, the color may fade rapidly, and the product will not be marketable.

The chemicals referred to above that are related to vitamin C are sodium erythorbate and sodium ascorbate. You will often see vitamin C or one of these two chemicals listed as an ingredient on packages of processed meat.

A person who processes meats as a hobby has little need for these chemicals, so they are not specified for use in this book. Nevertheless, their mention is deserved because some people have the mistaken impression that vitamin C (ascorbic acid) will function as a color developer (color fixer) in place of nitrites or nitrates. There is at least one book on sausage making and one book on food smoking that says ¼ teaspoon of vitamin C per 5 pounds of ground pork or ground beef will cause the pink or reddish color of the meat to be fixed. It won't; I tried it.

Apparently, someone in the past thought that a color accelerator was the same thing as a color developer. It is not. None of these chemicals will function as a color developer (color fixer). Furthermore, it must be emphasized that neither vitamin C nor the two related chemicals will provide protection against botulism.

If you need accelerated color development or improved color stability, you may, of course, use one of these three chemicals along with Prague Powder #1 or sodium nitrite. Vitamin C is the least desirable because it can cause depletion of nitrite. Either sodium erythorbate or sodium ascorbate is most often used.

Your pharmacist, or a chemical supply company, may be able to order some for you; such chemicals are not available at amateur sausage supply shops. If you must use vitamin C, be sure to use pure crystalline powder. No matter which one of the three is used, you should add ⅛ teaspoon (0.625 ml) to 2½ pounds (1.135 kg) of meat. The ⅛ teaspoon of the chemical should not be added directly to the meat. Instead, it should be thoroughly mixed with the seasoning ingredients first; this will result in a more uniform distribution.

# Liquid Smoke

Liquid smoke is something you may want to add to your list of supplies. It can be used in marinades, added to brines, or applied directly. Jerky recipes often have liquid smoke as an ingredient because many people use their kitchen oven to dry the meat. If a kitchen oven is used, the application of liquid smoke is the only way for the meat to get a smoke flavor.

Water smokers do not impart as much smoke flavor as a regular smoker, so you may want to use a little of the liquid smoke to boost the smoky aroma of a water smoked product. This is especially true if the smoking time is short.

Most large grocery stores offer Wright's Liquid Smoke, but liquid smoke other than this hickory aroma (mesquite, for example) can be obtained from some companies that offer sausage-making supplies.

# CHAPTER 6

# Health
# Matters

In this age, the average adult in any modern country is aware of germs and the most common diseases related to food. Most adults are aware that sanitation prevents the spread of disease, and they know that refrigeration retards spoilage. They are also aware, for example, that it is dangerous to eat raw or undercooked pork. This level of knowledge helps to keep us healthy.

The amateur food smoker, however, needs to have a bit more knowledge about such matters than the average person does. This is because food smoking involves subjecting the food to conditions that come close to the limits of safe handling. For example:

ᚦ Fresh meat and fish are refrigerated (while curing) for a period of time that may exceed the normal refrigeration time.

ᚦ Meat is commonly smoked in a warm smoker for several hours.

ᚦ Meat is cooked until it is safe to eat, but just barely safe. This is particularly true for some varieties of sausage.

Reading this chapter will not qualify a person to become a public health specialist, and it does not cover all of the health hazards related to food, but it will provide information that an amateur food smoker needs know.

Some of the following information may cause concern because it deals with potential health problems related to food. I hope that it will be reassuring for me to mention that in all of the years that I have smoked food, not once has the product spoiled during processing, and not once has a product caused food poisoning or any other health-related problem. If safe food-handling guidelines are practiced, food smoking does not pose any more of a health risk than common cooking.

# Trichinosis

The parasitic disease known as trichinosis is most often associated with eating undercooked pork. About 1 percent of hogs in the United States are infected, and one of the main reasons is that pigs are sometimes fed uncooked garbage containing raw pork scraps. Well-informed hunters usually know that bear meat can also harbor these nasty little larvae. Trichinae may be present in the meat of any warm-blooded omnivorous animal, and they exist even in the meat of some carnivorous animals and warm-blooded marine animals such as the seal.

The larvae in consumed meat will mature into adult roundworms in the small intestine of the host animal—or human host. Some of the females will bore a hole in the small intestine of the host and deposit eggs. The resulting larvae enter the bloodstream and burrow into the tissue of various voluntary muscles. The host, as a defense mechanism, forms a coating around each larva. This coating, with the roundworm larva inside, is known as a cyst. In time, the cysts usually become calcified on the outside. The larvae, inside the cysts, remain in the muscles in a dormant condition. If the raw or undercooked flesh of this animal is eaten, the cycle repeats itself.

The cysts, each containing a coiled larva, are about ⅟₅₀ inch (0.51 mm) long. That is about half the length of the comma in this sentence, more or less. Therefore, they are essentially invisible to the naked eye. The U.S. INSPECTED AND PASSED stamp means nothing as far as trichinosis is concerned: The inspection does not include microscopic examination of the flesh of each hog. Furthermore, even if the flesh of each animal were to be inspected by microscope, cysts may be overlooked.

A drug has been developed to treat trichinosis, but it is much better to avoid contracting the disease in the first place. Intestinal disorders followed by chronic muscular pain are two of the many possible symptoms. This is the bad news. The good news is that it is very easy to kill trichinae before they cause problems. There is no danger in eating pork that has been treated by cooking it properly or by freezing it according to USDA instructions that are described below.

The common way to protect positively against trichinosis is to heat each piece of meat (from susceptible animals) to a *minimum* internal temperature of 137° F (58.4° C) *throughout.* To be even safer, commercially produced "fully cooked" meats such as hams and sausages are usually heated to a minimum internal temperature of between 152° and 154° F (67° and 68° C). When we cook pork in the oven or in a frying pan, the internal temperature usually climbs even higher than this.

Another way to kill trichinae in pork is to freeze it according to USDA regulations. Any one of the following USDA-approved freezing procedures will definitely kill all the trichinae in pork:

- -20° F (-28.9° C) for 12 days.

- -10° F (-23.4° C) for 20 days.

- 5° F (-15° C) for 30 days.

You may freeze the pork in your home freezer if your freezer temperature is cold enough and you are able to accurately measure and monitor the temperature. Alternatively, you can ask your butcher to order some *Certified Pork.* Certified Pork has been frozen according to the USDA regulations, and it will not cause trichinosis even if it is eaten raw.

Chain grocery stores may not be able to provide you with Certified Pork because it is not on the list of items for which the butchers can make a special order. However, local meat distributors or meatpackers might be able to supply it, especially if they supply local sausage makers. An independently owned grocery store or butcher shop is another possible source. The most commonly available cut of Certified Pork is pork shoulder (Boston butt), and it is usually sold by the carton; one carton contains several frozen shoulders. Be sure that it has some kind of tag, label, or stamp that reads CERTIFIED PORK.

There is only one case where Certified Pork, or the equivalent, *must* be used: when the finished, ready-to-eat product contains uncooked pork. Examples of this are some varieties of fermented sausages. For all other products, use a meat thermometer to make sure that the pork is fully cooked.

Note that in the above discussions of freezing meat to kill trichinae, I used the word *pork.* Strains of trichinae found in some wild animals (especially those that live in cold or arctic climates) may be more resistant to freezing temperatures than the strains found in the domesticated swine. It is risky, therefore, to use the USDA freezing method to kill trichinae in the meat of susceptible *wild* animals such as bear. Kill the trichinae by making sure that the meat is heated to *at least* 137° F (58.4° C) throughout. Better yet—heat it to 160° F (71.1° C).

If you intend to process bear meat, you may be interested in the results of a study by a Montana State University researcher. The study was conducted from 1984 through 1989, and it consisted of inspecting the meat from 275 bears. *Bears infested with trichinae accounted for 15.6 percent of the total.* In another study, this time by the University of Washington, it was reported that trichinae in bear meat may survive the USDA freezing regulations for pork. Be safe: Cook meat from potentially infested wild animals; don't depend on freezing to kill those insidious roundworm larvae.

You should never put raw or undercooked meat from susceptible animals in your mouth, even though you intend to just taste it and spit it out. Furthermore, always wash the cutting board and knives with hot water and dish detergent if they have been exposed to such meat.

# Fish Parasites

Freshwater fish often harbor parasites that are harmful to humans. Harmful parasites in ocean fish exist, but humans are only rarely infected. Farmed ocean fish are less likely to have harmful parasites than wild fish. Use caution with wild salmon, in particular. It should be cooked or frozen as indicated below.

Parasites that exist in fish can be killed easily and rendered harmless. Two methods are available: Heat the fish to a minimum of 140° F (60° C), or freeze the fish at -10° F (-23.3° C) for seven days. If fish are hot smoked properly, any parasites present will be killed during the smoking process. If fish are only cold smoked (such as Scotch-style salmon), it is prudent to use commercially frozen fish because most home freezers will not freeze at -10° F (-23.3° C).

# Tularemia

Tularemia (also known as rabbit fever) is a disease of rodents. It is caused by a bacterium that can be transmitted to other animals and humans. If humans contract this disease, it is most often due to handling infected animals or eating the undercooked flesh of infected animals. Tick bites, or bites from bloodsucking flies, can also cause tularemia infection.

This disease can bring on a high fever, chills, headaches, vomiting, swollen lymph nodes, and various skin problems. Fortunately, it is not fatal, and antibiotics will bring about dramatic recovery.

Wild rabbits are the greatest source of tularemia infection for a person who smokes wild game. If you handle wild rabbits, be sure to wear rubber or plastic gloves with no holes in them; it is believed that these bacteria can penetrate even healthy and uncut human skin. After the rabbit meat is cooked as well as you would cook pork, it is perfectly safe to touch and, of course, eat.

# Food Poisoning

## SALMONELLA

Salmonella food poisoning is common. (It is sometimes mistakenly called ptomaine poisoning.) The U.S. Public Health Service estimates that there are as many as two million cases of salmonella food poisoning every year in the United States, and its incidence is increasing. It is rarely fatal, but it can cause death in infants, older people, and people who are in poor health. With a little care by those who handle, prepare, and process food, however, there is little need to fear this disease.

Salmonella has no connection with salmon. The physician who did most of the initial research on these bacteria was named Dr. Salmon, and the bacteria were named in his honor. There are about 400 kinds of bacteria in the salmonella family, and several of them cause the common salmonella food poisoning.

These bacteria cause gastrointestinal infection. The symptoms may range from mild intestinal cramps to very severe diarrhea. Symptoms usually begin 6 to 48 hours after eating the contaminated food, and they persist for 4 to 16 hours. The right kind of antibiotic for this bacterial infection can provide a very effective cure.

The salmonella organisms that cause food poisoning most often occur in eggs (especially eggs that have a crack in their shell). They can also be found in poultry, meat, and other kinds of animal products such as whipped cream, as well as in contaminated water. The bacteria cannot be detected by odor, and they can survive in frozen and dried foods. If salmonella bacteria are present, they will multiply at temperatures between 40° and 140° F (4.4° and 60° C). Temperatures that approximate the temperature of the human body are most favorable for their proliferation.

Salt and sugar help to prevent the growth of salmonella and other microorganisms. Furthermore, if the meat or fish is drying while it is being processed, the growth of microorganisms is further discouraged. Consequently, if a product is smoked at temperatures between 40° and

140° F (4.4° and 60° C), it should contain a substantial amount of salt and sugar, and it should not be smoked with humid air. Do not smoke foods in a water smoker below 140° F (60° C).

To prevent salmonella poisoning:

- Keep all utensils clean, especially the cutting boards. Be sure to wash them after they are exposed to raw meat.

- Avoid cracked eggs unless they will be heated to an internal temperature of 165° F (74° C).

- Store food at 40° F (4° C) or below.

- Thaw meat in a refrigerator, or use the cold water thawing method (see chapter 8, page 139). Microwave thawing is safe, but it is not recommended for the thawing of material that will be smoked.

- Do not let raw meat touch other foods.

- Keep hot foods hot.

- Refrigerate or discard leftovers immediately.

Following these simple precautions from the first stage of processing to the point of consumption will greatly reduce the risk of salmonella poisoning and poisoning from other varieties of bacteria. To reduce the risk to zero is impossible, even if you become a strict vegetarian.

Some other food poisoning diseases that are caused by bacteria are campylobacteriosis, listeriosis, perfringens, botulism, and *E. coli* O-157. The latter two require additional explanation.

## BOTULISM

*Botulism* is a word that was coined in 1896 when Dr. Emile van Ermengem was investigating the cause of food poisoning related to the eating of German sausages. *Botulus* means "sausage" in Latin.

Botulism is a form of food poisoning that is often fatal. Eating improperly canned foods is the common cause. Another cause is eating preserved foods that have been improperly processed and packed in an airtight plastic package or in an airtight casing. Commercially prepared foods rarely cause botulism because of the precautions taken by commercial processors. Foods improperly processed at home, particularly home-canned foods, are the main culprits.

There are no food-processing procedures in this book that may lead to the formation of botulin, the toxin that causes botulism. However, the processing of smoked sausage could result in botulism if the specified nitrite curing powder is not used.

*Clostridium botulinum* bacterium spores are everywhere. They are in the soil, on fruit and vegetables, and on meat and fish. Consequently, they are also found in the human intestines. The spores themselves are harmless; the poison, called botulin, is created only when the spores reproduce. In order for the spores to multiply, several conditions must exist *at the same time:* an airtight environment, a certain temperature range, a favorable chemical environment (nonacidic, for example), and a period of storage favorable for reproduction. The processed food will be free of the toxin if *any one* of these required conditions is eliminated.

None of the processes mentioned in this book specify packing the food in a perfectly airtight container such as a can or a sealed canning jar. Tightly sealed plastic bags or vacuum packs are suggested for use while cooking, refrigerating, or freezing the product; nevertheless, they are never suggested for storing or processing foods under conditions that might cause spores to reproduce. However, sausage casing that is packed tightly and sealed tightly can approximate an airtight container, so caution is prudent for sausages that will be smoked. The smoking temperature and lengthy smoking time could encourage spore reproduction.

Fortunately, there is a very easy way to make smoked sausage perfectly safe: Change its chemical composition in a way that will positively prevent toxin formation.

There are several ways to do this, but most of these approaches would make the sausage taste awful. There is one way, however, to change the chemical composition of the sausage and make it taste even better: Add a very small amount of sodium nitrite ($NaNO_2$). Toxin formation is positively prevented if a specified amount of this chemical is mixed with the raw sausage. *Not one person has ever been known to contract botulism after eating sausage properly treated with sodium nitrite.* You can feel confident that sausage properly treated with this chemical will be free of the toxin.

The commercially produced curing powder known as Prague Powder #1 is recommended for treating the sausage. Used as directed, it will impart exactly the right amount of sodium nitrite into the sausage. The sausage will be wholesome and free of botulin. (Commercial meat processors are required to use sodium nitrite in cooked sausage and luncheon meats, as mandated by the Federal Drug Administration.)

If you decide that you will not use chemical additives for processing your smoked products, you should also decide that you will not make *smoked* sausage. Untreated raw sausage (also called fresh sausage) can be made, cooked, and eaten safely—even if it is stuffed in casings. However, smoked sausage made without the above-mentioned nitrite may be deadly because, as mentioned above, the sausage is usually smoked for a long time in the temperature range that encourages spore reproduction and toxin formation.

### *E. COLI* O-157

I had never heard of this bacterium until the summer of 1996. In that year, it became headline news in Japan. Almost 10,000 Japanese became ill, and at least 11 people died. Later, I found out that 700 people suffered the same kind of food poisoning in the United States in 1993 after they ate undercooked ground beef at a hamburger sandwich chain.

*E. coli* O-157 is a new strain of the intestinal bacteria that are known collectively as *E. coli*. Most of these bacteria are either harmless or cause temporary intestinal discomfort and diarrhea. However, one of them acquired genes that enabled it to cause severe illness in human beings. In 1982, U.S. scientists isolated it and labeled this new strain. They called it *E. coli* O-157.

Food poisoning caused by *E. coli* O-157 is much more severe than that caused by salmonella food poisoning, and it is very difficult for doctors to treat; antibiotics can worsen the condition. Symptoms appear many days after consuming the contaminated food.

It is certainly not a common cause of food poisoning in the United States or in the world as a whole, but health authorities believe it will become much more common in the future. For this reason, it deserves a mention.

Continuing research will clarify much of the mystery surrounding this new health threat, but there are some useful facts available at this time. It appears that nonchlorinated water and almost any food can become contaminated with *E. coli* O-157 bacteria, but meat—particularly beef—deserves special attention. About 1 percent of healthy cattle have O-157 in their intestines. Improper slaughtering can cause contamination of the meat. If this contaminated meat touches other food, directly or indirectly, contamination can spread.

Fortunately, good food-handling practices can greatly reduce the risk of exposure to *E. coli* O-157. The same precautions used to reduce the risk of salmonella food poisoning are equally effective for *E. coli* O-157.

# Nitrites and Nitrates

At least as early as Roman times, impure salts that were mined from certain locations were used to cure meats. The salts from some of these locations were prized for their ability to flavor meats and to give them a reddish or pink color, even when they were fully cooked. A few hundred years ago, it was realized that nitrates were the impurities in those salts that caused the unique flavor and the color fixing effect noted by the ancients. Since then, nitrates have been added to pure salt to cure meats. The most commonly used nitrate was potassium nitrate ($KNO_3$, commonly called saltpeter), but sodium nitrate ($NaNO_3$, also known as saltpeter or, less confusingly, as Chile saltpeter) has also been widely used. The Federal Meat Inspection Act of 1906 officially authorized the use of nitrates for the curing of commercial meat products.

Later, in the early 1900s, scientists discovered that the nitrates used for curing would slowly break down into nitrites. It was also discovered that those nitrites were the chemicals that led to the color fixing and flavor changes. Consequently, the U.S. government permitted the direct use of nitrites to cure meats, but placed a limit on the amount that could be used.

In the late 1960s, it became clear that the use of nitrates and nitrites could cause nitrosamines to be formed under certain conditions, and nitrosamines in *substantial* amounts were known to act as carcinogens in test animals. Therefore, there was much research and discussion about this in the early 1970s. Tentative conclusions and a set of guidelines regarding nitrite and nitrate usage were issued in 1975, and there have been no significant changes in the guidelines since that time—despite continuing research.

Several problems confound this research: Nitrates and nitrites occur naturally in the human saliva, in vegetables, and quite often in drinking water. As an example, celery, beets, and radishes contain between 2,700 and 1,600 PPM (parts per million) of nitrites. The ham and sausages commonly available at a grocery store will contain no more than 156 PPM of nitrites.

Below is a summary of the most important considerations and conclusions made by researchers and government policy makers:

◊ The risk of botulism in some kinds of cured meat is very great. Nitrates and nitrites are the only palatable additives presently available that will positively prevent this often deadly form of food poisoning.

◊ Though nitrosamines can cause cancer in test animals, it is not clear whether they will cause cancer in humans.

◊ Tests on commercially prepared products occasionally show trace amounts of nitrosamines, but the amounts detected are much lower than what would be required to cause cancer in test animals.

The net result is that botulism would be a real danger if these chemicals were banned. The degree of risk from nitrosamines posed by the continued use of these chemicals is unknown. Actually, there may be none at all. Considering these points, it was decided to continue to permit these chemicals to be used in some products (bacon, for example), and to mandate that they be used when there is a clear botulism hazard (smoked sausage in casing, for instance). At the same time, however, many restrictions were placed on the usage of these chemicals in order to minimize the risk of exposure to nitrosamines. This approach allowed the continued production of traditionally cured products, preserved the protection against botulism offered by nitrates and nitrites, and minimized the exposure to carcinogens.

One significant restriction is that nitr*ates* (not nitr*ites*) are banned for all products except fermented sausage and products cured with traditional dry cure. (Such products undergo a lengthy curing process, so the slower dissipation rate of nitrates is required.) Another change was that the amount of nitrites permitted in various categories of foods was reduced.

Of course, the U.S. government cannot prevent an amateur smoker from using nitrates and, furthermore, can't regulate the amount of *any* additive he or she uses. Nevertheless, since the federal regulations for the commercial use of nitrites and nitrates are intended to protect our health, it is in our interest to follow those regulations to the extent possible. Consequently, nitrates are not specified for use in any curing procedure in this book because classical dry cure and fermented sausage formulations and processes are not presented.

Government regulations for commercial products specify nitrite content in *parts per million* (PPM), and the required or allowable amount is different according to the product. For example, more nitrite is required in sausage than is allowed in bacon. Since few of us have the equipment or expertise to measure nitrite in PPM, we will rely on the commercial curing powders—which must also meet federal regulations. Used as directed, they are formulated to give you a product that will be within government regulations—a product that will positively prevent botulism and pose zero to minimal risk from nitrosamine exposure. When pure sodium nitrite is specified for brines, USDA guidelines for amateur curing are used. These guidelines are found in government publications that describe how to process meats on the farm (for example, Farmers' Bulletin Number 2265—*Pork Slaughtering, Cutting, Preserving, and Cooking on the Farm*, published by the USDA).

When adding sodium nitrite to brine, do not use more than 1½ teaspoons (7.5 ml) of sodium nitrite per gallon (4 liters) of water. This amount is slightly less than that recommended in the USDA bulletin mentioned above. In this book, only 1 teaspoon (5 ml) of sodium nitrite per gallon of water is used. Color fixing is easily accomplished with this amount, and reducing the amount to 1 teaspoon causes no hazard because botulism is not a concern with brine-cured products. Actually, I have achieved good color fixing with as little as ½ teaspoon (2.5 ml) of sodium nitrite per gallon of brine.

Potassium nitrite and potassium nitrate can be used instead of their sodium counterparts. Either the potassium or the sodium chemicals will produce the same effect and provide the same protection. However, in recent years, the sodium-based nitrites and nitrates have become favored because the lighter weights of the sodium chemicals allow less of the chemicals (in terms of weight) to be used.

# CHAPTER 7

# Curing and Marinating

Man has been applying salt, sweeteners, and other flavorings to food for eons. Our ancestors discovered that some of these seasonings, applied in sufficient quantity, help to preserve food. The application of salt, sweeteners, and other flavorings to meat, fowl, and fish came to be known as curing when it was done to help preserve food.

If salt was used for preservation, it was essential for a considerable amount to be infused into the product. Much dry salt was applied directly, and it was left on the food for a long time. Another method was to soak the flesh in a strong brine solution—and soak it long enough to ensure deep penetration of the salt.

The infusion of salt caused moisture to be extracted. Reduced moisture content and a high salt content created an environment very unfavorable to the proliferation of microorganisms that cause decay. Thus, preservation was accomplished. Cured meat was often smoked and dried, which made it even less perishable. The food could be kept at room temperature without spoiling for as long as a year, or even longer. In the days before the technology of canning and refrigeration were developed, this salt curing (often combined with smoking and drying) saved many people from starvation.

Most of these cured foods were very salty, so some of the salt had to be extracted before eating. Often it was extracted as part of the cooking process. Extracting salt from hard-cured foods is called *freshening* or, occasionally, *desalting*. Corned beef is a good example of a heavily salted, cured meat that is freshened by cooking in water.

Curing, smoking, drying, and freshening is a lot of work compared with the ease of using canned, frozen, or refrigerated foods. Consequently, as the new preservation techniques became widely available, the production and consumption of hard-cured meats and fish declined proportionately.

However, in various countries around the world, some of these cured and smoked products continue to be well appreciated, so they are still produced. In effect, each of them has become a cultural treasure of its country. Two examples are the hard-cured hams of our southern states, and the salted, dried, and smoked bonito fish of Japan. Jerky, made of many kinds of meat from wild and domesticated animals—and even made from fish—is perpetually popular in many countries of the world. These products will still be around when your grandchildren become grandparents.

The private production of hard-cured foods by individuals was largely replaced by the production of mildly cured meats and fishes by commercial processors. These foods require refrigeration, but they need not be freshened (desalted) because the relatively low salt content is pleasing to the average palate. Good examples of these mildly cured products are the common types of cured ham, sausage, and bacon found in our grocery stores.

Most people appreciated the lowering of the salt content. Unfortunately, while the salt content was being lowered, other changes were taking place to reduce the production cost. These changes—or shortcuts—made the products cheaper and more competitive, but the flavor suffered. For example, the use of liquid smoke often replaced actual smoking. Nowadays, not even liquid smoke is used on much of the ham and bacon produced by the large processors.

People like you and I know that products tastier than those available at the supermarkets can be made. Custom smokers do it—at a very high price. You can do it, too—at a very low price. Making delicious smoked foods, however, involves more than just exposing meats and fish to smoke. We must learn how to season the food. For some products, this means learning the "secrets" of curing.

It would be wonderful if we could dust off our grandparents' or great-grandparents' curing recipes and use them. Unfortunately, if you are looking for a mild cure, you are unlikely to find it among the recipes of our ancestors. The amateur food smoker of today normally wants old-time flavor with a modern mild-salt cure. If that is your goal, read on! Three curing techniques will be discussed on the following pages. The latter two will help you to obtain that old-time flavor you are looking for, and will provide you with the mild-salt cure to which we have become accustomed.

# Dry Curing the Classical Way

*Note:* I am using the phrase *classical dry cure* in this book to distinguish this curing method from the *modern dry cure* method, which will be described later in this chapter.

The classical dry cure method is the least popular curing method used by hobbyists. It results in products that must be freshened (desalted) before eating.

A large quantity of dry salt (usually combined with a sweetener, spices, and a nitrate color developer) is applied to the meat. If it will not be aged, about 1½ tablespoons (22.5 ml) of salt per pound (454 g) of meat will be applied. If it is to be aged (a southern-style ham, for example), about 2½ tablespoons (37.5 ml) of salt per pound is used. If the meat is thick, or if it has a bone in it, it is usually injected (pumped) with a brine solution, too. A tool that resembles a large hypodermic needle (called a *meat pump*) is used for this purpose.

For a 16- to 18-pound ham, the cure (the mixture of salt and other curing ingredients) is piled on the fresh, chilled meat, and it is cured in a cold environment for up to 35 days. A 4-pound fish fillet is cured for about eight hours. Trying to limit the salt absorption by reducing the recommended curing time will yield unpredictable results.

The classical dry curing of boneless meat that is not over about 6 inches (15 cm) thick is not difficult to do. Pumping is not required. Moreover, because it is boneless, spoilage due a problem known as *bone marrow sour* will not occur. Nevertheless, the classical dry cure method will result in a very salty product.

One of the primary goals of this book is to show how to make smoked products with just the right amount of salt. Consequently, the details of how to hard cure specific meat or fish products will not be explained.

Nevertheless, trying to make a distinguished product such as an authentic southern-style smoked ham is, in my opinion, an admirable goal. If that is where your interests lead you, I encourage you to look at appendix 5 for a source of information on this subject. The information available will provide you with the detailed directions you need.

When you gather information on how to cure and smoke the ham, be sure to look for information on how to store, desalt, and cook it. Such information is every bit as important as instructions about how to cure and smoke it.

# Brine Curing or Wet Curing

Brine curing (also known as wet curing or sweet pickle curing) is widely used by professionals and hobbyists alike. This method is adaptable to cure the flesh of any creature that walks, flies, swims, hops, or crawls. Mild cures with a low salt content, or hard cures with a high salt content, are possible. Brines can be custom-seasoned to meet your expectations and taste.

The strength of the brine (the ratio of water to salt) and the time that the meat is left in the brine are the two most important factors controlling the amount of salt that will be present in the finished product. The seasonings that you add to the brine will give the product a special flavor. You are the boss, and you can control the process.

As mentioned above, an important factor in brining foods is the concentration of salt in the brine. Nevertheless, there is no broad agreement on what the concentration should be. Some argue that strong brine is the only kind that should be used. Others favor a medium-strength or weak brine.

Also, there is lack of agreement on the best way to indicate the strength of the brine. The *weight* of the salt as a percentage of the *weight* of the water is one method that is used to indicate brine strength. Using this system, 13.5 ounces (384 g) of salt added to a gallon (3,840 g) of water would make a 10 percent brine solution. (This is because the weight of the salt is $\frac{1}{10}$ the weight of the water; the metric weight measurements—384 g of salt and 3,840 g of water—make this readily apparent.)

However, indicating the brine strength by indicating the *percentage of salt saturation* is the most commonly used method, so this method will be employed in this book. At 68° F (20° C), 100 parts by weight of water will dissolve 35.8 parts by weight of salt. No more salt than this can be dissolved in the water—it will be 100 percent saturated with salt. This is called 100 percent brine. Water at the same temperature containing half that amount of salt would be called 50 percent (saturated) brine, and so on. Using this system, the 10 percent brine mentioned in the previous paragraph would be called 40 percent (saturated) brine. From this point on, whenever the strength of brine is mentioned, please understand the percent number to mean percent of salt saturation.

There are two ways to make a brine solution of any desired strength. One way is to consult a table, and then add the specified amount of salt to the specified amount of water (see appendix 3). The other way is to use an instrument to measure brine strength (a salinometer), and slowly add salt until the salinometer indicates that the desired strength has been reached. (The upper stem of a salinometer has a scale that indicates percent of saturation.) Unfortunately, a commercially manufactured salinometer is awkward to use and fragile because it is made from a long glass tube. (See page 82.)

Instead of using a manufactured salinometer to measure brine strength, an egg or a potato will do very nicely as a makeshift salinometer. The egg should be fresh, and it is preferable that it be a large egg. Any size of potato will do, but it should be fresh. A dried and wrinkled potato contains less moisture than a fresh one, so it will be more buoyant and, therefore, will produce weaker brine. The same thing can be said for an egg that is less than fresh—it will contain less moisture. If all of your potatoes happen to be a little dried and wrinkled, peel one of them deeply and use it.

Slowly add salt to the water, and stir the mixture constantly to dissolve it. Stop adding salt when the egg or potato floats, and it just barely breaks the surface of the brine. This method of measuring the brine strength will produce brine with about 50 percent saturation—the strength used by many smokers. A concentration of 50 percent lies about midway between the extremes of 90 percent and 15 percent used by some people, so it is a good place to start. Our ancestors used this egg or potato method, and it continues to be widely used by food smokers all over the world.

However, rather than using an egg or potato, you can easily make salinometers to blend *any* strength of brine. (See How to Make a Salinometer in chapter 4, page 82.) In this book, either homemade salinometers or the brine charts will be used to make brines.

Although a 50 percent brine solution is a good place to start, it might be a good idea to keep in mind some of the pros and cons of using a stronger or weaker solution.

Some people use the strong solution of 80 to 90 percent because it gives a faster cure, and because it extracts more moisture from the flesh. Those who use a 15 to 25 percent brine solution claim that the raw material is more uniformly cured, and that salt content is easier to control. There does seem to be a general agreement that weak brines are not good for brining fish because the flesh can become waterlogged, soft, difficult to handle, and easy to tear.

It is not necessary to use the same strength of brine for every product you make. For example, you may find that you like strong brine for your fish, but weaker brine for chicken.

It is important, however, to use the same strength of brine each time you make a specific product. When you use brine to wet cure trout, for example, the strength of the brine should be the same every time. If this strength is always different, it will be difficult to determine the best curing time. After several trout-curing sessions, there might be a good reason to change the brine strength, but this will change the curing time. The new curing time will be somewhat of an educated guess until you get some experience with the new brine strength.

If the brine strength is kept constant for each product, once you learn the required curing time to get the perfect flavor, you will be able to produce the same delicious product repeatedly. This is assuming that you recorded all of the conditions in your notebook, and all conditions remain the same.

To transform the "art" of brining into a skilled craft, all you need to do is:

ℓ Record the brine formula for each product. If changes in the formula or curing time are necessary, record the changes and the results.

ℓ Record all the smoking conditions for the first try on a new product: the drying method, the smoking time, the smoke chamber temperature, the kind of smoking fuel, and other conditions unique to your product. Record any changes in these conditions in future sessions for the same product. (The smoking conditions can affect salt concentration. For example, prolonged smoking at a high temperature will cause drying, and drying will increase salt concentration.)

ℓ Date all records with the full date: June 1, 2005, for example. After a few years pass, it is sometimes difficult to distinguish between the original process and the improved process unless you have the full date—including the year.

ℓ Record the *honest* taste impressions of anyone who samples the product. Recording flattery will get you nowhere.

ℓ Note what changes are needed to improve the brine cure formula. (Initially, you should avoid making changes in the strength of the brine; instead, try to make changes in the salt content of the product by increasing or decreasing the cure time.) Change seasonings such as spices and sweeteners as you see fit, but be sure to record the changes. If used, don't increase the recommended maximum amount of sodium nitrite (1½ teaspoons per gallon of water—7.5 ml per 4 liters of water), but it may be decreased or eliminated.

Three approaches to making brine are outlined below. All of them should produce the same result. One of these approaches might be more suitable for your situation or for the raw material you are using.

## FRESH-BLEND METHOD

For the fresh-blend method, the basic idea is that enough brine of the desired strength is made up (and other ingredients are added) to cure all of the meat or fish at one time, and then *the brine is discarded after a single use.*

This method is best for experimentation because each batch of brine is made from scratch. The basic sweet pickle cure is described below. However, this is for illustration only. For your first attempt at brine curing, it would be best to try one of the brine-cured products described in other chapters; they will be more flavorful because additional seasonings will be suggested.

## SWEET PICKLE CURE (ABOUT 50 PERCENT SATURATION)

1 gallon (4 liters) quality water, preferably boiled and chilled
2 cups (480 ml) noniodized fine-grain salt
½ cup (120 ml) granulated white sugar
1 tsp. (5 ml) sodium nitrite (optional)
(normally, other seasonings of your choice would be added)

Sugar may be increased or decreased, but it is best not to eliminate it. Sugar counteracts the toughening effect of salt, and it mellows the harsh salt flavor. It also acts as a preservative.

Sodium nitrite is optional, but you should never use more than 1½ teaspoons per gallon (7.5 ml per 4 liters) of water (this is the maximum amount recommended by the USDA for amateur curing). Sodium nitrite can be used with pork or with chicken legs, for example, if you want the finished product to have the pink color and taste typical of cured ham. Used on beef, it will give the meat a reddish color similar to corned beef. There will be no color fixing during the curing; this takes place during the smoking or cooking of the product. If the meat contains sodium nitrite, the pink or reddish color will be fixed when the flesh reaches about 135° F (57° C).

Other seasonings can be added to the brine, as you desire. Fresh onions, fresh garlic, and bay leaves, for example, are commonly used. Personalize the brine by adding any of your favorite spices. Go easy on seasonings that have a strong flavor. Try to avoid combinations that might clash with each other. Many people boil the spices in a small amount of water for a few seconds, then chill this paste and add it to the brine. The boiling seems to release the flavor. Powdered spices are preferred.

The time that the raw material is left in the brine is determined by several factors: the thickness of the meat, the fat content, the extent and type of skin covering, and the degree of saltiness you desire. When the curing is finished, the sweet pickle cure should be discarded because the water that the salt extracted from the raw material has diluted it. The brine has also been weakened due to absorption of salt and flavorings by the raw materials.

Considering the ratio of the salt to the water, the sweet pickle cure described above will be about a 50 percent saturated cure. However, if the strength of the cure is measured with a salinometer, it will read higher than 50 percent because the dissolved sugar and other ingredients are influencing the reading. If you want a stronger or weaker brine, you can consult appendix 3 to determine how much salt is required to get a certain brine strength, or just change the amount of salt as you see fit, and make a record of that change.

Of course, the salt can be weighed instead of being measured by volume. Alternatively, salt can be added to the water until the salinometer, egg, or potato indicates that the proper strength has been reached. Volume measurement of rock salt is not accurate.

In summary, this fresh-blend method is useful for experimentation, and it is a very good method for those who have had little experience with wet curing. It is the favorite wet cure method for most amateurs because it is very simple, and it will produce an adequate amount of product for family and friends.

However, if you perfect a product and decide to make the same product repeatedly, the following method may be better for you.

## BULK-BLEND METHOD FOR BRINE CURING

The basic idea behind the bulk-blend method is that a large amount of the dry ingredients is prepared and blended in advance. That is, the salt and all other powdered or granular ingredients for a certain kind of brine are prepared in bulk. If this is done, each ingredient need not be measured individually for each batch of brine. To make a batch of brine, the prescribed amount of bulk-blend is added to the prescribed amount of water.

The formula for the same sweet pickle cure (the formula that was used for the fresh-blend method) will be used again to demonstrate how to make it in bulk. Each ingredient in that formula was multiplied by 12 in order to obtain the result indicated below. If 12 is used as a multiplier: ¼ tsp. becomes 1 Tbsp., ½ tsp. becomes 2 Tbsp., 1 tsp. becomes ¼ cup, and 1 Tbsp. becomes ¾ cup. How easy!

Multiplication by 12 is best when the American system of measurement is being used. The reason for this is due to the number 12 being factorable by 2, 3, or 4. These are the same numbers that are used to divide the gallon into quarts, cups, tablespoons, et cetera—all the way down to ⅛ teaspoon. Multiplication by 10 is best if you are using the metric system.

## BULK SWEET PICKLE CURE
## (ABOUT 50 PERCENT SATURATION)
## FOR 12 GALLONS OF BRINE

24 cups noniodized fine-grain salt
6 cups white sugar
6 Tbsp. sodium nitrite (optional)
(normally, other seasonings of your choice would be added when
the brine is blended)

Measure and blend the dry ingredients. To determine the amount of blend to add to each gallon of water, calculate the sum of the volume of all dry ingredients in the *basic* nonbulk formula. In this case, it would be 2 cups + ½ cup + ½ teaspoon (see the previously described Sweet Pickle Cure).

Consequently, to make a gallon of brine using the bulk mix, 2½ cups + ½ teaspoon of bulk-blend would be added to a gallon of water. Actually, the "+ ½ teaspoon" is not significant and can be ignored. Store the bulk-blend in a plastic bag or in a glass or plastic container that has a rustproof lid.

### RECYCLED-BRINE METHOD

A batch of brine can be used several times. First, make one batch of brine by adding the required amount of bulk-blend to the required amount of water. Add nonpowdered or nongranulated ingredients (chopped onions or grated ginger, for example). Cure the first batch of material. Remove that material from the brine, and then add more of the bulk-blend to bring it up to the original strength. Cure the second batch of meat or fish. In this way, the same brine can be used several times if is brought back up to the original strength after each use. (*Caution:* The brine can't be stored for extended periods between each use because it will contain particles of meat or fish.)

As mentioned previously, the brine needs to be brought back up to the original strength because each batch of meat or fish will absorb some of its salt and flavorings. Furthermore, the brine will extract moisture from the raw material, and the moisture will cause dilution of the brine.

The best way to determine how much bulk-blend is required to bring the brine up to original strength is to make and use a homemade salinometer described in chapter 4, page 82. First, make a batch of brine by adding the prescribed amount of bulk-blend to the prescribed amount of water. Next, make a homemade salinometer which will float just enough to break the surface of this brine. After you use the brine to cure a batch of product, bring it back to its original strength by adding enough bulk-blend to make the salinometer break the surface of the brine again, as it did initially.

Obviously, this homemade salinometer is usable only for the specific kind of brine that you are making, so write the name of the brine directly on the salinometer with a permanent marker. Mark it with a unique brine name so that you will be certain of its application. This same salinometer may also be used to make the first batch of brine. If it is used to make the first batch, bulk-blend is added to any amount of water until the salinometer floats.

Using the homemade salinometer to maintain consistent brine strength will enable you to make a good product every time. Consistency is very important for any kind of curing. The exact strength of the brine in terms of dissolved salt is not very important. Knowing the exact strength of the brine will not make you an expert in brine curing. Being consistent will make you an expert.

# Modern Dry Curing

Even if you have read other books on the subject of smoking foods, the term *modern dry curing* will be unfamiliar. Modern dry curing is a name for an excellent curing process that has never, to my knowledge, been defined or described. I will explain how the term came about.

Many years ago, when I first started smoking food, one of my first goals was to make some truly good bacon. This goal seemed to be within the grasp of a know-nothing beginner. After all, bacon had been made on innumerable farmsteads in America and Europe, so it couldn't be difficult to make—I thought.

The first disappointment was that books on food smoking available to me didn't even discuss the subject of curing and smoking bacon. In two of the books, the only thing that was said about bacon was that *store-bought* bacon could be made more flavorful by cold smoking it for an hour or two. Eventually, I got some detailed descriptions of the old-fashioned bacon curing and smoking processes, and I tried them—all of them. I followed the instructions carefully. The result was always the same: awful. Without freshening (desalting) the cured-and-smoked bacon in water for a long time, it was so salty that it was inedible. Moreover, if the bacon was freshened, much of the smoky flavor was washed out with the salt. The desalting time was considerable (often a matter of several hours), and the result was unpredictable.

These repeated failures at making bacon that met my expectations caused me to admit defeat for the time being. I turned my attention to making smoked sausage. To my delight, the sausage I made was usually quite good, irrespective of the source of the recipe. However, what impressed me most of all was that the salt content was usually just about right. When it was not just right, I could adjust it by changing the quantity of the salt in the recipe. Gradually, I realized that between 2 and 3 teaspoons (10 and 15 ml) of salt (depending on the kind of sausage being made) was the perfect amount to season 2½ pounds (1.135 kg) of ground meat.

The success with sausage gave me an idea: *Control the salt content in the bacon in about the same way as it is controlled in the sausage.* Therefore, I decided that I would not cure bacon with the old-fashioned dry cure method that uses lots of salt; nor would I cure it for a long time in strong brine. Instead, I decided to rub on 3 teaspoons (15 ml) of salt per 2½ pounds (1.135 kg) of pork belly (about the same ratio used for sausage), and then give adequate time for the salt to be absorbed by the pork belly.

I tried it. I weighed the trimmed pork belly and rubbed on exactly 3 teaspoons (15 ml) of salt per 2½ pounds (1.135 kg) of belly. Of course, this was mixed with sugar, some other seasonings, and ½ teaspoon (2.5 ml) of Prague Powder #1 per 2½ pounds of belly. The thickest part of the pork belly was about 1½ inches (4 cm), and I estimated that 10 days would be required for the cure to migrate to the center of the slab. (This estimate was based on my research of data regarding the rate of salt absorption for the classical dry cure.) The curing process was carried out in a cold refrigerator (about 38° F, or 3.3° C), and the meat was over-hauled (rubbed again and restacked) daily to ensure uniform distribution of the cure. After the curing was finished, the surface was rinsed and dried, and then I gave the belly a few hours of cold smoking followed by two or three hours of smoking at 145° F (69° C) to impart a reddish brown color to the surface.

After all the previous disappointments, I was very pleased with the result. It tasted better than commercially produced bacon, and it had a delightfully smoky flavor. Most importantly, the salt content was just right!

Over the years, I have used this special dry cure method to cure all varieties of fresh meats and fowl, many kinds of fish, and some wild meat as well. Without doubt, it is my favorite curing method, and I have no hesitation about recommending it for most curing projects.

When recording the results of my many smoking sessions, I soon found that I needed to have a name for this new dry curing process in which the salt was reduced and carefully measured according to the weight of the raw material. In some ways, it is similar to the technique called *dry rub* that is used by culinary buffs, but *dry rub* did not convey the concept well. After much thought, I decided to call it *modern dry curing* and call the conventional method *classical dry curing*.

The modern dry curing method does not replace the classical dry curing method, and it does not replace the brine (wet) cure method. It is simply a third option that may give the result you want, may be easier to do, or may offer better control of salt content. The modern dry cure will produce results quite different from the classical dry cure. The brine cure, however, can be used in various ways that will give essentially the same results as either the modern dry cure or the classical dry cure. Below are some points worth considering when you are trying to decide whether to use the brine cure or the modern dry cure:

◊ Since the modern dry cure requires no water, it is better than the brine method when the water supply is heavily chlorinated or has a high mineral content (such water can taint the raw material).

◊ The brine cure requires much more salt and seasoning, making it less economical than the modern dry cure method.

◊ The brine method is faster; mild brine curing can often be accomplished in minutes or hours. Modern dry cure times are measured in days.

◊ The modern dry cure is preferable if a nitrite cure is used. This is because the slower curing will result in uniform penetration, complete color development, and better color stability.

◊ Brine curing can sometimes be accomplished without refrigeration. Modern dry curing requires space in a cold refrigerator having a temperature range of 36° to 40° F (2.2° to 4.4° C).

◊ A beginner can do a good job of modern dry curing on his or her first try. Brine curing for a person without experience can be an unpredictable operation because there are several variables to consider: time, thickness, fat content, type of raw material, and skin covering. The more variables there are, the greater the chance that control of salt content will be lost.

◊ If the material consists of *a large number of uniformly sized pieces* (such as many whole chicken legs or many fish of the same size), the curing may be less tedious if the whole lot is immersed in brine at one time. The items can also be rinsed easily at one time when the cure is finished. Modern dry curing requires more work to ensure that each piece is thoroughly covered with cure mixture and thoroughly rinsed at the end of the cure. If a large number of pieces are involved, the overhaul, too, might be more difficult with the modern dry cure.

◊ In most cases, the modern dry cure method will give better control over the amount of salt absorbed into the raw material. The high degree of control is realized because the amount of salt you apply is the only important variable. Time is not so important if the time is adequate for the salt to penetrate to the very center of the product.

## MAKING THE MODERN DRY CURE MIXTURE

The basic idea of the modern dry cure process is that the amount of salt, sweetener, curing powder (if used), and seasonings applied is determined by the weight of the raw material. The raw material is then refrigerated until the cure migrates to the center of the product.

The simplest cure is a mixture of salt and sugar. If you want a mild salt taste, mix 3 teaspoons (15 ml) of salt together with 1 teaspoon (5 ml) of sugar. Blend very well. This will provide you with 4 teaspoons (20 ml) of curing mixture that will cure 2¼ pounds (1 kg) of meat, fowl, or fish. (The reason for the 2¼-pound unit rather than a 2½-pound unit will be explained shortly.)

If you just happen to have 3⅓ pounds (1.5 kg) of raw material, for example, you will have to do a little arithmetic to figure out that you would need 6 teaspoons of curing mixture. (Don't be concerned about the arithmetic at this time; it will be greatly simplified.) You could blend exactly the amount you need, or you could double, triple, or quadruple the basic cure mixture recipe, use 6 teaspoons (30 ml) of that, and store the remainder for future use.

In reality, you will most likely want other seasonings (and, possibly, a nitrite curing powder) in your curing mixture. If you know that you will use the same curing mixture repeatedly, it is most convenient to make the mixture in bulk so that it will be ready when you need it. (This approach is similar to preparing bulk-blend for brining.) On the other hand, if you are making a certain product for the first time, it is wise to blend just the amount you will need for the job at hand. In most cases, you will want to make one or two changes in the mixture when you make the product the next time.

## A PRACTICAL EXAMPLE OF A MODERN DRY CURE PROJECT

As an example of how to blend and apply the modern dry cure mixture, we will go through the process required for bacon, step by step. If you actually want to make smoked bacon, be sure to read the specific directions for curing and smoking bacon in chapter 9. The following instructions are only for illustrating the modern dry cure process.

*Note:* Prague Powder #1 is used for fixing the color of cured sausage and for preventing toxic botulin development in cured sausage. The manufacturers of this curing powder specify 1 level teaspoon of Prague Powder #1 per 5 pounds of ground meat. Of course, ½ teaspoon would be used for 2½ pounds of ground meat. However, the modern dry cure process is for curing solid meat, not ground meat. Furthermore, the meat is rinsed at the end of the modern dry cure process; this rinsing will remove the small amount of Prague Powder that has remained on the surface of the meat. To compensate for this inevitable loss of Prague Powder caused by rinsing, the modern dry cure process specifies ½ teaspoon of Prague Powder #1 per 2¼ pounds of meat, rather than ½ teaspoon per 2½ pounds of meat. If you feel that 2¼ pounds is an awkward unit to use, change it to 2½ pounds—or double everything, and use 5 pounds as your standard. The difference will be insignificant.

## MODERN DRY CURE MIX FOR 2¼ POUNDS (1 KILOGRAM) OF BACON (MAPLE SYRUP CURED)

3 tsp. (15 ml) noniodized salt
½ tsp. (2.5 ml) Prague Powder #1
½ tsp. (2.5 ml) onion powder
½ tsp. (2.5 ml) garlic powder
½ tsp. (2.5 ml) white pepper
2 Tbsp. (30 ml) maple syrup (blend the syrup with the dry
    ingredients at time of application)

Total dry ingredients: 3 + ½ + ½ + ½ + ½ = 5 tsp.
Total dry ingredients, metric: 15 + 2.5 + 2.5 + 2.5 + 2.5 = 25 ml.

### CURE MIX MEASURING CHART
5 tsp. (25 ml) per 2¼ lbs. (1 kg) of belly + 2 Tbsp. (30 ml) of syrup
2½ tsp. (12.5 ml) per 1 lb.* (500 g) of belly + 1 Tbsp. (15 ml) of syrup
1¼ tsp. (6.25 ml) per ½ lb. (250 g) of belly + 1½ tsp. (7.5 ml) of syrup
½ tsp. (2.5 ml) per ¼ lb. (125 g) of belly + ¾ tsp. (4 ml) of syrup

*This should read "per 1⅛ lbs.," but the difference is not significant.

If, for example, the total weight of the pork belly is 4 pounds, you would use 5 + 2½ + 1¼ + ½ = 9¼ teaspoons (refer to the chart above). Metric for the same amount of pork belly would be 25 + 12.5 + 6.25 + 2.5 = 46.25 ml of modern dry cure mixture.

To this amount of modern dry cure mixture, add 6 + 3 + 1½ + ¾ = 11¼ teaspoons (30 + 15 + 7.5 + 4 = 56.5 ml) of maple syrup. The maple syrup and the modern dry cure mixture are blended to form a thick liquid, and this liquid is then rubbed on the meat. (Most modern dry cures are actually dry, but this cure is a thick liquid because of the liquid sweetener.)

It is a good idea to measure the dry cure mixture carefully, but you need not be so careful when measuring the maple syrup. In this example, 11¼ teaspoons is just a little less than ¼ cup, so measure out ¼ cup of the syrup. There will be some syrup adhering to the measuring cup after you empty it. Give that measuring cup and a small rubber spatula to the nearest kid, and he or she will finish off the remaining ¾ teaspoon of syrup. (For people using metric measure, 60 ml is close enough.)

All of this calculation may give you a headache, but the first bite of your homemade bacon will cure that instantaneously.

Let's say, for example, that you made the maple-syrup-cured bacon described in chapter 9, page 153 (which uses the same curing formula described here), and you are completely satisfied. That is, you fully intend to make the same product repeatedly. In this case, it would be convenient to mix up a large quantity of the cure and store it for future use. To make the modern dry cure in bulk, multiply all the ingredients (except for the maple syrup) by some multiplier—12, for example. (For the American measuring system, using 12 as a multiplier is easier than using 10. Please refer to the explanation earlier in this chapter: Bulk-Blend Method for Brine Curing, page 122.) Using the Cure Mix Measuring Chart, measure out the amount of bulk-blend you need whenever you want to make bacon. Below, for example, is the formula to make the bacon-curing mixture in bulk.

## MODERN DRY CURE—BULK-BLEND FOR 27 POUNDS (12 KILOGRAMS) OF BACON (MAPLE SYRUP CURED)

¾ cup (180 ml) salt
2 Tbsp. (30 ml) Prague Powder #1
2 Tbsp. (30 ml) white pepper
2 Tbsp. (30 ml) onion powder
2 Tbsp. (30 ml) garlic powder

At the time of application, blend the maple syrup with the proper amount of dry ingredients. Use 2 tablespoons (30 ml) of maple syrup per 2¼ pounds (1 kg) of pork belly.

## HOW TO DESIGN YOUR OWN MODERN DRY CURE

Creating your own modern dry cure is very easy. If you follow a few guidelines, the chances of turning out a superb product on your first try are extremely high.

Before you formulate your customized modern dry cure, it is best to get experience using some of the suggested cures in this book. Such experience will enable you to design your customized cure so that the amount of salt and other seasonings will probably match your preferences perfectly.

In this book, the basic formulation of the modern dry cure is always based on 2¼ pounds (1 kg) of raw material—meat, fowl, or fish. As previously mentioned, you need not base your formulations on 2¼ pounds of raw material, but you should base all of them on a certain unit of weight; use 2½ pounds or 5 pounds, if you wish. If you always use the same weight of raw material as a standard, you will soon be able to predict the degree of flavor that will be imparted by, say, 1 teaspoon (5 ml) of oregano.

The amount of salt to be used is easy to determine. If you have tried any of the modern dry cures suggested in this book, then you know the degree of salinity that will be imparted by 3 teaspoons (15 ml) of salt per 2¼ pounds (1 kg) of raw material. For your customized formulation, you should increase or decrease the salt according to your taste. Keep in mind, however, that a great reduction of the salt could result in spoilage during the curing and smoking operations. Food poisoning is another possibility if there is a great reduction of salt and sugar.

Prague Powder #1 is optional unless there is a danger of botulism poisoning (when smoked sausages are being prepared, for example). Otherwise, the most significant effects of a curing powder are the color fixing (pink or red) and the special flavor imparted. If you don't need these special effects, eliminate the Prague Powder #1. If it is used, never use more than ½ teaspoon (2.5 ml) per 2¼ pounds (1 kg) of raw material. Since Prague Powder #1 contains over 93 percent common table salt, its use affects the salinity of the finished product.

The use of spices and herbs is a very personal thing. Use the varieties and amounts that you judge to be appropriate. Information in cookbooks, together with your accumulated experience, is the best guide for the kinds and amounts of spices to use. Good cookbooks (such as *Joy of Cooking*) will indicate which spices are commonly used with the various raw materials. Descriptions of the commonly used seasonings, along with their most common applications, are also given in appendix 1.

Selecting from a variety of sweeteners can do much to customize your cure. Commonly used sweeteners are discussed in chapter 5. Because sweeteners tenderize in addition to adding flavor, I recommend their use. Start with somewhere between 1 and 6 teaspoons (5 and 30 ml) per 2¼ pounds (1 kg) of raw material.

You may wish to use some seasonings that are fresh, or some seasonings that are not in powdered or granulated form. Examples include fresh onions, fresh garlic, fresh herbs, soy sauce, and maple syrup. Such seasonings must be prepared separately, after the weight of the raw material is known.

After the formulation has been decided, calculate the sum of the volume measurements of all of the various powdered and granulated ingredients. This total will be the amount of blended curing mixture that should be applied to your standard unit of raw material (2¼ pounds, 2½ pounds, or 5 pounds, for example). (The standard unit for metric people will most likely be 1 kg.)

To make your modern dry cure in bulk, multiply each ingredient in your basic formula by 12. (To make bulk-blend in the metric system, multiply each ingredient by 10.)

The sodium nitrite in Prague Powder #1 can degrade and become ineffective when it is mixed with certain seasonings and stored for a long period. Consequently, if the bulk formula contains Prague Powder #1, it should be kept in an airtight container and used within a few months.

# Marinating

### WHY MARINATE?

Seasoning meats with marinades, before smoking them, opens a new world of flavor. Every general cookbook and barbecue book will have a few recipes for marinades. Many of them can be used to season foods in preparation for smoking. Besides greatly increasing the range of flavors that come out of your smoker, there are two more points worthy of consideration. First, marinades normally contain less salt than salt cures—many contain no salt. Second, they usually contain no nitrates or nitrites.

About 20 percent of humans are sensitive to the sodium contained in salt, and this sensitivity can contribute to high blood pressure. Such people may be able to eat normal amounts of marinated (and then smoked) foods if the salt is reduced, eliminated, or replaced with a salt substitute. However, sodium-sensitive individuals would be able to eat only small amounts of the common salt-cured products.

The second point—the fact that marinades usually do not contain nitrates or nitrites—is important for those who don't want to put additives in their smoked products.

If you want to try marinades—and you really should—there are some basic guidelines presented below.

### BASIC GUIDELINES FOR MARINADES

A marinade is a liquid that always contains some kind of a liquid acid and one or more seasoning ingredients. It will often contain oil, as well.

Wine, citrus juice, beer, vinegar, and sherry are some examples of acids used. Because of the acid content, marinades must be mixed and applied in an acid-resistant container such as those made of glass, glazed ceramic, stainless steel, or food-grade plastic. Never use aluminum, copper, common steel, or cast iron. For the same reason, acid-resistant implements made of materials such as stainless steel or plastic should be used for stirring or turning over the meat.

The size and shape of the marinating container is not important. Furthermore, it is not necessary for the raw material to be completely covered with marinade. It is important, however, to mix or turn over the material from time to time. About 1 cup (240 ml) of marinade liquid is usually sufficient for 2 pounds (about 1 kg) of meat.

Meat absorbs the flavors of the marinade in which it is immersed. The acid in the marinade tenderizes the meat. Oils, if used, help to prevent the meat from drying when it is cooked or smoked. Immersion time normally varies from less than an hour to many hours. In this book, however, an immersion time of several days is suggested for some of the products. If the meat is to be marinated more than one hour, it should be refrigerated to retard proliferation of bacteria.

Some marinades are cooked. Cooked marinades are made sterile by the cooking process, so it is a little safer to use them for an immersion time that exceeds 12 hours. Of course, cooked marinades should be well chilled before using.

The warmer the marinade and the warmer the raw material, the faster the penetration of the flavor. Any marinade at room temperature, for example, will penetrate the meat faster than one at refrigerator temperature. However, as mentioned previously, marinating for over an hour at room temperature might cause a dangerous proliferation of bacteria.

There are no strict rules for the length of the immersion time. Obviously, a strong flavor requires more time than a mild flavor. Thick pieces of meat require more time than thin pieces. If tenderization and deep penetration are the goals, longer times are more effective. As a general guideline, you will need to marinate 1-inch (2.5 cm) cubes of meat for two or three hours, at a minimum. However, a hunk of meat 4 to 6 inches (10 to 15 cm) thick would probably be marinated overnight, minimum. If you use a marinade recipe from a cookbook, the instructions will usually offer guidelines.

I believe that long marinating times are best for preparing raw material for smoking. Consequently, if a cookbook recipe suggests overnight, I might marinate for two or three days. When marinating material that will be smoked, I tend to consider the marinade to be a type of cure; hence, I extend the marinating time to ensure thorough penetration of the flavor. Obviously, the refrigerator should be in the proper temperature range if marinating times are extended significantly. Spoilage might result if the refrigerator is too warm.

The taste of the finished product will be a reflection of the taste of the ingredients that you use. If you don't like the taste of any ingredient, don't use it. If wine is called for in the recipe, use a wine that tastes good to you. If you can't stand burgundy, use another variety of wine that agrees with your palate. It does not have to be expensive; a table wine that you would enjoy drinking is fine. The so-called cooking wines are a poor choice.

Many recipes for marinades call for soy sauce. If you do use soy sauce, use a good brand. Kikkoman is good. Yamasa soy sauce, made in Oregon, is excellent. If you want to try imported brands, you should be able to find some good ones at Chinese, Japanese, or Korean grocery stores. In East Asian countries where soy sauce is used daily, there are many special-purpose varieties. So if you buy imported soy sauce at an ethnic grocery store, ask the shopkeeper to help you select a general-purpose type. If you do go to an ethnic grocery store, consider purchasing some imported Japanese Worcestershire sauce for seasoning your smoked products; in my opinion, it is much better than our domestic brands. The Japanese sauce will probably have WORCESTER SAUCE written in English on the label.

Complete directions for processing several marinated-and-smoked products will be found in this book. Each product will appear in the chapter dealing with the kind of meat being processed in that chapter— red meat, poultry, fish, what have you. However, you should not limit yourself to the marinade recipes found herein; explore the numerous marinade recipes that appear in cookbooks and barbecue books.

It is best to hot smoke marinated foods at temperatures greater than 140º F (60º C). Spoilage, or proliferation of microorganisms, might result if the product is smoked at lower temperatures. This is because marinades typically impart less salt and sugar than does a salt curing process, and this reduced salt and sugar makes the proliferation of microorganisms more likely.

# CHAPTER 8

# Techniques

![flame icon] Whenever a technique or an explanation relates to only one chapter, it will normally appear in that chapter. However, a number of techniques have application in more than one chapter. Such techniques are explained here. It is a good idea to become familiar with the contents of this chapter so you can refer to whatever may be helpful.

## Hanging with a Skewer and Twine Loop

If you wish to hang a hunk of meat for drying or smoking, one of the best methods is to use a skewer and a loop of butcher's twine. It is fast and easy, and it disfigures the meat much less than hooks. Furthermore, if the meat is thin, the skewer may prevent horizontal curling.

♭ Select a bamboo or stainless-steel skewer at least 1 inch (2.5 cm) longer than the width of the meat. (Asian grocery stores usually stock bamboo skewers of assorted lengths.)

♭ Cut a piece of butcher's twine about four times the width of the meat.

♭ Push the skewer through the meat near one end of the hunk.

♭ Tie the two ends of the twine together, and then pass the

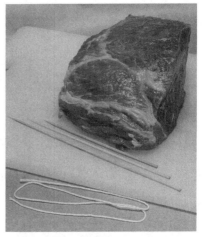

**Twine and skewers—materials to prepare meat for hanging.**

twine over the skewer ends and under the loop, as illustrated in the photo. The meat can now be hung directly on a support rod, but the use of an S hook on which to hang the twine is more convenient.

## Net-Tying

Net-tying is a good way to hang meat in the smoker, and it makes a very attractive finished product. For some reason, a net-tied prod-

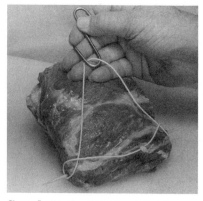

**Cured meat—prepared for hanging in the smoker.**

uct looks like "the real thing." It is particularly attractive on beef tongue, hunks of ham, or large sausages. It does have one disadvantage: It takes more time to net-tie than it does to lay the product on a smoking rack or to hang it with a skewer and a loop of twine. However, net-tying will become faster and easier as you gain experience.

The irregular shape of a beef tongue makes it one of the more difficult items to tie, so the beef tongue will be used to illustrate the procedure. You can practice this technique without using meat. Instead of meat, use a block of wood or any other object.

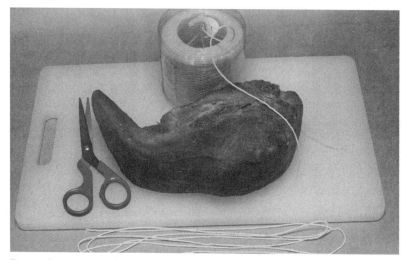

**Preparing to net-tie a cured beef tongue.**

🔥 Cut a piece of butcher's twine about eight times the length of the tongue.

🔥 Hold the twine over the tip of the tongue, leaving about 6 inches (15 cm) of twine to spare. Bring the long end of the twine about 2 inches (5 cm) from the tip of the tongue (on the top), and put your left thumb on top of the twine (if you are right-handed). If you press the twine with your thumb, you can bend the twine 90 degrees and wrap it completely around the front part of the tongue.

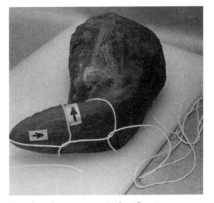

**Beginning to net-tie the tongue.**

🔥 Feed the long end of the twine under the bend (at the point where you were pressing with your thumb).

🔥 Again, bring the twine along the top until it is about 4 or 5 inches (10 to 12 cm) from the tip the tongue. Do just as above: Press down with the thumb, wrap around, and feed the long end under the bend in the twine. Do the same thing two more times.

**Net-tying the bottom (root) of the tongue.**

🔥 On the bottom (root) of the tongue, feed the long end of the twine over and under each place that the twine has been wrapped around the tongue.

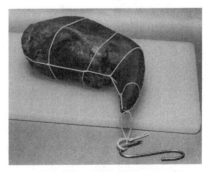

**Net-tie of the cured tongue is complete. It is ready to smoke.**

❧ Make a knot at the tip of the tongue. Then tie the two loose ends together about 2 or 3 inches (5 to 8 cm) from the tip of the tongue. If desired, make a loop, and insert a hook in that loop.

❧ To prevent slippage, use eight short pieces of twine to tie a knot at each of the eight points where the twine intersects. (The knots are not shown in the photograph.)

# Expelling Air from Plastic Bags

After putting raw material or product in a plastic bag, it is advisable to expel most of the air before sealing. This is especially true in the following situations:

❧ The product or raw material will be frozen.

❧ The finished product will be cooked using the hot water cooking method described later in this chapter.

❧ The raw material will be thawed using the cold water thawing method.

A simple technique will expel almost all of the air. First, fill a deep pan with cold water. Put the material in a plastic bag, and then immerse the bag in the water while keeping the open end of the bag above the waterline. Push the bag down until the water pressure has forced the air out; twist the bag closed, and seal it.

# Thawing

Instead of using fresh material, frozen meat, frozen fowl, and frozen fish are often thawed, cured, and smoked. Smoked products made of thawed raw material are usually indistinguishable from those made of fresh material. However, it is best if the raw material has been properly frozen, properly thawed, and used as soon as possible.

Microwave thawing is widely used for general household and commercial food preparation, especially for foods that are to be cooked soon. However, it is not suitable for most of the processing described in this book:

❧ A microwave oven causes uneven thawing.

❧ Some parts of the material are warmed excessively, especially the edges.

♭ The material is sometimes partially cooked.

Removing raw material from the freezer and thawing it at room temperature is another bad way to thaw; the surface and the thin parts of the material will thaw quickly, and they will remain at a relatively warm temperature while the thicker parts continue thawing. Bacteria could begin to multiply on the warmer parts of the raw material. The conditions might not be bad enough to cause food poisoning, but the quality of the finished product will suffer. It is best to use one of the recommended thawing methods that are explained below.

## REFRIGERATOR THAWING

If the raw material is to be thawed in a refrigerator, the refrigerator should be set to between 36° and 40° F (2.2° and 4.4° C). Thawing in a refrigerator is a very good method for most kinds of food. There is one disadvantage, however: Refrigerator thawing may require considerable time. Four days, or more, might be required to thaw a turkey, for example.

## COLD WATER THAWING

If cold water thawing is employed, the pieces of raw material must be sealed in plastic bags to prevent absorption of water (this is important). It is best to put only one piece of raw material in each bag. Remove as much air as possible. Place the bagged material in a deep container, and fill the container with cold tap water. The material should be pressed below the surface of the water. Set the container in a sink, and allow a thin stream of cold tap water to run into the container—or change the water in the container from time to time.

A large joint of meat (a primal cut of top sirloin, for example) might require only a number of hours to thaw in cold water, but the same joint of meat might require several days to thaw in the refrigerator. This will be true even if the temperature of the water in the container is the same as the temperature of the air in the refrigerator. Why does cold water thaw more effectively? The heat conductivity of water is much greater than that of the air in the refrigerator. Consequently, thawing is much faster in water—even if the thawing temperatures are the same.

Cold water thawing can be used in combination with refrigerator thawing. Even if you began the thawing in the refrigerator, you can finish it quickly in cold water. This is especially useful when you have underestimated the refrigerator thawing time, and you need to begin your processing schedule.

Finally, some people (like me) believe that fish should always be thawed quickly in cold water. Deterioration of the flesh begins to occur when fish starts thawing. Consequently, quick thawing in cold water will result in fresher fish.

# Surface drying

Traditional smoking requires that the surface of the product be reasonably dry before smoking begins. If the surface is not dry, smoke will dissolve in the surface moisture, and this will cause an uneven coloration and an unpleasant taste.

Food smoking books often suggest that the product be hung, unwrapped, in a refrigerator overnight. I do not suggest this method of drying in this book because it is troublesome and because most people, including myself, usually do not have enough refrigerator space to accommodate all of the product.

The technique for surface drying that I have developed requires the use of paper towels and newspaper. The product is not hung; it is stacked on the refrigerator shelf after being wrapped with paper towels and newspaper. If this technique is used, very little refrigerator space is required.

The next morning, the paper is removed and discarded. Almost all of the surface moisture will have been absorbed by the paper. After subjecting the product to about 140° F (60 ° C) for about an hour or so, the surface will be dry and smoking may begin.

# Hot Water Cooking

Sausages are commonly cooked in hot water. I use a method of hot water cooking for cooking various kinds of smoked meats, including medium- and large-diameter sausage. The technique is a useful alternative to cooking the product in a steamer, a hot smoker, a water smoker, or a kitchen oven. The method of hot water cooking described below is suitable for red meat and for fowl that is being processed in pieces. It is not a good method for cooking fish.

Hot water cooking has many advantages:

**↟** Hot water cooking between 170° and 200° F (76.7° and 93.3° C) does not dry the product nearly as much as cooking it in an oven or in a hot smoker without a water pan.

🔥 If the product is cooked in hot water, shrinkage is less than cooking it in a kitchen oven or cooking it in a hot smoker without a water pan.

🔥 Cooking in hot water is much faster than cooking in a smoker (with or without a water pan) because the heat conductivity of water is much better than that of air.

🔥 It is very easy to avoid overcooking if hot water cooking is used. The hot water temperature can be kept just high enough for cooking to take place; as soon as the product has become fully cooked, it can be removed from the hot water. (Because a meat thermometer is used, it is easy to determine when the product is fully cooked.)

A hot water cooker (enamelware stockpot) with a lid, a lid weight (stone), an alcohol-in-glass water thermometer, and a baby-dial sausage thermometer. The recessed lid was made from a plastic tray that is normally used under large flowerpots. This pie-pan-shaped lid is about 1 inch (2.5 cm) deep.

The method described below requires the product to be placed in plastic bags before cooking in hot water. Use of plastic bags will prevent dissolving of the seasoning and smoke flavor into the cooking water. Your kitchen will smell wonderful if plastic bags are not used, but the product will taste flat because much of the flavor and aroma will be dissolved in the hot water used for cooking. For sausages, the natural or synthetic casing gives some protection from the water. Nevertheless, it is recommended that sausages, too, be put into plastic bags prior to cooking in hot water.

Rather than using common plastic food bags, vacuum-packing plastic may be used. This plastic is strong, and the air is almost completely removed. However, vacuum-packing is more expensive.

## HOT WATER COOKER

The basic elements of a hot water cooker are:

🔥 A large pan, pot, or kettle made of any kind of metal normally used for pots and pans (including cast iron or aluminum). A large stockpot is ideal.

🔥 A recessed lid that is shaped like a pie pan. The rim of this lid rests on the top edge of the cooker pot. The recessed area of this lid has holes bored in it, and this recessed area will sink slightly below the water surface when the pot is nearly full of hot water. The primary purpose of the lid is to press the meat down, below the surface of the hot water. The thermometer for the hot water is inserted into one of the small holes in the recessed lid, and a baby-dial meat thermometer protrudes from the large hole in the lid. This recessed lid can be made of any material that can withstand the temperature of very hot water.

🔥 A clean stone, brick, or other heavy object to place in the center of the recessed lid. The heavy stone functions to keep the lid from being pushed upward by the buoyancy of the meat or sausage.

🔥 A liquid-in-glass or dial thermometer that will read at least as high as 212º F (100º C). This thermometer is used to measure the temperature of the hot water.

🔥 A baby-dial sausage thermometer (shown in the photograph). As mentioned above, this thermometer protrudes from the large hole in the lid. The diameter of this large hole should be slightly greater than the diameter of the dial on the baby-dial thermometer. Secure the thermometer to the pot handle with twine.

## HOW TO COOK WITH HOT WATER

If a recipe in this book suggests that the product be cooked in hot water, the basic instructions for doing so will be indicated. Nevertheless, the more detailed explanation given below may be helpful in the beginning.

🔥 Fill the cooking pot about half to three-quarters of the way with water. Put the water-temperature thermometer in the pot, and begin to heat the water to the suggested cooking temperature.

🔥 While the water is heating, inspect each piece of smoked meat for sharp corners or projections that could punch a hole in the plastic bag (the plastic bag that will be used to encase the meat). Scissors can be used to snip off any sharp projection (a sharp, dried fiber of meat, for example).

𝄐 Select the thickest piece of meat, and insert a sausage thermometer into the center of the thickest part. Be sure the tip of the thermometer does not touch bone, and be sure it is not embedded in fat. (If either one of these conditions exists, the thermometer reading may not be accurate.)

𝄐 Wrap this thickest piece of meat with plastic food wrap. Twist the plastic wrap around the sausage thermometer stem at the point where it projects from the meat. Wrap all the other pieces with plastic food wrap. (The main reason for wrapping with plastic food wrap is to give additional protection against the plastic bag being punctured by a sharp point on the smoked meat. A second purpose is to reduce the dissolving of the flavor, even if the plastic bag leaks despite the precautions taken.)

𝄐 Put the remaining pieces of meat in individual plastic bags, expel the air, and twist the neck closed. Seal the neck with a short piece of butcher's twine or a wire bread-bag tie. If butcher's twine is used, it is convenient to use something like a piece of cellophane tape or a clothespin to keep the bag twisted shut while it is being tied. A bagging tape machine could be used instead of using cellophane tape (see the bagging tape machine photo in chapter 4). The thickest piece of meat (the piece with the thermometer embedded in it) is sealed in a similar way. Of course, the neck of the plastic bag should be twisted around the stem of the thermometer.

𝄐 When the hot water is approximately the correct cooking temperature, put all the meat in the pot except the piece with the thermometer. (If the water is a few degrees above the correct cooking temperature, there is no need to be concerned about it; the meat is cooler than the water, and it will bring the temperature down.)

𝄐 Place the recessed lid on the pot, and add hot tap water to bring the water level to the bottom of the recessed lid. On the other hand, if there is excess water, it needs to be removed to prevent the pot from overflowing.

𝄐 Tie another piece of twine on the thermometer protruding from the thickest piece of meat (tie this twine at about the same place that you previously sealed the bag). This twine should be long enough to tie to the handle of the pot.

◊ Remove the lid, and pass the dial of the sausage thermometer through the bottom of the large hole in the lid. Feed the twine through the same hole. Put this piece of meat in the hot water while replacing the lid. Tie the twine to the pot handle.

◊ Insert the hot water thermometer through a small hole in the lid. If necessary, use twine to tie it to a handle on the pot. Weight the lid with a large stone so that the meat will be pushed below the surface of the water. It is desirable for some water to come up through the holes in the lid. Adjust the water level again, if necessary.

◊ Bring the temperature of the water to the specified cooking temperature, and try to maintain that temperature. *Important:* Before reading the hot water thermometer, it is best to move it back and forth a few times to make sure that it is not resting against a relatively cool piece of meat.

◊ Cook the meat until the specified internal temperature is reached. Depending on the thickness of the meat and other factors, this may require an hour or more. If you want the finest quality possible, avoid the temptation to speed up the cooking by raising the temperature of the hot water.

◊ After the product has been cooked, put all the pieces in a colander, open the bags, and drain. There will be some juice in the bags because a little juice is squeezed out when the meat shrinks during cooking. (Sausages should be cooled quickly in cold water before the plastic bags are opened.) Cool at room temperature for two hours. Refrigerate overnight, uncovered (to facilitate drying of the surface). The pieces should be sealed in plastic bags the following morning.

*Caution:* Be particularly careful when cooking at a rather high temperature: 190° F (87.8° C), for example. If the temperature of the water should accidentally reach the boiling point, the bags will balloon, and some may burst. In addition, the meat will shrink more than it normally does. Worst of all, the ballooning bags will cause the hot water to overflow the pot, and you will have a very watery mess to clean up. I made this mistake once, but I do not think I will make it again.

# Cooking with a Steamer

Cooking with a steamer produces results almost as good as the hot water cooking method described above. Furthermore, steamer cooking is simple, fast, and effective. The use of a special technique described below results in a succulent product that is bathed in its own juices.

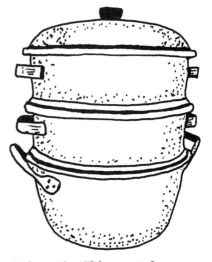

A steamer with a minimum internal diameter of 11 inches (28 cm) is recommended. Any kind of steamer can be used, but I like to use a large aluminum Chinese steamer. Chinese steamers usually have three tiers. Water boils in the pan in the lowest tier. Each of the steamer baskets has numerous holes punched in the bottom. Steam from the boiling

**A three-tier Chinese-style aluminum steamer. The bottom tier is for water. Stacked on the water pan are two steamer baskets and a lid.**

water passes up, through these holes, and escapes from the top of the steamer.

After pieces of red meat, sausage, or fowl are cured and cold smoked, wrap each piece very well with plastic food wrap. (This will cause the product to be bathed in the juices that are squeezed out when the meat cooks and shrinks.) Insert the cable probe of an electronic meat thermometer in the thickest piece. The probe may be stuck through the plastic wrap. Place all of the meat in the steamer baskets.

Bring the water to a boil, and steam the meat until the internal target temperature is reached. If the thermometer's audible alarm is switched to the ON position, you need not monitor the cooking process—watch TV, if you like, and wait for the alarm to sound.

# Sharpening Knives

Various kinds of electrical and mechanical knife sharpening gadgets are on the market. Most of them promise a razor-sharp edge with little or no effort. However, none of them will put a better edge on your knife than an old-fashioned sharpening stone. Furthermore, many of these gadgets will destroy or damage knives very quickly. Admittedly, sharpening knives by hand is not at the top of my list of interesting things to do, but it is the best way to get a truly sharp knife.

When sharpening a knife, it is best to use a lot of water on the stone to wash away the metal dust and abrasive particles. I sharpen my knives in the kitchen sink with the whetstone placed on top of an inverted plastic dishpan. A fine stream of water constantly flows on the stone. The samurai warriors of feudal Japan used water on the whetstone when sharpening their swords. In modern Japan, this technique is still used when the Japanese sharpen their culinary knives.

Some people use mineral oil on the stone, but this is very messy, and it is certainly no better than water. If oil has ever been used on the stone, it is best to buy a new stone, and use nothing but water on it.

Use the whetstone described in chapter 4, page 86. First, use the coarse side of the stone. Hold the knife blade at an angle of about 20 degrees to the stone. The blade may be pushed, pulled, or sharpened in a circular motion; it makes no difference—the motion used to sharpen the knife is not important. Do what is comfortable for you. It is important, however, to maintain an angle of about 20 degrees on both sides of the blade.

Stroke the right side of the blade for about 15 seconds, then turn it over and stroke the left side for about 15 seconds. The sharpening should begin at the tip of the blade and proceed slowly to the hilt, or vice versa.

Continue sharpening on the coarse side of the stone until the knife feels very sharp. If the knife was quite dull, this may require five minutes or more. Stainless-steel knives are made of hard steel, so more time is required to sharpen them than to sharpen carbon-steel knives. Long knives require more time to sharpen than short knives.

When the knife feels sharp, turn the stone over so that the fine side is up. Continue sharpening at the same angle but with lighter pressure. This will remove the burrs and the edge curl, and it will put a fine edge on the knife.

Between sharpening sessions, a butcher's steel should be employed to remove the edge curl and burrs that develop when a knife is used.

# CHAPTER 9

# Smoking Red Meat

## Smoked Pork Loin

In the 1970s, I worked for Hammond Organ Company, a manufacturer of electronic organs in Chicago. One of my duties was to look after some of the foreign guests who visited the company from time to time, and this included taking them out for lunch or dinner. One establishment that we frequented was a cozy German restaurant that served delicious and authentic cuisine. A permanent feature on the menu was cured-and-smoked pork loin (*kassler rippchen*). A slice at least 1 inch (2.5 cm) thick was served with a mountain of sauerkraut.

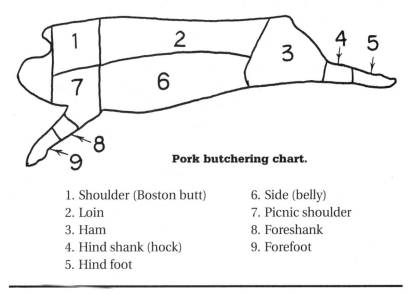

**Pork butchering chart.**

1. Shoulder (Boston butt)
2. Loin
3. Ham
4. Hind shank (hock)
5. Hind foot
6. Side (belly)
7. Picnic shoulder
8. Foreshank
9. Forefoot

That smoked pork loin was truly unforgettable. I never dreamed I would be able to make it myself. However, a few years later when I became interested in smoking foods, I recalled the smoked pork loin, and I decided that making it would be one of my goals—and I did it! It comes out of my smoker three or four times a year, and my family and friends never seem to tire of it. The only disappointing thing about smoked pork loin is that it is just too easy to produce. Something so good should require more work!

## PORK LOIN

All of us are familiar with the pork chop. The pork chop is cut from the long muscle (the loin) that lies on both sides of the pig near the backbone and between the foreleg and the hind leg. The best pork chops are cut from the center section of the loin. The

**Cured pork loin (modern dry cure), ready to smoke.**

front part of the loin (toward the shoulders of the pig) has fat marbled in the red meat, and it is most often used for pork roasts or country-style ribs. The most attractive smoked pork loin will be made from the same section of the loin that is used for high-quality pork chops—the center. Nevertheless, don't hesitate to use the front or back of the loin if economy is more important than appearance. Pork from the cheaper front part of the loin is pictured in the Cured Pork Loin (Modern Dry Cure) photograph.

Bone-in loin may be cured and smoked if you want authentic *kassler rippchen*, but you may prefer boned material since it is easier to cure and easier to slice after the smoking and cooking have been completed. Boned pork loin is very easy to buy nowadays.

It seems logical to me that more cure mix should be applied to a pound of boned meat than to a pound of bone-in meat. To my way of thinking, the bone-in meat would require less curing mix because the bone does not need to be cured. But, alas, it seems that my logic is flawed. The same amount of cure applied to either a pound of boned meat or a pound of bone-in meat seems to produce the same taste. (It may be that the bones are absorbing about the same amount of cure as the meat.) Consequently, if you use bone-in meat, I recommend that you weigh the meat and apply the cure accordingly, disregarding the fact that the meat contains bones.

## TRIMMING, CUTTING, AND PIERCING

A pork loin usually requires very little trimming. Cut off loose flesh, if any exists, and remove blood clots. If you like, you may shave off excess fat on the top part of the loin.

A whole, uncut pork loin can be processed if it will fit in your curing containers, refrigerator, and smoker. However, if you intend to give pieces of the smoked loin as gifts, the finished product will be more attractive if the loin is cut into hunks about 4 to 6 inches (10 to 15 cm) long. In addition, the loin is easier to weigh, handle, cure, smoke, and freeze if it is cut into pieces of a more manageable size. The following instructions assume that the loin has been cut into hunks.

Wash each piece of the loin in cold water, and drain in a colander. Blot them with a paper towel. Pierce well (especially any surface that is covered with fat). While the curing mix and curing equipment are being readied, refrigerate the meat.

## CURING

The total curing time required depends on the thickness of the thickest part of the loin. Measure the thickest part, and allow seven days of curing time for every inch (2.5 cm) of thickness. Consequently, about two weeks of curing time is required if the thickest part of the loin is 2 inches (5 cm) thick.

### CURE MIX FOR 2¼ POUNDS (1 KILOGRAM) OF PORK LOIN

1 Tbsp. (15 ml) salt
1 Tbsp. (15 ml) brown sugar—packed in the spoon
¾ tsp. (3.75 ml) onion powder
½ tsp. (2.5 ml) Prague Powder #1 (curing powder)
½ tsp. (2.5 ml) garlic powder
½ tsp. (2.5 ml) white pepper
¼ tsp. (1.25 ml) allspice

Total: 8½ tsp. (42.5 ml).

### CURE MIX MEASURING CHART

8½ tsp. (42.5 ml) per 2¼ lbs. (1 kg) of pork loin
4¼ tsp. (21.25 ml) per 1 lb. (500 g) of pork loin
2 tsp. (10 ml) per ½ lb. (250 g) of pork loin
1 tsp. (5 ml) per ¼ lb. (125 g) of pork loin

## BULK MIX FOR 27 POUNDS (12 KILOGRAMS) OF PORK LOIN

¾ cup (180 ml) salt
¾ cup (180 ml) brown sugar—packed in the cup
3 Tbsp. (45 ml) onion powder
2 Tbsp. (30 ml) Prague Powder #1
2 Tbsp. (30 ml) garlic powder
2 Tbsp. (30 ml) white pepper
1 Tbsp. (15 ml) allspice

1. Weigh the pork loin. If more than one curing container must be used, calculate separately the total weight of meat that will be put into each container. The curing containers should have tight-fitting lids. Prepare, calculate, and measure the required amount of curing mixture for each container (use the Cure Mix Measuring Chart).
2. Place the loin in the curing container(s). Rub the curing mix evenly on all surfaces of the meat. Cover the pork and refrigerate.
3. Overhaul the pieces of loin after about 12 hours of curing (remove from the container, rub all surfaces, and return to the container). If there is liquid in the bottom of the curing container, be sure to wet the meat with that liquid. This meat will be cold, so the use of rubber gloves is recommended.
4. Overhaul the meat about once a day for the first week, and then overhaul it every other day until the required curing time has elapsed.
5. When the curing has been finished, rinse each piece of loin *very well* in lukewarm water. Drain. Wrap each piece in a paper towel, and then wrap again with newspaper. Refrigerate overnight.

### SMOKING THE LOIN

1. If you intend to hang the loin in the smoke chamber, you should prepare the meat for hanging (see chapter 8). Net-tying is very attractive for any pieces you intend to use as a present. Hanging with skewers and string loops is the easiest method.
2. Hang the loin in the smoke chamber, or place it on smoking racks. Dry at about 140° F (60° C) until the surface feels dry (about an hour). Do not use smoke during the drying period. Using smoke when the meat is wet could cause bitterness and an uneven, mottled coloration.
3. When dry, cold smoke at less than 85° F (30° C) for three to six hours, depending on how smoky you want the meat. Raise the tem-

perature of the smoker to about 145º F (63º C), and continue to smoke until the pork takes on a reddish brown color (two to three hours). Remove the meat from the smoker. *Note:* If your equipment will not operate at these low temperatures, you should dry and smoke the meat as close as possible to the suggested temperatures.

**COOKING THE LOIN**

The pork is not fully cooked when it comes out of the smoker. Of course, it may be cooked by any conventional method used to cook meat. It can be sliced and fried, oven roasted, or cut up and added to boiled foods for seasoning. A water smoker can be used for the cooking, or the special hot water cooking method can be employed. Another good option would be steam cooking. Instructions for hot water cooking and steam cooking are in chapter 8.

The pork loin is fully cooked when the internal temperature is 160º F (71º C). The special hot water cooking conditions that are best for pork loin are as follows:

♨ The water temperature is 175º F (80º C).

♨ The cooking time will probably be one to two hours.

After cooking, this cured and smoked pork loin can be used as you would use fully cooked, cured ham. In fact, any lean pork from any part of the pig can be processed and used in the same way.

# Honey-Cured Ham

The meat from the rear leg of a hog is called ham. If this meat is not processed, it is called *fresh ham.* Cooked fresh ham will be the same color as a fried pork chop, and the taste will be the same. Normally, however, when we use the word *ham,* we mean the pink *cured ham* with the slightly salty taste.

Honey-cured ham is famous, delicious, and easy to make. There is one minor restricting factor, however: You cannot process a whole ham with the curing techniques presented in this book. If you were to try to cure a whole leg without injecting the flesh with strong brine, the meat would probably spoil due to a problem called *bone marrow sour.* Nevertheless, you can produce ham that will be very much like the ham you buy at the supermarket, but it will have three significant differences: This will not be a whole ham; it will have a smokier aroma; and it will taste better. If you do not need to have a whole ham in the round, this product is worth a try.

## PREPARING THE FRESH HAM

If economy is important, you can buy irregularly shaped hunks of pork that are often packed in large plastic tubes—most of this meat is cut from the rear leg or the loin. It is suitable as the raw material, and it may be cheaper than a whole rear leg. Wholesale grocery stores are much more likely to stock these large bags of pork hunks than a common supermarket.

If you want to use the conventional fresh ham as the raw material, you will probably have to place an order with your butcher. Almost any butcher will be happy to order a whole fresh ham for you. To prepare the ham, the first step is to remove the bone. Next, remove the skin and the excess fat. Butterfly the meat or cut it into slabs; the goal is to cut the meat so that the thickest piece is not more than 3 inches (7.5 mm) thick. Save and freeze the scraps and trimmings to make sausage sometime in the future.

*Note:* If you do not have butchering experience, ask the butcher to remove the bone for you. Many butchers will do this free of charge. They might be willing to remove the skin, too. It is best if you do the rest of the trimming and cutting yourself so that you can be assured of getting the thicknesses that you want.

Use a fork with sharp tines or a meat piercing tool to pierce the meat thoroughly. Next, measure the thickest piece of meat. One week of curing time will be required for each inch (2.5 cm) of thickness, so three weeks will be required if the thickest piece is 3 inches (7.5 cm) thick.

## CURE MIX FOR 2¼ POUNDS (1 KILOGRAM) OF FRESH HAM

> 1 Tbsp. (15 ml) salt
> 1 tsp. (5 ml) onion powder
> ½ tsp. (2.5 ml) Prague Powder #1
> ½ tsp. (2.5 ml) white pepper powder
> ⅛ tsp. (0.625 ml) clove powder (optional)
> 3 Tbsp. (45 ml) honey (add to the dry ingredients at the time of
>     application)

Total: 5⅛ tsp. (25.625 ml)—excluding honey. (The "⅛ tsp." and "0.625 ml" are insignificant and may be eliminated.)

### CURE MIX MEASURING CHART

5 tsp. (25 ml) per 2¼ lbs. (1 kg) of pork + 3 Tbsp. (45 ml) honey

2½ tsp. (12.5 ml) per 1 lb. (500 g) of pork + 4½ tsp. (22.5 ml) honey

1¼ tsp. (6.25 ml) per ½ lb. (250 g) of pork + 2¼ tsp. (11.25 ml) honey

½ tsp. (2.5 ml) per ¼ lb. (125 g) of pork + 1 tsp. (5 ml) honey

### BULK MIX FOR 27 POUNDS (12 KILOGRAMS) OF FRESH HAM

¾ cup (180 ml) salt

¼ cup (120 ml) onion powder

2 Tbsp. (30 ml) Prague Powder #1

2 Tbsp. (30 ml) white pepper

1½ tsp. (7.5 ml) clove powder (optional)

3 Tbsp. (45 ml) honey per 2¼ lbs. (1 kg) of fresh ham (add to the cure at the time of application)

### CURING, SMOKING, AND COOKING THE HAM

The curing, smoking, and cooking of this honey-cured ham are exactly the same as for the previous product, smoked pork loin. Enjoy!

# Maple-Syrup-Cured Bacon

Bacon was normally hard cured in the old days, and then smoked and dried for a lengthy period so that it could be kept without refrigeration for months—or even as long as a year. Urbanization and improved refrigeration put the job of making bacon into the hands of commercial meat processors.

These meat processors have developed mechanized curing methods for meats that home smokers cannot duplicate. For example, commercial meat processors can cure a slab of pork belly in just a few hours. A machine with hundreds of hypodermic-like needles injects the liquid cure in the pork belly in about the same amount of time that it would take you to dial a telephone number. The slab of belly is ready to smoke after it sets overnight.

Even though some of the commercially produced bacon is rather good, you can make much better bacon than that sold at a common grocery store. The bacon resulting from the process described below will probably be among the best you have eaten. With a little adjustment of the seasoning to match your taste, you can produce the best bacon you have ever eaten. You can control all the seasonings, the smokiness, and the salt content. Moreover, with a little care you will be able to produce the same exquisite product every time. It requires a little work, but not much—and most of that work is fun because it is creative.

## PORK BELLY

When a pig is butchered, the belly meat that extends from the chest to the hind leg is cut down the middle into two belly slabs. The belly meat that comes from the area of the chest is called brisket, and the meat that is nearest the hind leg is called flank. The brisket end of the belly is thicker than the flank, and it is preferred for making bacon. Bacon made from the flank will taste the same, but it will not be as attractive. If you are able to select between the two halves, you may find that the flank half is cheaper. Frozen belly works just as well as fresh belly.

It is recommended that the skin be removed from the belly before processing it into bacon. Both the cure and smoke flavor will penetrate the belly more easily if the skin is removed. However, the skin need not be discarded; it can be cured and smoked with the bacon. Cured and smoked pork skin makes excellent flavoring when boiling dried beans or making soup. If the skin will be processed with the pork belly, be sure to include the weight of the skin when you calculate the amount of cure mix.

## TRIMMING, CUTTING, AND PIERCING

1. The belly slab should be thawed, but well chilled. Remove the skin, and use a sharp boning knife to trim out cartilage remaining where the rib bones used to lie. Cut off loose flesh, and remove blood clots. If you like, you may trim the edges of the slab to give it a squared appearance. If the trimmings are free of blood clots and gristle, you may freeze them to use when you make sausage sometime in the future.

2. At this point, you should decide whether you want to cure and smoke the bacon as one whole slab, or process the belly after it is cut into several rectangles. The instructions will be for processing the rectangles. They are much easier to handle, weigh, cure, smoke, and freeze.

3. Cut the slab into rectangles. Wash each rectangle in cold water, and drain them in a colander. Blot each piece with a paper towel, and pierce it well. While the curing mix and curing equipment are being readied, refrigerate the pork belly.

## CURING

The total required curing time depends on the thickness of the thickest rectangle. Measure the thickest rectangle; allow seven days of curing time for every inch (2.5 cm) of thickness. If the thickest rectangle measures 1½ inches (4 cm), for example, the curing time will be a week and a half.

### CURE MIX FOR 2¼ POUNDS (1 KILOGRAM) OF PORK BELLY

1 Tbsp. (15 ml) salt
½ tsp. (2.5 ml) onion powder
½ tsp. (2.5 ml) Prague Powder #1
½ tsp. (2.5 ml) garlic powder
½ tsp. (2.5 ml) white pepper
2 Tbsp. (30 ml) maple syrup (add to the ingredients above at the time of use)

*Note:* If about 1 teaspoon of imitation maple flavor is added to the maple syrup, the bacon will have a stronger maple aroma.

Total: 5 tsp. (25 ml)—excluding maple syrup and the optional maple flavor.

### CURE MIX MEASURING CHART

5 tsp. (25 ml) per 2¼ lbs. (1 kg) of belly + 2 Tbsp. (30 ml) of syrup
2½ tsp. (12.5 ml) per 1 lb. (500 g) of belly + 1 Tbsp. (15 ml) of syrup
1¼ tsp. (6.25 ml) per ½ lb. (250 g) of belly + 1½ tsp. (7.5 ml) of syrup
½ tsp. (2.5 ml) per ¼ lb. (125 g) of belly + ¾ tsp. (3.75 ml) of syrup

### BULK MIX FOR 27 POUNDS (12 KILOGRAMS) OF PORK BELLY

¾ cup (180 ml) salt
2 Tbsp. (30 ml) onion powder
2 Tbsp. (30 ml) Prague Powder #1
2 Tbsp. (30 ml) garlic powder
2 Tbsp. (30 ml) white pepper
2 Tbsp. (30 ml) maple syrup per 2¼ lbs. (1 kg) of belly (add to the cure at the time of use)

1. Weigh the pork belly rectangles. If more than one curing container must be used, calculate separately the total weight of meat that will be put in each container. The curing containers should have tight-

fitting lids. Prepare, calculate, and measure the required amount of curing mixture and maple syrup for each container (use the Cure Mix Measuring Chart).

2. Place the rectangles in the curing containers. Blend the curing mix and the maple syrup to form a thick liquid. Rub the liquid on the meat evenly to ensure equal distribution of the cure. Cover and refrigerate.

3. Rub again, and rearrange the rectangles after about 12 hours of curing.

4. Overhaul (rub and rearrange) the bacon rectangles once a day during the curing period.

5. When the curing time has elapsed, rinse each rectangle very well in lukewarm water. Drain in a colander. Wrap each rectangle in a paper towel, and then wrap again with newspaper. Refrigerate overnight.

## SMOKING THE BACON

1. If you intend to hang the rectangles of pork belly in the smoke chamber, you should prepare the meat for hanging (see chapter 8). If you want to smoke a whole pork belly slab at one time, special hangers are available from mail-order supply companies. These hangers have several nail-like spikes on which the slab is impaled. A similar slab hanger could be constructed with a short board and stainless-steel or chrome-plated spikes. Zinc-dipped nails may also be used.

2. Hang the rectangles in the smoke chamber, or place them on smoking racks. Dry at about 140° F (60° C) until the surface is dry—about an hour. Do not use smoke during the drying period.

3. When dry, cold smoke at less than 85° F (30° C) for three to six hours, depending on how smoky you want the bacon. (If you do not have a cold smoker, keep the temperature as low as possible.) Raise the temperature of the smoker to about 145° F (63° C), and smoke until the bacon takes on a reddish brown color (two to three hours).

4. Cool the meat at room temperature for about two hours, and then refrigerate, uncovered, overnight. Put the bacon rectangles in individual plastic bags and seal them. Freeze the bacon that will not be consumed within one week. If bacon is to be frozen, it is best to wrap it in plastic food wrap before it is sealed in a plastic bag. The bacon will keep well in the freezer for at least two months.

*Note:* This bacon is not a fully cooked product. Smoking at about 145° F (63° C) for two or three hours might not protect against trichinosis. All bacon should be fully cooked before it is consumed.

*Hint:* If you intend to fry or broil the bacon, it is a good idea to make about five scores across the top of the bacon rectangles before you slice it. Each score should be approximately 1/16 inch (1 mm) deep, and it should be perpendicular to the direction of slicing. These scores will help to prevent the bacon from curling when it is being cooked. Also, keep in mind that maple-syrup-cured bacon is a type of sugar-cured bacon, so it should be fried slowly at a low temperature and turned frequently. Frying sugar-cured bacon at a high temperature will cause it to caramelize and char.

# Other Bacon Varieties

By making changes in the seasoning ingredients, the sweetener, or even the raw material, many other bacon varieties can be made.

### CANADIAN BACON

Canadian bacon is popular in the United States, but it is expensive. You can make it yourself cheaply. In Canada, there is a similar product called *peameal bacon,* or peameal back bacon.

Peameal bacon is made from the *eye of the loin,* as is our Canadian bacon. (The eye of the loin is the well-trimmed core of a boneless pork loin.) However, the peameal bacon is rolled in yellow cornmeal, and it is never smoked. Our Canadian bacon is usually smoked, and it is never rolled in yellow cornmeal.

Why is the Canadian product called peameal bacon? Well, in the old days, it was rolled in a meal made from dried yellow peas; it was thought that the peameal would help to preserve the bacon. Yellow cornmeal was cheaper, and it seemed to work as well, so they changed the coating to cornmeal. Apparently, the name *cornmeal bacon* never caught on.

To make Canadian bacon as it is made in the United States, process the eye of the loin exactly as the maple-syrup-cured bacon is processed. However, instead of 3 tablespoons of maple syrup as the sweetener, use 1 tablespoon (15 ml) of common white sugar.

Commercially produced Canadian bacon is round because it is processed in a sleeve. This homemade product will have an oval shape.

When the eye of the loin is trimmed in preparation for curing, it is a traditional practice to leave about ⅛ inch (3 mm) of fat on the top.

## IRISH BACON

Irish bacon is similar to Canadian bacon. The main difference is that Irish bacon is made from exactly the same part of the loin used to make boneless pork chops. Consequently, after Irish bacon is cured, smoked, and thinly sliced, it will have the same teardrop shape and the same percent of fat as a pork chop, but it will be boneless.

To make this bacon, process a boned pork loin in the same way that maple-syrup-cured bacon is processed. However, it would be more traditional to use about 1 tablespoon (15 ml) of brown or white sugar instead of syrup.

One custom smoke shop in New York cures Irish bacon with a wee bit o' Irish whiskey. Hmmm—if Irish bacon tastes better with a little Irish whiskey in the cure, I wonder what a little Canadian whiskey would do for Canadian bacon?

## PEPPER BACON

Cure the pork belly by using the maple syrup cure, or use whatever seasonings and sweetener you like. However, before you put it in the smoker, press black pepper on the surface of the bacon slab or the bacon rectangles. Use very coarsely ground black pepper or cracked peppercorns.

You may want to use the following technique to make the pepper stick better: Before applying the pepper, paint the surface of the bacon very lightly with a mixture of 1 part honey, diluted with 3 parts of water. Let the surface dry until it becomes sticky, and then apply the pepper. The same thing can be accomplished with undiluted maple syrup or corn syrup.

## JOWL BACON

Bacon that is made from the cheek of the pig is called jowl bacon. Use the maple syrup cure or any other bacon cure that you like. Jowl bacon looks similar to belly bacon, but the slices are shorter. It is a little tougher, but the taste is the same as belly bacon. The Italians make jowl bacon; they call it *guanciale*.

### SPICY BACON

Try adding your favorite spices to the curing mix. For example, I have found that the addition of allspice makes an interesting flavor variation. A few people enjoy smoked pork that has been seasoned with cinnamon. I do not. Furthermore, sage is an excellent spice for fresh country sausage and many smoked poultry products; however, for me, it has an unpleasant taste in smoked pork products.

### CAJUN BACON

The curing process for Cajun country-style ribs that appears later in this chapter can be used to produce Cajun bacon—a well-seasoned bacon that is famous in Louisiana. Use the same Cajun-style curing process, but smoke the belly according to the instructions for maple-syrup-cured bacon.

### FATBACK BACON

The fat on the back of a pig is called fatback. It is hard fat, which means that it does not melt as easily as regular pork fat. Rural people sometimes process fatback in the same way as belly bacon. Of course, they call it *fatback bacon*. Obviously, this bacon is very high in cholesterol.

### COUNTRY BACON

Recently, I saw a product called *country bacon* in the butcher shop of a large grocery store. It was made from lean pork that had been cut to the same thickness as bacon slabs; then these slabs were processed as bacon. Of course, it was sliced like bacon.

If you like bacon but are concerned about the fat, you may wish to use lean slabs and make country bacon. To the extent possible, it is best to cut the slabs of lean meat *with the grain*. If the slabs are cut with the grain and the finished product is thinly sliced across the grain, the bacon will be tender.

### GYPSY BACON

Gypsy bacon is a Hungarian specialty. It is a method of cooking bacon rather than a method of curing and smoking it. The first step is to process the pork belly into bacon. Next, roast unsliced bacon hunks in a common oven at 350° F (175° C) until the internal temperature reaches 160° F (71° C). Sprinkle the roasted bacon liberally with paprika, preferably the flavorful Hungarian paprika. Slice the bacon thinly, and serve it on rye bread.

For a campfire treat, you may skewer a very thick slice of bacon in the same way a frankfurter is skewered. Cook it over the campfire, sprinkle it liberally with paprika, and serve on rye.

### BEEF BACON

Beef bacon is not as popular as it used to be. However, if you like it, you can make it. Simply use the parts of the beef brisket that resemble the red and white layering of pork belly.

If you want to be kind to your heart, use all lean meat. However, just as for the previously described country bacon, it would be best to cut the slabs of lean meat *with the grain* before curing, and then slice it thinly across the grain after it is smoked.

## Ham Hocks

Cured and smoked ham hocks are commonly used in southern-style cooking, and they are commonly used as a flavoring for cooking dried beans and peas. Pinto beans, navy beans, lima beans, black-eyed peas, split peas, and lentils, for example, taste very good when cooked with smoked ham hocks.

Cured and smoked ham hocks are sold at grocery stores, but you can easily make your own. All you have to do is process the fresh ham hocks in the same way as smoked pork loin is processed. When measuring the cure, disregard the fact that the hocks contain a lot of bone; weigh the hocks and apply the suggested amount of cure accordingly.

The raw material (fresh, uncured ham hocks) can be found in many grocery stores, especially in ethnic grocery stores. If you do not see them on display, ask the butcher if he or she can obtain them. Local meat-packers that retail to the public can provide them. If they do not retail to the public, they will be able to tell you where to find fresh ham hocks.

## Chinese-Style Barbecued Pork

Almost everyone has eaten *cha shu*—a flavorful Chinese-style barbecued pork that originated in the Hong Kong area of China. This delicacy is usually red on the outside. As an appetizer, it is thinly sliced and served with a small dish of hot mustard and toasted sesame seeds. A small amount of hot Chinese mustard is smeared on the pork, which is then dipped in sesame seeds. *Cha shu* is also used in fried rice, or in other dishes, as a seasoning ingredient.

The pork is marinated for a rather long time. It is traditionally barbecued, but it is even better when it is water smoked. If you like pork, this product will probably become one of your favorites. My friends appreciate the taste imparted by the ingredients listed below, but the recipe is not carved in stone—change it as you see fit. The pork can be either lean or fatty.

*Cha shu* is traditionally used as an appetizer, but it can also be served as a main course. As a main course, you may wish to use boneless pork chops or pork steak as the raw material. It can also be used for gourmet sandwiches.

In China, the Chinese use red-orange powdered food color in the marinade. However, the red liquid food color available anywhere in the United States works perfectly. I know of one professional Chinese cook here in Oregon who uses the American liquid food color, and I suspect that many other Chinese cooks do the same.

Below, you will see that clear honey is required. If your honey has crystallized, it may be clarified quickly in a microwave.

## MARINADE FOR 2¼ POUNDS (1 KILOGRAM) OF PORK

⅓ cup (80 ml) honey (clear)
¼ cup (60 ml) sugar
¼ cup (60 ml) sherry, or *shao hsing* wine
3 Tbsp. (45 ml) soy sauce
1 Tbsp. (15 ml) grated fresh ginger, or 1 tsp. ginger powder
1½ tsp. (7.5 ml) salt
½ tsp. (2.5 ml) red food color (liquid or powder)
¼ tsp. (1.25 ml) finely ground white pepper
2 cloves garlic, minced, or ¼ tsp. (1.25 ml) garlic powder

### DAY 1, MORNING

Prepare the amount of marinade appropriate for the weight of pork to be seasoned. Cut the pork into long rectangles about 1½ inches (4 cm) thick and 2 to 3 inches (5 to 7 cm) wide—the length is not important. It is best to pierce the pork to encourage deep penetration of the marinade. Begin to marinate the pork; keep it refrigerated. Shake the container several times a day. Marinate until the morning of Day 3.

**DAY 3, MORNING**
1. Remove the meat from the marinade and drain. *Do not rinse.*
2. Smoke the pork in a water smoker at about 240º F (115º C). After about an hour, baste the meat with peanut oil or common salad oil.
3. Smoke until the internal temperature reaches 160º F (71º C). The actual cooking time depends on several factors, but it will probably require about two hours. To prevent excessive drying, it is best to remove the thinner pieces as soon as they are cooked.

# Cajun Country-Style Ribs

This product is made from the very meaty and very economical cut of pork called country-style ribs. Actually, these are not ribs at all. These rib-shaped cuts usually come from the end of the loin that is located just above the shoulder blade. Consequently, they are sometimes called shoulder blade ribs. Boston butt is also cut into country-style ribs.

Cajun bacon is well known in the Cajun area of the Deep South, and that bacon inspired this product. Seasonings used in Cajun cooking were selected to flavor the pork. If you like highly seasoned foods, I believe that you will like this product. The Prague Powder #1 is optional. If it is used, the pork will be the same pink color as cured ham.

**CURE MIX FOR 2¼ POUNDS (1 KILOGRAM) OF COUNTRY-STYLE RIBS**

2 tsp. (10 ml) salt
2½ tsp. (12.5 ml) brown sugar—packed in the spoon
1 Tbsp. (15 ml) paprika
1½ tsp. (7.5 ml) onion powder
1 tsp. (5 ml) garlic powder
1 tsp. (5 ml) black pepper
1 tsp. (5 ml) cayenne
¾ tsp. (3.75 ml) ground oregano
½ tsp. (2.5 ml) ground thyme
½ tsp. (2.5 ml) Prague Powder #1 (optional)
¼ tsp. (1.25 ml) coriander powder

Total: 14 tsp. (70 ml) = 4 Tbsp. + 2 tsp.

### CURE MIX MEASURING CHART

4 Tbsp. + 2 tsp. (70 ml) per 2¼ lbs. (1 kg) country-style ribs

2 Tbsp. + 1 tsp. (35 ml) per 1 lb. (500 g) country-style ribs

3½ tsp. (17.5 ml) per ½ lb. (250 g) country-style ribs

1¾ tsp. (8.75 ml) per ¼ lb. (125 g) country-style ribs

### BULK MIX FOR 27 POUNDS (12 KILOGRAMS) OF COUNTRY-STYLE RIBS

½ cup (120 ml) salt

½ cup + 2 Tbsp. (150 ml) brown sugar—packed in the cup

¾ cup (180 ml) paprika

¼ cup + 2 Tbsp. (90 ml) onion powder

¼ cup (60 ml) garlic powder

¼ cup (60 ml) black pepper

¼ cup (60 ml) cayenne

3 Tbsp. (45 ml) ground oregano

2 Tbsp. (30 ml) ground thyme

2 Tbsp. (30 ml) Prague Powder #1 (optional)

1 Tbsp. (15 ml) coriander powder

The country-style ribs are cured, smoked, and cooked in the same way as the previously described smoked pork loin. Water smoking or steaming are good methods for cooking the pork.

# Wild Boar

In a hilly area near my former home in Japan, a friend grows Oriental pears for a living. Several years ago, when I was still living there, he trapped four wild boar sucklings that were playing in one of his orchards. He raised them as you would raise domesticated piglets. Sweet potatoes were their main food. He slaughtered them when they got just the right size to eat, and he asked me to smoke the loins, hams, and shoulders of one of them. I did so, with pleasure.

Since the wild boar is related to our domesticated swine, I decided to cure and smoke the meat in the same way that I smoke pork loin. I skinned and boned all the meat, and then cut the thicker pieces into slabs so that they would cure in 14 days. Before smoking the meat, I net-tied all of the cured hunks individually to make them as attractive as possible. The result was exceptional, and my friend was delighted. In fact, he was so pleased with the result that he asked me to smoke one more wild boar.

The taste was much like cured and well-smoked pork, but with a hint of something wild. The color of the finished product was a deep rose, rather than pink.

Considering this experience, I suggest that wild boar be processed in the same way as common pork. Use your favorite curing and smoking process for pork. If you do have the privilege of processing wild boar, you will notice that the animal has much less fat than a porker. In some places, there is almost no fat between the skin and the red muscle tissue. According to what I have read, a wild boar under one year old is the tastiest.

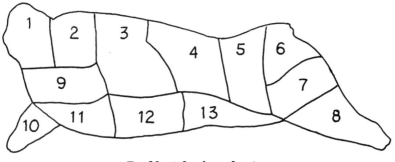

**Beef butchering chart.**

1. Neck
2. Chuck
3. Rib
4. Short loin
5. Sirloin
6. Rump
7. Round

8. Shank
9. Shoulder
10. Foreshank
11. Brisket
12. Short plate
13. Flank

# Beef Jerky

In times gone by, wild game was the only meat available. When a kill was made, people would gorge themselves on the fresh meat and hope that they could make another kill before they starved to death. Under such circumstances, they would wish that they could preserve meat when there was more than they could eat. It was not long until they discovered that they could postpone decay by *jerking* the meat (drying it in the sun). By putting a lot of salt on the meat before it was jerked, the meat could be preserved for a long time. Thinly slicing the meat and drying it with fire helped to make the process more effective and more predictable.

Jerky made in this way was very hard and very salty. It was often eaten after boiling it together with other foods. The boiling of the jerky extracted much of the salt, made the meat moist, and seasoned the other food in the pot.

We now have other methods of preserving meat, and we do not depend on jerked meat to live. Nowadays, we make jerky because we want a good-tasting snack. Commercial processors of jerky use preservatives, so they are able to reduce the salt and still make a product that has a long shelf life. When we make jerky at home, I believe our primary goals are to make a product that tastes better and costs less than that we can buy. For some people, a third goal is to make a product that is not loaded with preservatives. We can do all of these things—but we must be willing to accept a shorter shelf life.

The two jerky products described below will taste better than commercial jerky, and they will certainly cost less. In fact, if all of the jerky you have eaten has been commercially prepared, this will probably be the best jerky you have ever eaten. If the salt content or seasoning is not exactly right, you can change it. However, because the salt content is comparatively low, and because there are no preservatives other than a modest amount of salt and sweetener, the shelf life at room temperature is not more than about two weeks. This is a small sacrifice, because the shelf life can be extended far beyond the two weeks by refrigerating or freezing the jerky.

Directions for making California jerky and Wild West jerky are given below. The basic processing directions for making either product are the same. Only the seasoning is different. Beef is specified, but any meat can be used. Pork, or any meat that may contain trichinae, should be heated until the internal temperature is at least 160° F (71° C).

Lean meat, such as beef *bottom round* or *top round*, is preferable because fatty meat processed into jerky turns rancid quickly. Keep in mind that there will be a 40 to 50 percent weight loss when making jerky. Ten pounds (4.5 kg) of raw meat will become 5 to 6 pounds (2.25 to 2.75 kg) of jerky.

The following jerky seasoning formulas are not true marinades, and they are not true brines, either. They are somewhere in between.

Nevertheless, these cures work very well for jerky, and they can be used as models to make countless other jerky seasoning formulas.

A small amount of Prague Powder #1 is used in both of the seasoning mixtures. Because this curing powder is used, the finished product will have an eye-pleasing reddish color. If you choose not to use the Prague Powder, the finished product will be the same brown color that is characteristic of cooked beef.

## PREPARATION AND SEASONING

1. Begin with hunks of meat, rather than with meat that has been cut into steaks or chops. (Steaks and chops are cut across the grain of the meat. This makes them unsuitable for jerky.) Chill the meat thoroughly. Cold meat is easier to cut, and bacterial growth is retarded.

2. Trim the fat from the meat. It is impossible to remove the streaks of fat that are marbled into the meat, but you should remove all fat that can be removed easily.

3. Use a long slicing knife or an electric meat slicer to slice ¼-inch-thick (7 mm) strips. The strips should be 1 to 2 inches (2.5 to 5 cm) wide. The meat must be cut *with the grain*, not across. If the meat is cut across the grain, it will be too fragile after it dries. You can determine if the strip has been correctly cut with the grain by pulling on the ends of the strip. If it has been properly cut with the grain, the strip will stretch; if not, the muscle fibers will separate, and the strip will tear.

4. Chill the meat again while preparing the seasoning mixture.

5. There are two jerky marinade recipes: California jerky and Wild West jerky. Select and prepare one of these marinades. Stir the marinade well until all ingredients are dissolved. Add the meat strips and stir them from time to time, especially during the first few hours of curing. Refrigerate overnight.

6. During the morning of the second day, use a colander (or the like) to drain the curing liquid from the meat. *Do not rinse!*

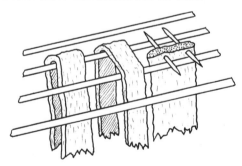

**Bad and good ways to hang jerky.**

The strip of meat that is hanging on the left in the drawing demonstrates a bad way to hang jerky. There will be poor air circulation because the slice of meat is almost touching itself. Drying will be uneven.

Better ways to hang jerky are indicated by the jerky strips hanging in the middle and on the right: It could be hung with toothpicks, or it could be hung over two bars.

### OPTION 1—SMOKER DRYING

1. Hang the strips, place the strips on smoker racks, or lay the strips in wire-mesh smoking baskets. (I prefer the wire-mesh baskets. Hanging the strips will allow more of the product to be processed, but the use of baskets makes processing easier and faster.) If the suggested high temperatures and long processing times are followed, beef, pork, or any other kind of meat will be thoroughly cooked. You may use a common smoker with a heat source inside or a water smoker with the water pan removed. To facilitate drying, the smoker chimney damper should be fully open.

2. Dry at 140º F (60º C) with no smoke until the surface is dry. This will require at least one hour. If the strips are on wire mesh, turn them over after 30 to 45 minutes to prevent sticking.

3. Raise the temperature to 160º F (71º C), and smoke for two or three hours.

4. Raise the temperature to 175º F (80º C)—for poultry, raise the temperature to 185º F (85º C)—and continue to dry with no smoke until done. This final drying and cooking step will require about three hours. When the jerky is done, it will be about half the thickness of the raw jerky, and it will appear to have lost about 50 percent of its weight. The jerky will not snap when it is bent, but a few of the muscle fibers will fray. If the jerky is dried until it snaps when it is bent, the jerky will have a longer shelf life, but it will not be as tasty. Let the jerky cool to room temperature, and either freeze or refrigerate it.

### OPTION 2—OVEN DRYING

Place the drained jerky on racks in the oven. A drip tray must be placed under the jerky. Heat the oven to 150º F (65º C). If the temperature can't be set that low, then set the oven to the lowest setting. Dry for about three hours, and then raise the temperature to 175º F (80º C). For fowl, however, the temperature should be raised to 185º F (85º C). Continue drying for another two to four hours. Let the jerky cool to room temperature, and then freeze or refrigerate it.

### CALIFORNIA JERKY

Processing instructions appear above.

### SEASONING FOR 2¼ POUNDS (1 KILOGRAM) OF SLICED BEEF

> 1 Tbsp. (15 ml) salt
> 2 Tbsp. (30 ml) brown sugar—packed in the spoon
> 2 tsp. (10 ml) ginger powder
> 2 tsp. (10 ml) garlic powder
> 2 tsp. (10 ml) black pepper
> ½ tsp. (2.5 ml) Prague Powder #1 (optional)
> ½ tsp. (2.5 ml) MSG (optional)
> ½ tsp. (2.5 ml) hickory smoke flavor (optional)
> ¾ cup (180 ml) orange juice
> 3 Tbsp. (45 ml) soy sauce
> 2 cups (480 ml) cold water

### WILD WEST JERKY

Processing instructions appear above.

### SEASONING FOR 2¼ POUNDS (1 KILOGRAM) OF SLICED BEEF

> 1 Tbsp. (15 ml) salt
> 1 Tbsp. (15 ml) honey
> 2 tsp. (10 ml) black pepper
> 1 tsp. (5 ml) garlic powder
> ½ tsp. (2.5 ml) Prague Powder #1 (optional)
> ½ tsp. (2.5 ml) MSG (optional)
> ½ tsp. (2.5 ml) hickory smoke flavor (optional)
> ½ tsp. (2.5 ml) cayenne
> ½ tsp. (2.5 ml) coriander
> ½ tsp. (2.5 ml) chili powder
> 3 Tbsp. (45 ml) soy sauce
> 2 tsp. (10 ml) Worcestershire sauce
> ¾ cup (180 ml) apple juice
> 2 cups (480 ml) cold water

# Smoked Beef Tongue

Old-fashioned smoked tongue is hard cured in the same way as corned beef. Because of the high salt content, it must be placed in a large kettle, covered with water, and simmered for about an hour per pound (450 g). This long period of simmering extracts the excess salt.

The excellent refrigeration available nowadays allows you to use a mild cure that does not require simmering to extract excess salt. The modern dry cure method infuses just the right amount of salt to match your taste.

If you have ever tasted old-fashioned smoked tongue, you will most certainly say that the smoked tongue produced by the following process tastes much better. This is because the smoke flavor, the meat flavor, and the seasonings are not dissolved out of the tongue by a long period of simmering in water.

This mildly cured, smoked tongue is quite easy to make, but the whole process will require about two weeks of curing and about six hours of smoking.

Normally, meat is cured and smoked before it is cooked. This smoked tongue is unusual because it is cooked before it is smoked. (You *cure* first, then *cook*, and then *smoke*.) This is done because the skin should be removed before smoking, and it is most easily removed from the tongue after cooking has taken place.

Of course, if the skin is removed from the raw tongue in the beginning, the more common order (cure, then smoke, and then cook) could be employed. A raw tongue can be skinned if it is first frozen solid. A razor-sharp knife must be used, and work must begin at the tip of the tongue while the tip is still frozen and stiff. I have skinned a frozen tongue many times, but it is extremely dangerous and not recommended. However, if you do try it, make sure that there is *never* anything in front of the cutting edge of the knife other than the tongue itself. The knife *will* slip and leap forward *many* times. Also, be sure to count your fingers before and after this procedure. Japanese butchers frequently use this method to skin tongues, but I don't think a reasonably sane American butcher would consider it. Safety matters aside, skinning a raw tongue is a labor-intensive and time-consuming operation.

### THE TONGUE

Any size of beef tongue can be used, but tongue lovers claim that tongues weighing less than 3 pounds (1,400 g) are best. Another consideration is that small tongues cure faster than large ones. Frozen tongues work just as well as fresh.

If there is a meatpacker or distributor in your area, you might be able to buy frozen Grade 2 beef tongues. The price will be about half the price of fresh tongues sold at a common supermarket. Grade 2 tongues are cheaper because they have a hook mark or a knife slash that distracts from the appearance.

Scrub the tongue very well with a vegetable brush under lukewarm water. Drain, and refrigerate it while preparing the cure.

## CURING

The total curing time depends on the thickness of the tongue. Measure *across the top* of the tongue at the thickest point (from the right side to the left, where the big taste buds are located). Allow seven days of curing time for every inch (2.5 cm) of thickness.

## CURE MIX FOR 2¼ POUNDS (1 KILOGRAM) OF TONGUE

1 Tbsp. (15 ml) salt
1 tsp. (5 ml) granulated sugar
¾ tsp. (3.75 ml) onion powder
½ tsp. (2.5 ml) oregano
½ tsp. (2.5 ml) Prague Powder #1
½ tsp. (2.5 ml) black pepper
½ tsp. (2.5 ml) garlic powder
¼ tsp. (1.25 ml) red pepper, or cayenne
1 shredded bay leaf (do not mix with the ingredients listed above)

Total: 7 tsp. (35 ml)—excluding the bay leaf.

### CURE MIX MEASURING CHART
7 tsp. (35 ml) per 2¼ lbs. (1 kg) of tongue + one bay leaf
3½ tsp. (17.5 ml) per 1 lb. (500 g) of tongue + ½ bay leaf
1¾ tsp. (8.75 ml) per ½ lb. (250 g) of tongue + ¼ bay leaf
¾ tsp. (3.75 ml) per ¼ lb. (125 g) of tongue

## BULK MIX FOR 27 POUNDS (12 KILOGRAMS) OF TONGUE

¾ cup (180 ml) salt
4 Tbsp. (60 ml) sugar
3 Tbsp. (45 ml) onion powder

2 Tbsp. (30 ml) oregano
2 Tbsp. (30 ml) Prague Powder #1
2 Tbsp. (30 ml) black pepper
2 Tbsp. (30 ml) garlic powder
1 Tbsp. (15 ml) red pepper
1 shredded bay leaf per 2¼ lbs. (1 kg) of tongue (do not mix with
   the ingredients listed above)

1. It is very important to pierce the tongue thoroughly. To get even better cure penetration, slice some of the skin off the top of the tongue where it has the most bulk. This will greatly improve the cure penetration.
2. Weigh the tongue. Prepare, calculate, and measure the required amount of curing mixture (use the Cure Mix Measuring Chart).
3. Place the tongue in a curing container having a tight-fitting lid. Sprinkle on the curing mixture, and rub the meat well to ensure equal distribution of the cure. Cut the required amount of bay leaf into very thin strips (scissors work well for this). Sprinkle the bay leaf strips on the tongue, and rub again. Cover, and refrigerate the tongue.
4. Overhaul the tongue after about 12 hours of curing. When it is being overhauled, reapply any juices that may have oozed from the meat.
5. Overhaul the tongue once a day for the first week, and then overhaul it every other day until the required curing time has elapsed.

## COOKING IN HOT WATER—OPTION 1

1. Rinse the cured tongue *very well* in lukewarm water. Put it in a sturdy and watertight plastic bag (two plastic bags, one inside the other, are even better). Remove as much air as possible. Seal the bag(s) tightly with a wire bread-bag tie, and cook in water heated to 200° F (93° C). Make sure that the tongue is pressed below the surface of the hot water. *Caution:* If the water reaches the boiling point, the bags may balloon and burst.
2. Cook from an hour to an hour and a quarter per pound (450 g). The longer time will result in a very tender product; the shorter time will produce a tongue with a little more resistance to the bite.
3. Open the plastic bag(s), and drain the tongue in a colander (juice from the cooked tongue will have accumulated in the plastic bag—this may be discarded). Skin the tongue, and trim the root (the

underside) with a sharp knife. Because the tongue has been cooked, the skin can now be sliced off easily. Rinse and drain again. (When slicing off the skin, you will notice that the tongue is a beautiful maroon color. The heat from the cooking, together with the small amount of sodium nitrite in the Prague Powder #1, has caused the color to be fixed.)

4. Wrap the tongue in paper towels, and then wrap it again with newspaper. Refrigerate overnight.

## COOKING IN A STEAMER—OPTION 2

1. Rinse the cured tongue very well in lukewarm water. Wrap it tightly with plastic food wrap.
2. Insert the probe of an electronic meat thermometer into the thickest part of the tongue; stick the probe through the food wrap. (The electronic meat thermometer should be the type that has a cable attached to an external temperature-monitoring unit.)
3. Place the tongue in a steamer, and steam it until the internal temperature reaches 170° F (77° C). Continue to steam for 45 minutes more so that the tongue will become tender.
4. Remove the tongue from the steamer, place it in a colander, and remove the plastic food wrap. Use a sharp knife to shave off the skin. Rinse the tongue again and drain it.
5. Wrap the tongue in paper towels and newspapers. Refrigerate it overnight.

## SMOKING

1. Dry the tongue in front of an electric fan. Blotting it from time to time with a paper towel will help the drying process go faster. Depending on the ambient humidity and other factors, the surface will become dry in one or two hours. During this time, it is best to make sure that dogs, cats, skunks, raccoons, or other animals cannot gain access to it.
2. If you intend to net-tie the tongue and hang it in the smoke chamber, you should tie it at this point. A net-tied tongue will make a more attractive product than one that has been hung by hooks or placed on a rack. (See chapter 8.)
3. Rub the entire tongue with olive oil, peanut oil, or any other cooking oil. (The oil helps to prevent the surface from drying excessively, and it gives the tongue an eye-pleasing sheen.) Begin smoking.

**4.** Ideally, cold smoking at about 80° F (27° C), or less, is best. Six hours of cold smoking will impart a medium smoky flavor. The tongue may be smoked at higher temperatures, but the smoking time might have to be reduced to prevent excessive drying of the surface. If smoking is done at higher temperatures, reapplication of cooking oil from time to time is advised.

**5.** Chill overnight, uncovered, in the refrigerator. Place the tongue in a plastic bag. Refrigerate or freeze the tongue until it is consumed.

Smoked tongue is gourmet fare, and it is very tasty when it is served either hot or cold. Slice it thinly, and serve it as an appetizer. Try it for sandwiches. Try it on crackers, or mince it and add it to scrambled eggs or salad. Mustard and horseradish are traditional dressings for tongue, but I find them too harsh for the subtle flavors of this product.

# Pastrami

The Slavic Jews created pastrami. It is related to pork *pastrama*, a highly seasoned, smoked pork that is famous in Romania. This similarly seasoned beef pastrami became very popular in the Jewish delicatessens throughout Europe. Eventually, it found its way to the United States with the Jewish immigrants. Today, it is available in numerous countries of the world, and its origins are almost forgotten.

The international popularization of pastrami led to significant variations in seasoning and processing, but the following points are generally true for the various products known as pastrami:

Pastrami is made of beef that has been cured and highly seasoned with salt, sugar, garlic, black pepper, and a nitrate or nitrite color fixer. Depending on the processor, numerous other seasonings are used: Allspice, onions, ginger, red pepper, cloves, coriander seeds, oregano, paprika, and pickling spices are some of the more common additions. The black pepper is coarsely ground and pressed onto the surface of the meat before smoking.

Inexpensive cuts of meat are usually used to make pastrami. Almost any cut of beef can be used, but the most common cuts are brisket, plate, and shoulder. To be authentic, pastrami must be smoked.

Pastrami is thoroughly cooked. Depending on the processor, it is steamed, hot smoked, boiled, oven roasted, or possibly even grilled. (A modified form of hot water cooking is one of the methods suggested below, but other methods may be employed. If it is hot smoked, water smoking should be used to prevent severe drying. Oven roasting, too, can cause excessive drying unless precautions are taken.)

The following procedure for making pastrami will give you a consistently tasty product. A fellow teacher and friend in Japan—a Jewish woman from New York—regularly bought this pastrami from me whenever I made a batch. I consider her approval of this product to be a great compliment. I hope you will like it. Make changes in the seasonings if you need to tune the product to your taste buds.

### BEEF: TOP SIRLOIN, PLATE, OR BRISKET

The primal cut (a large hunk) of top sirloin is my favorite for making pastrami. A good grade of beef plate is my second choice. (Plate is the part of the beef belly that lies between the brisket and the flank.) Exceedingly fat meat, or exceedingly lean meat (beef round, for example), should be avoided.

1. Cut off loose flesh, and remove bloody spots and gristle to the extent possible. Remove excess fat.
2. Cut the meat into the sizes that you want to process. Remember that thick meat requires longer curing time.
3. Rinse all of the pieces of beef in cold water, and drain them in a colander. Blot them with a paper towel. Pierce all surfaces deeply. Place the meat in the curing container(s) you will use, and refrigerate it while the cure mix is being readied.

### CURING

Measure the thickest hunk, and allow six days of curing time for every inch (2.5 cm) of thickness.

**Pastrami—overhauling the beef plate with rubber gloves.**

## PASTRAMI CURE MIX FOR 2¼ POUNDS (1 KILOGRAM) OF BEEF

1 Tbsp. (15 ml) salt
1 tsp. (5 ml) garlic powder
1 tsp. (5 ml) onion powder
1 tsp. (5 ml) granulated sugar
½ tsp. (2.5 ml) Prague Powder #1
½ tsp. (2.5 ml) red pepper
½ tsp. (2.5 ml) white pepper
½ tsp. (2.5 ml) oregano
½ tsp. (2.5 ml) paprika
¼ tsp. (1.25 ml) allspice
¼ tsp. (1.25 ml) ginger powder

Total: 9 tsp. (45 ml) = 3 Tbsp.

### CURE MIX MEASURING CHART

3 Tbsp. (45 ml) per 2¼ lbs. (1 kg) of beef
4½ tsp. (22.5 ml) per 1 lb. (500 g) of beef
2¼ tsp. (11.25 ml) per ½ lb. (250 g) of beef
1 tsp. (5 ml) per ¼ lb. (125 g) of beef

## BULK MIX FOR 27 POUNDS (12 KILOGRAMS) OF PASTRAMI

¾ cup (180 ml) salt
¼ cup (60 ml) garlic powder
¼ cup (60 ml) onion powder
¼ cup (60 ml) granulated sugar
2 Tbsp. (30 ml) Prague Powder #1
2 Tbsp. (30 ml) red pepper
2 Tbsp. (30 ml) white pepper
2 Tbsp. (30 ml) oregano
2 Tbsp. (30 ml) paprika
1 Tbsp. (15 ml) allspice
1 Tbsp. (15 ml) ginger powder

1. Weigh the beef. If more than one curing container will be used, cal-culate separately the total weight of the beef that will be placed in each container. Prepare, calculate, and measure the required amount of curing mixture for each container (use the Cure Mix Measuring Chart).
2. Place the beef in the curing container(s). Rub the cure mix on the meat evenly. Cover, and refrigerate the meat.

3. Overhaul the pieces of beef after about 12 hours of curing. Be sure to wet the meat with any liquid that may have accumulated in the bottom of the curing container.

4. Overhaul the meat once a day until the required curing time has elapsed.

5. When the curing is finished, rinse each piece of beef *very well* in lukewarm water. Drain in a colander, and blot with a paper towel.

6. On all surfaces of each piece of pastrami, sprinkle and press on coarsely ground pepper. A light coating of pepper is recommended for the first time you make pastrami; too much pepper is worse than not enough.

7. Wrap each piece of beef in a paper towel, and then wrap again with newspaper. Refrigerate overnight.

## OPTION 1—TRADITIONAL SMOKING AND HOT WATER COOKING

1. If the meat will be hung in the smoke chamber, you should prepare the meat for hanging by net-tying or by using the skewer-and-loop method (see chapter 8).

2. Hang the pieces in the smoke chamber, or place them on smoking racks. Dry at less than 140° F (60° C) until the surface is dry (about an hour). Do not use smoke during the drying period.

3. To avoid excessive drying and excessively dark coloration, smoke at less than 85° F (30° C), if possible. Smoke the pastrami for three to six hours, depending on how smoky you want the meat. Raise the temperature to about 145° F (63° C) for an hour or two toward the end of the smoking time if darker coloration is desired.

*Note:* The following steps are for hot water cooking. Instructions unique to pastrami are given below, but it might be helpful to review the general instructions for hot water cooking in chapter 8.

1. Begin heating water in your hot water cooker. Raise the water temperature to 200° F (93° C).

2. While the water is heating, wrap each piece of pastrami in plastic food wrap, and then put it in a plastic bag. Expel as much air as possible from each bag before tying or sealing it.

3. Put all of the meat in the hot water cooker at one time, and press it below the surface. Maintain the hot water temperature as close to 200° F (93° C) as possible. Cook the meat about two and a half hours. This long period of cooking at high temperatures is to make

the meat tender; even gristle will be tender. A thermometer inserted into the thickest piece of meat is not required given the cooking time and rather high temperature. *Caution:* Raising the temperature to the boiling point will cause the plastic bags to balloon, the water to overflow the pot, and the meat to shrink excessively.

4. Remove the meat from the hot water cooker, open the plastic bags, remove the plastic wrapping, and drain in a colander.

5. Cool at room temperature for about two hours, and then refrigerate, uncovered, overnight. The next morning, the pieces of pastrami should be put in plastic bags and sealed. Freeze the portion that will not be consumed in one week.

### OPTION 2—TRADITIONAL SMOKING, THEN STEAMING OR ROASTING

Use the traditional cold smoking (as explained in Option 1) to smoke the pastrami. However, instead of cooking with the hot water method, roast the pastrami in an oven, or steam it. In either case, the pastrami is done when the internal temperature is 170° F (77° C). An aluminum-foil tent should be used if the pastrami is cooked in an oven. If it is steamed, wrap each piece of pastrami in plastic food wrap before steaming, and use an electronic meat thermometer with a cable probe to monitor the internal temperature.

### OPTION 3—WATER SMOKING

Water smoking is an easy way to smoke and cook the cured pastrami. The disadvantages are that the external coloration will not be as good, and the product will not have as much smoky flavor as that imparted by traditional cold smoking.

The first step to water smoke the cured pastrami is to preheat the water smoker to about 240° F (115° C). Next, water smoke the meat until the internal temperature is 170° F (77° C). The thinner pieces will cook faster, and they should be removed from the smoker as soon as they are cooked.

# Deer, Elk, Moose, and Other Big Game

Venison, elk, moose, and other meats from big-game animals are commonly made into jerky. These meats also make excellent pastrami; try processing in the same way as beef pastrami. The numerous spices present in the jerky marinades and in the pastrami cure will subdue the wild taste. Yet another popular way to use wild game is to process it into sausage; see chapter 12.

Wild game is drier than meat from domesticated animals, so meat from wild animals will benefit from the application of cooking oil. When making any product other than jerky or sausage, it is a good idea to oil the wild game frequently during smoking and cooking. Also, cooking these meats with moist heat is better than cooking them with dry heat.

# Lamb Ham

Scandinavian peoples began settling Iceland over 1,000 years ago, and they brought numerous sheep with them. Descendants of those sheep still roam the island, and they are a principal source of food. Smoked leg of lamb is part of the Icelandic culture: About 90 percent of the households serve smoked leg of lamb on Christmas Day.

I would like to say that the following product is authentic Icelandic smoked leg of lamb—but it is not. There are three reasons for this. First, the traditional product is hard cured, so it is very salty—it must be freshened (desalted) before it is eaten. Second, Icelanders do not use plain hot water to freshen the smoked leg of lamb; they simmer it in very stinky water that was used to boil skate (a fish-like creature related to the ray). The third reason is that the Icelanders use dried sheep dung as the smoking fuel, and I could not obtain any dried dung to test the process—but I must admit that I did not look very hard for it. The product described here will be mildly cured, and it will be smoked with hard wood—not hard dung.

Many Americans avoid lamb because it can have a gamy taste if it is not prepared properly. If leg of lamb is processed as indicated below, I believe that you will detect no gamy taste, whatsoever.

## THE RAW MATERIAL

Lamb is becoming more popular in the United States, and good-quality lamb is now available throughout the year. For this product, boned and butterflied leg of lamb is required. Buy a small leg of lamb, and ask the butcher to butterfly it for you. Get the sirloin half of the leg (the upper half), not the shank half (the lower half). When it is butterflied, the meat will lie flat, and the thickness will usually vary between 1 and 2½ inches (2.5 to 6.3 cm).

Boned leg of lamb is easy to buy. If you need to butterfly it yourself, it is not hard to do. Put the boned leg on the counter with the skin side down. The meat will be thin in the middle where the bone was removed, but it will be thick to the left and right. Hold the knife horizontally, parallel with the top of the counter. Cut the middle of one of the thick parts almost to the outside edge, and open the meat, as you would open a book. Do the same with the thick part on the other side.

The leg of lamb is now butterflied—you now have one large slab of lamb. To make it easier to process, it is best to cut it into two or four smaller slabs.

Most of the fat should be removed. If the skin side of the meat has parchment-like membrane on it, it should be removed. This membrane is called *fell*, and it will make the meat taste gamy. Normally, the fell is removed by the meat processor before it is shipped to the retailer.

## CURING

The total curing time depends on the thickness of the thickest part of the butterfly. Allow seven days of curing time for every inch (2.5 cm) of thickness.

### CURE MIX FOR 2¼ POUNDS (1 KILOGRAM) OF LEG OF LAMB

1 Tbsp. (15 ml) salt
1 Tbsp. (15 ml) sugar
1½ tsp. (7.5 ml) garlic powder
1 tsp. (5 ml) onion powder
½ tsp. (2.5 ml) Prague Powder #1
½ tsp. (2.5 ml) oregano powder
½ tsp. (2.5 ml) black pepper
¼ tsp. (1.25 ml) thyme powder
¼ tsp. (1.25 ml) rosemary powder

Total: 10½ tsp. (52.5 ml).

#### CURE MIX MEASURING CHART

10½ tsp. (52.5 ml) per 2¼ lbs. (1 kg) lamb
5¼ tsp. (26.5 ml) per 1 lb. (500 g) lamb
2½ tsp. (12.5 ml) per ½ lb. (250 g) lamb
1¼ tsp. (6.25 ml) per ¼ lb. (125 g) lamb

### BULK-BLEND FOR 27 POUNDS (12 KILOGRAMS) OF LAMB

¾ cup (180 ml) salt
¾ cup (180 ml) sugar

6 Tbsp. (150 ml) garlic powder
¼ cup (120 ml) onion powder
2 Tbsp. (30 ml) Prague Powder #1
2 Tbsp. (30 ml) oregano powder
2 Tbsp. (30 ml) black pepper
1 Tbsp. (15 ml) thyme powder
1 Tbsp. (15 ml) rosemary powder

1. Weigh the slabs of lamb. Prepare, calculate, and measure the required amount of curing mixture (use the Cure Mix Measuring Chart).
2. Pierce all of the surfaces thoroughly. Place the lamb in the curing container. Rub the curing mix evenly on the meat. Cover the lamb, and refrigerate.
3. Overhaul the pieces of lamb after about 12 hours of curing.
4. Overhaul the meat about once a day for the first week, and then overhaul every other day until the required curing time has elapsed.
5. When the curing is finished, rinse each piece of lamb *very well* in lukewarm water. Drain. Wrap each piece in a paper towel, and then wrap again with newspaper. Refrigerate overnight.

## SMOKING THE LAMB

1. Place the slabs on smoking racks with the skin side down. Dry at less than 140º F (60º C) until the surface feels dry (about an hour). Do not use smoke during the drying period.
2. When the meat is dry, cold smoke it at the lowest possible temperature for three to six hours. Raise the temperature of the smoker to about 145º F (63º C), and smoke the lamb until it takes on a reddish brown color (about two hours). Remove the meat from the smoker.

## COOKING THE LAMB

The lamb is not fully cooked when comes out of the smoker. It needs to be cooked by any conventional method used to cook meat. Roasting in an oven, steaming, water smoking, or hot water cooking can be employed. Below are the basic instructions for cooking with a hot water cooker.

🌡 The water temperature is about 185º F (85º C).

🌡 The lamb is well done when the internal temperature is 170º F (76.6º C).

# CHAPTER 10

# Smoking Poultry and Wildfowl

Chicken is a very good raw material for learning smoking skills. Chicken can be dry cured, wet cured, or marinated. Salt and other seasonings sprinkled on the surface before smoking will also give good results. If the product is cured with either curing powder or sodium nitrite, the dark meat will taste a little like cured ham. Either a whole chicken or a cut-up chicken can be processed. It can be cold smoked, hot smoked, or water smoked. Jerky can be made from the boned thighs and drumsticks. Ground chicken can be made into sausage. If the seasoning and smoking are done properly, chicken produces high-quality, exquisitely flavored smoked food.

Besides all of these good points, chicken is also very economical. Indeed, it is difficult to find a good raw material for smoking that is more economical than chicken. When learning how to smoke foods, just as with learning how to do anything else, you will make mistakes at first. Mistakes made with chicken are less distressing than those made with the more expensive beef, pork, and fish.

Because of their larger size, turkeys are a little more difficult than chickens to cure, smoke, and cook. However, nowadays, small turkeys are available—some of them are less than 10 pounds (4.5 kg). When turkeys are processed whole, these small birds are easier to use as a raw material than the monster birds. Turkey has become more economical, and it has become easier to buy specific parts of the turkey.

When you buy either a whole turkey or turkey parts, be careful about one important point: Make sure that the meat has not been injected with broth, salt, seasonings, or the like. Pumped turkey meat is not suitable for making the products described in this book. Nationally advertised brands of turkey are often pumped. Generic turkeys usually are not.

Many people like the taste of domesticated ducks and geese. These birds will also produce gourmet-class smoked products.

Wildfowl are much more difficult to process with consistently good results than are domesticated birds. The main reason for this is that there are great variations in quality even within the same species. This is true even if they were harvested on the same day and at the same location. One bird might be young, and the other might be old. One bird might have had access to an ample amount of good food, but the other might have gotten just enough to survive. Nevertheless, good wildfowl that are skillfully seasoned and smoked are something that you might expect to find gracing the table of the Sultan of Brunei.

The products in this chapter use domesticated birds as the raw material, but wild birds can be used as well. Pheasant, for example, can replace chicken as the raw material; wild geese and wild turkeys can replace their domesticated cousins.

# Techniques for Smoking Whole Birds

Special techniques are required when whole birds are smoked.

### STUFFING AND WRAPPING WITH NEWSPAPER

After a fowl is cured, the instructions will often indicate that the bird is to be rinsed and the body cavity is to be stuffed with crumpled newspaper that has been wrapped in paper towels. In all cases, the paper towels and newspaper must be discarded prior to smoking or cooking.

### TRUSSING A BIRD

When a whole bird is smoked, the wings and legs should be secured; this is called trussing. Trussing makes the bird more attractive and easier to handle.

### MOUNTING OR HANGING THE BIRD WITH THE TAIL UP

When a whole bird is smoked, it is advisable to mount or hang it vertically—with the tail pointing up. There are two reasons for this. First,

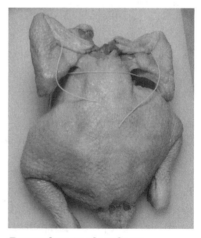

**Preparing to tie wings.**

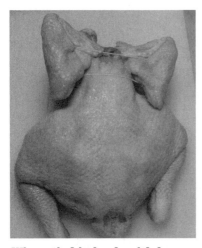

**Wings tied in back with loop of twine.**

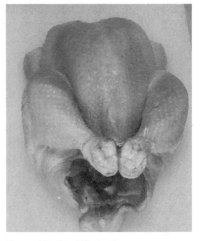

**Legs tied with twine.**

the heat and smoke can easily flow upward, through the open body cavity. Second, the juices and oils will drip out of the bird, and these liquids will not accumulate inside the body cavity; this is particularly important for fat birds such as domesticated ducks and geese.

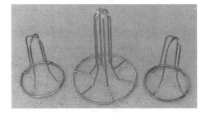

**Chicken racks (left and right) and turkey rack (center).**

Special steel racks can be purchased for chickens and turkeys (shown in the photograph). The tower of the rack is inserted into the hole in the breast that is located just under the neck. The result will be that the breast is pointing down and the tail is pointing up. Although the racks are made for chickens and turkeys, they can be used for other kinds of domesticated poultry and for wildfowl. For example, the turkey rack can be used for a goose, and the chicken rack can be used for a duck or pheasant. (If you wish to purchase racks, see appendix 5.)

If the steel chicken and turkey racks are not available, the technique explained below can be used to hang the bird with the tail pointing up.

**1.** This stainless-steel or hardwood rod is for twisting the twine that passes through the body cavity. It also supports the weight of the bird when it is in the tail-up position; consequently, there will be no stress on the legs.

2. Twisted twine that pulls the legs toward the body.

3. Twine to tie the legs together.

4. Twine or cord to hang the bird with the tail up.

**Bird prepared for hanging with the tail up.**

First, tie the legs together. To restrain the legs and relieve stress on them, pass a length of twine through the front of the body cavity and around the twine that is holding the legs together. Bring the twine back through the body cavity, and tie both ends to the rod that is placed across the opening at the front of the bird. Twist the rod and string like a tourniquet. The ends of the legs will be pulled toward the bird. The purpose of this procedure is to secure the legs in an attractive position and to prevent the legs from being stretched when the bird is dried and smoked with the tail pointing up.

# Whole Smoked Chicken—Brine Cure

This product tastes as good as it looks—and it looks great! You will want to serve it to guests as the main course for dinner. The salt content will suit the average palate, but if you desire a milder or stronger salt taste, change the brining time. Try to use about the same weight of bird every time, if possible. If birds of the same weight are used, you will be able to determine rapidly the curing time that produces a product with the perfect salt content. A small bird brined for the same time as a large bird, for example, will be a little saltier.

Use young, tender, well-chilled chickens that are suitable for frying or broiling. The bird should be as fresh as possible so that it will withstand the rigors of curing and smoking. Chickens frozen while fresh are excellent candidates. The instructions below, for the most part, mention only one bird, but you will probably want to brine and smoke at least two at a time.

### CURING

Select a curing container just large enough to accept the whole bird (or birds), but deep enough to permit the brine to cover the bird completely. Using the brine more than once should be avoided because it will have been diluted by the moisture extracted from the meat during the first use. *Hint:* To determine how much brine you will need, put the bird in the curing container, and measure the amount of cold water required to cover it. (The chicken must be completely covered with brine.) You may use the same cold water to make the brine.

The formula will make 8 quarts (8 liters) of brine; you may need to cut this in half or double it. The amount you will need depends primarily on the shape and size of the curing container.

The instructions suggest cold smoking and then roasting in a kitchen oven, but the bird may also be processed in a portable electric smoker or a water smoker.

Sodium nitrite is an optional ingredient. If you use it, the product will have a different flavor and appearance; the fully cooked dark meat will be pink, and it will have a taste similar to cured ham.

## BRINE

8 quarts (8 liters) cold water
4 cups (960 ml) salt
1⅓ cups (320 ml) brown sugar—packed in the cup
2 tsp. (10 ml) sodium nitrite (optional) (see chapter 5, page 97)

Add the salt, brown sugar, and optional sodium nitrite to the water, and stir well with a large wooden, plastic, or stainless-steel spoon or paddle until these ingredients are dissolved.

## SEASONING FOR 8 QUARTS (8 LITERS) OF BRINE

4 tsp. (20 ml) garlic powder
1 tsp. (5 ml) onion powder
1 tsp. (5 ml) rubbed sage—packed in the spoon
1 tsp. (5 ml) marjoram, or oregano
1 tsp. (5 ml) poultry seasoning—packed in the spoon
4 bay leaves, cut into thin strips

1. Boil the seasonings for a few seconds in just enough water to make a thin paste. Cool the paste in a freezer for a few minutes, and then add it to the brine. Refrigerate the brine while the chicken is being readied. (If there is not enough space in the refrigerator, put ice cubes in jars or in strong plastic bags, and float these in the brine.)
2. Clean and rinse the bird, then drain it in a colander. Next, pierce the chicken well, especially the legs and breast. Put a clean stone (previously sterilized by boiling) in the body cavity so that the bird will not float. The stone should have a diameter of about 2½ inches (6

cm). If the brine does not cover the bird, put some more clean rocks—or tightly sealed jars of water with plastic lids—in the brine. The rocks, or sealed jars of water, will raise the brine level. Brine for one and a half hours, stirring from time to time.

3. After the brine cure is finished, give the bird a quick rinse and drain it. Blot the bird inside and out. Stuff the body cavity with a clean cloth or with a wad of crumpled newspaper that has been wrapped in paper towels. Finally, wrap the whole bird with paper towels, and then wrap it again with newspaper. Put several layers of newspaper and a paper towel under the bird to absorb water. Store in a refrigerator overnight with the tail pointed upward so that it will drain and dry. (Storing overnight while wrapped in paper will get rid of much excess moisture, and it allows the salt and other flavorings to migrate within the meat and become uniform.)

## DRYING AND SMOKING

1. The next morning, you will need to set up the smoker to finish drying the chicken. Preheat it to about 140º F (60º C).

2. Mount the bird on a chicken rack, or prepare it for hanging with the tail pointing up (see the instructions earlier in this chapter).

3. Dry the bird in a vertical position in the smoker at 140º F (60º C). After the skin is dry to the touch (about an hour), cold smoke it for three hours at 85º F (30º C) or below, if possible. This will provide a mild smoke flavor. If you like a stronger flavor, smoke the chicken for about six hours.

4. Apply salad oil to the skin. Hot smoke at 145º F (63º C) until the bird takes on a beautiful reddish brown color (probably two more hours).

## ROASTING

Remove the chicken from the smoker. Apply salad oil to the skin again. Cover well with foil, but do not seal the foil tightly—leave a few small openings in the foil for steam to escape. (Because the chicken has been browned in the smoker, additional browning is undesirable, and the foil prevents this. The loose wrapping of foil allows some steam to escape, but it also prevents excessive drying.) Add about 2 Tbsp. (30 ml) of water to the inside of the foil, and roast the bird in a kitchen oven at 350º F (176º C) for about two hours. Use a meat thermometer to test for doneness. When the internal temperature is 180º F (82º C), it is done.

# Whole Smoked Chicken—
# Modern Dry Cure

This product will look as good as the whole smoked chicken that was produced by the brine cure method (above). The taste will be different because both the seasonings and the curing techniques are different. The dark meat will be pink even when it is fully cooked, and this dark meat will taste a little like cured ham. The color of the breast meat, however, will not be affected by Prague Powder #1. The salt content of this product will suit the average person, but if you desire a milder or stronger salt taste, change the amount of salt in the curing formula.

You may use any size of bird, or you may mix different sizes. All the birds, regardless of size, may be processed in the same curing container. The sizes are not important because the amount of cure is measured and applied to each bird according to its weight. Use young, tender, well-chilled chickens that are suitable for frying or broiling.

Instead of using whole chickens, legs or breasts may be used—weigh all the chicken parts together, and apply the proper amount of cure accordingly. However, if cut-up chicken is used, reduce the salt in the curing formula from 1 tablespoon to 2 teaspoons. (Cut-up chicken absorbs salt more readily than whole birds.)

## CURING

### CURE AND SEASONING FOR 2¼ POUNDS (1 KILOGRAM) OF CHICKEN

1 Tbsp. (15 ml) salt
1 Tbsp. (15 ml) granulated sugar
1 tsp. (5 ml) poultry seasoning—packed in the spoon
1 tsp. (5 ml) onion powder
½ tsp. (2.5 ml) MSG
½ tsp. (2.5 ml) garlic powder
½ tsp. (2.5 ml) Prague Powder #1
½ tsp. (2.5 ml) rubbed sage—packed in the spoon
½ tsp. (2.5 ml) oregano
½ tsp. (2.5 ml) white pepper
½ tsp. (2.5 ml) paprika
¼ tsp. (1.25 ml) dill powder
¼ tsp. (1.25 ml) bay leaf powder

Total: 12 tsp. = 4 Tbsp. = ¼ cup (60 ml).

### CURE MIX MEASURING CHART

¼ cup (60 ml) per 2¼ lbs. (1 kg) of chicken

2 Tbsp. (30 ml) per 1 lb. (500 g) of chicken

1 Tbsp. (15 ml) per ½ lb. (250 g) of chicken

1½ tsp. (7.5 ml) per ¼ lb. (125 g) of chicken

## BULK-BLEND SEASONING MIX FOR 27 POUNDS (12 KILOGRAMS) OF CHICKEN

¾ cup (180 ml) salt

¾ cup (180 ml) granulated sugar

¼ cup (60 ml) poultry seasoning—packed in the cup

¼ cup (60 ml) onion powder

2 Tbsp. (30 ml) MSG

2 Tbsp. (30 ml) garlic powder

2 Tbsp. (30 ml) Prague Powder #1

2 Tbsp. (30 ml) rubbed sage—packed in the spoon

2 Tbsp. (30 ml) oregano

2 Tbsp. (30 ml) white pepper

2 Tbsp. (30 ml) paprika

1 Tbsp. (15 ml) dill powder

1 Tbsp. (15 ml) bay leaf powder

1. Rinse and clean the bird, and then let it drain in a colander. Next, pierce the chicken all over, especially the legs and breast. Prepare the proper amount of cure according to the weight of the bird. (If you are curing more than one bird, prepare the proper amount for each bird.) Apply the cure uniformly; a shaker with large holes works well for this. Be sure to apply the cure to the inside of the body cavity as well as to the outside skin. Cure in the refrigerator for at least four days. Rub all surfaces (overhaul) once a day during this period.

2. At the end of the curing period, rinse the bird very well in cool water, and blot it inside and out. Stuff the body cavity with paper towels that have been wrapped around crumpled newspaper. Store it in the refrigerator overnight, preferably with the tail pointed upward. Put a paper towel and several layers of newspaper under the chicken to absorb the water.

## SMOKING

Set up the smoker the next morning to finish drying the chicken. Preheat it to about 140º F (60º C). Dry, smoke, and cook the chicken in the same way as previously described for whole smoked chicken (brine cure). Alternatively, it may be water smoked or processed in a portable electric smoker. In any case, the bird must be cooked until the internal temperature is 180º F (82º C).

## Peking-Style Chicken

Peking-style chicken? Unheard of? That's right. There is no such thing. Correctly speaking, there was no such thing until a few years ago. Here's how it came about.

A Japanese acquaintance took up the hobby of raising unusual chickens. One breed that he is especially proud of is a small Chinese chicken that has feathers as black and shiny as a lump of coal. The comb is colored a dark gunmetal gray. The eggs from this species of chicken retail for about $4 each in Japan, but he gives them away to his friends. The most interesting thing about this chicken is that the meat—all of the meat, including the breast and even the skin—is darker than the darkest meat you have ever seen; it is almost black.

He decided that he wanted to learn how to smoke these black chickens so that he would have something even more unusual to give away to his friends. He asked me to help him design a homemade smoker and teach him how to smoke whole chickens. When his homemade water smoker was almost complete, I started thinking about how to season this very unusual Chinese chicken.

Well, there are many ways to season or cure a chicken. I thought, however, that the chicken should have a Chinese-style seasoning because the breed originated in China. The first thing that popped into my mind—in fact, the only thing that popped into my mind—was to season it in the same way that Peking duck is seasoned. I had made Peking duck several times, and I was very satisfied with it, so I was confident that the same approach would work on the black chicken. It worked very well.

The Chinese consider black chicken to be a delicacy, and I have seen frozen black chickens in large Asian food stores in the United States. However, they are hard to find, and they are expensive. For these reasons, I tried using common chicken. Surprisingly, despite the unusual coloration of the flesh, the Chinese black chicken tastes about the same as common chicken. Common chicken works very well, so that is what I use to prepare this product.

The seasoning suggested below is the same as for the Peking duck that appears later in this chapter, but there are some significant differences in processing. For example, the skin of the chicken is not scalded—chicken skin is too delicate to withstand such treatment. Another processing difference is that cooking in a water smoker is suggested, but you may smoke it, and then cook it in a kitchen oven like the Peking duck.

## THE CHICKENS

Young birds such as broilers or fryers should be used. Birds that weigh 4 to 5 pounds (2 kg, more or less) work well. Stewing chickens are too tough. I suggest that two chickens be processed at the same time. If there is any meat left over, it will not be left over for long. The instructions below are for two chickens.

### DAY 1, MORNING—Preparing and Seasoning the Chickens

1. Thaw the chickens, if necessary, and refrigerate the hearts, gizzards, and necks. They will be used to make a special kind of chicken soup.
2. Inspect the skin, and pull out pinfeathers. Remove the excess skin and fat from around the neck and from the rear end of the birds, but leave adequate skin to prevent the flesh from drying during smoking and roasting. Rinse the chickens well.
3. Blot the birds inside and out with paper towels. Pierce the chickens deeply, especially the breast, drumsticks, and thighs.

### SEASONING FOR TWO CHICKENS

    2 Tbsp. (30 ml) salt
    2 Tbsp. (30 ml) soy sauce
    2 Tbsp. (30 ml) honey
    2 Tbsp. (30 ml) sesame seed oil
    4 tsp. (20 ml) ginger powder
    ½ cup (120 ml) sherry, or *shao hsing* wine
    1 Tbsp. (15 ml) black pepper

Place the chickens in a curing container, and rub them inside and out with the seasoning mixture. Turn the breasts down. Do not wrap the birds or place a lid on the curing container while they are being cured. Refrigerate.

### DAY 1, EVENING

Overhaul the chickens. (Rub them again to redistribute the seasoning mixture.) Turn the breasts up.

## DAY 2, MORNING

Overhaul the chickens. Turn the breasts down.

## DAY 2, EVENING

1. Rinse the chickens briefly in cool water, inside and out. Use paper towels to pat dry.
2. Stuff the body cavities with crumpled newspaper that has been wrapped with paper towels. Place the birds on a paper towel with newspaper underneath and refrigerate, uncovered, overnight.

## DAY 3, MORNING—Smoking and Cooking the Chickens

Below are instructions for smoking and cooking if a water smoker is to be used. However, if you prefer, follow the instructions for smoking and cooking Peking duck (see page 202). For chicken, the fully cooked internal temperature is 180º F (82.2º C).

1. Truss the wings: Twist the wing tips behind the shoulder joints, and tie the upper parts of the wings together, behind the body.
2. Truss the legs: Tie the ends of the drumsticks together with butcher's twine.
3. Dry the chickens with an electric fan for 15 to 30 minutes until the skin feels somewhat dry. It need not be perfectly dry.
4. Apply salad oil to the birds.
5. Smoke the birds in a water smoker at about 250º F (120º C). This will require three to five hours. Make sure that the water pan does not go dry—the resulting fumes will taint the chickens.
6. The chickens are fully cooked when the juices run clear and the legs move easily. The internal temperature should be at least 180º F (82.2º C).

## GLAZE (OPTIONAL)

2 Tbsp. (30 ml) honey
2 Tbsp. (30 ml) soy sauce

Apply glaze to the chickens, if desired. Remove the water pan after applying the glaze. Raise the smoker temperature to a little higher than normal, and roast the birds about 15 minutes more. The glazing is finished when the color becomes medium or dark brown. Wait 15 minutes before carving. After carving, save the bones to make a special chicken soup.

**SAUCE BLEND (OPTIONAL)**

Make the same sauce as suggested for Peking duck. (See page 203.)

**CHICKEN SOUP**

If you wish to make chicken soup, make it in the same way that duck soup is made (see page 204).

# Chicken Legs—Brine and Sodium Nitrite Cure

I was the only foreigner living in Yasu Town, Fukuoka Prefecture, Japan (my wife is Japanese, so she does not qualify as a foreigner). After living there for many years, I gradually became well known (or notorious—opinions differed on this matter).

A few years ago, when I was still living there, the town officials decided to begin holding an annual festival in order to attract people to the town. They named it the Scarecrow Festival. The organizers from city hall pressured me to operate a concession stand at the festival to sell smoked food. They even offered the concession stand free of charge!

I would like to think that my smoked food had become so famous that the officials were convinced it would draw many people to the festival. However, I believe that the truth of the matter is that they were having a hard time filling enough concession stands to make the festival interesting; therefore—in desperation—they pressured the foreigner to do his thing.

In addition to being civic minded, I am also very easy to manipulate, so I agreed to operate the concession. I decided to offer smoked chicken legs because they could be sold for a reasonable price, and because they are easy to produce in quantity. I asked my friend, who does a good job on smoked trout, to share the stand with me. I smoked and sold about 275 chicken legs, and my friend, Mr. Nakamura, sold about 75 smoked trout. We did not make a lot of money because we sold the food only slightly above cost. Nevertheless, we had a lot of fun. Below is the procedure that I employed for the chicken legs. Because the product is cured with sodium nitrite, the flesh of the fully cooked product will be rosy pink and have a ham-like taste.

This procedure is for 40 chicken legs. Please modify the formula appropriately for the quantity you desire. If the legs are frozen, thaw them in your refrigerator before beginning. The legs are processed whole; the drumsticks are not separated from the thighs.

**Setting up the concession stand at the Scarecrow Festival. From left to right: Mrs. Nakamura, the trout-smoker's wife; Quinton Anderson, the author's son; the author.**

## DAY 1

Make the brine. A strong brine (about 80 percent) is being used in order to give a fast cure. If you wish, you may use weaker brine and increase the curing time.

### BRINE FOR ABOUT 40 CHICKEN LEGS

> 2 gallons (8 liters) cold water
> 3.5 cups (840 ml) salt
> 1⅓ cups (320 ml) brown sugar—packed in the cup
> 2 tsp. (10 ml) sodium nitrite (see chapter 5, page 97)

Add the salt, sugar, and sodium nitrite to the water, and stir with a wooden, stainless-steel, or plastic paddle until the ingredients are dissolved.

### SEASONING

> 4 tsp. (20 ml) garlic powder
> 1 tsp. (5 ml) onion powder
> 1 tsp. (5 ml) rubbed sage—packed in the spoon
> 1 tsp. (5 ml) oregano
> 1 tsp. (5 ml) poultry seasoning—packed in the spoon
> 4 bay leaves, cut into thin strips

1. Boil the seasonings for a few seconds in enough water to make a thin paste. Cool the paste, and add it to the brine.

2. Trim the chicken legs (but not excessively). Rinse and drain. Pierce the skin-covered *drumstick portions only*. Pierce them thoroughly. (The thighs should not be pierced because a large area of raw flesh is exposed, so the cure will penetrate

**Brine-cured chicken legs layered in paper towels and newspaper to absorb water after rinsing.**

the thighs easily.) Brine for exactly 30 minutes; stir frequently. After 30 minutes in the brine, give a quick rinse, and drain again. Blot the legs with paper towels. Pack the legs in plastic containers with each layer of legs separated by a layer of paper towels and newspaper. Refrigerate. The period of refrigeration will allow the excess water to be absorbed by the paper. It will also allow the cure to migrate to the center of the meat and become uniform.

## DAY 2, EVENING

If you wish to hang the legs in the smoker, the following technique may prove useful. This step may be ignored if the legs are going to be placed on racks.

Remove the legs from the containers, and discard the paper. Cut twine to about 14 inches (35 cm), and tie the ends together to form a loop. Wrap one end of the loop around the end of the drumstick, then feed the other end of the loop through that "eye" and pull it tight. Return the legs to the containers, and refrigerate again.

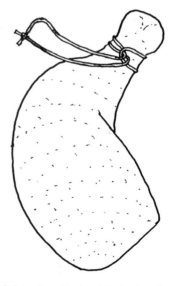

**Chicken leg tied with twine for hanging.**

**DAY 3, MORNING**

Dry in the smoker for about one hour at 140° F (60° C)—no smoke. The legs are dry when they no longer feel clammy. Cold smoke the legs for three hours at about 85° F (30° C). Water smoke the legs at 250° F (120° C) until they are cooked. Approximately an hour after a good color appears, take one leg out to determine if it is fully cooked—or use an electronic meat thermometer to determine when the fully cooked temperature of 180° F (82° C) has been reached.

# Tokyo Turkey—Marinated, No Nitrite

It seems to me that if the Chinese can season a duck with Chinese-type seasonings and call it Peking duck, then you or I can use Japanese-type seasonings on a turkey and call it Tokyo turkey. That is what we are going to do.

Peking duck has a long tradition, and it is most certainly eaten in China. On the other hand, turkeys are not raised in Japan in significant numbers, and most Japanese have never eaten turkey. Nevertheless, this is a great product, and the name *Tokyo turkey* has a nice ring to it!

When considering the adventure of smoking Tokyo turkey, keep in mind that the following process works equally well for chicken. The only thing you will have to change is the name. The marinade formula will process two large chickens. Cut the marinade in half if you want to process only one chicken.

### DAY 1, MORNING—Preparing and Seasoning the Turkey

Begin with a thawed or fresh turkey weighing about 10 pounds (4.5 kg). (When you buy the turkey, make sure that it has not been injected with salt, broth, or seasonings.) Check the skin for pinfeathers. Remove excess skin and fat from around the neck and at the rear of the bird, but leave adequate skin cover to prevent the flesh from drying excessively during smoking and roasting. Rinse well. Pierce the turkey well and deeply, especially the breast and legs. Prepare the following marinade:

### MARINADE FOR ONE 10-POUND (4.5-KILOGRAM) TURKEY

¼ cup (60 ml) salt
¼ cup (60 ml) sesame seed oil, or sesame seed oil/salad oil blend
¼ cup (60 ml) sugar

1 cup (240 ml) shredded ginger, or 2 Tbsp. (30 ml) ginger powder
2 cups (480 ml) chopped onions
4 cloves garlic, minced
1 cup (240 ml) saké (Japanese rice wine), or common white wine
2 tsp. (10 ml) *togarashi* (Japanese red pepper),
    or 1 Tbsp. (15 ml) cayenne
½ cup (120 ml) Kikkoman soy sauce, or general-purpose soy sauce

Blend the marinade in the curing container. Stir it until the salt and sugar have dissolved. Place the turkey in the container. Rub the bird inside and out with the seasoning mixture. Refrigerate. (Instead of using a curing container, a large, strong plastic bag may be employed.)

### DAY 2, MORNING AND EVENING

Overhaul the turkey. (If the bird is in a plastic bag, just slosh around the marinade, and turn the bird over a few times.)

### DAY 3, MORNING

Overhaul the turkey.

### DAY 3, EVENING

Rinse the bird briefly in cool water inside and out. Pat dry. Wad newspaper, wrap the wad with paper towels, and stuff this in the body cavity. Put the bird on a paper towel with newspaper underneath. Refrigerate overnight, uncovered.

### DAY 4, MORNING—Smoking the Turkey

1. Truss the wings: Lock the wings in place by twisting the wing tips behind the shoulders. Use twine to join the wings in back. See Trussing a Bird earlier in this chapter.
2. Truss the legs: Tie together with butcher's twine. Place the bird on the smoker rack with the breast up. Better yet, use the type of turkey rack illustrated earlier in this chapter.
3. Partially dry the bird in the water smoker for about 15 minutes at low heat. Use the empty water pan to catch grease. Do not use smoke. After drying, apply about ¼ cup (60 ml) of salad oil to the skin.

**4.** Fill the water pan with boiling water. Smoke and cook the bird in the water smoker at about 250° F (120° C). This process may take up to eight hours. If the turkey begins to darken excessively, or if you need to cook the bird faster, wrap the turkey in aluminum foil and move it to an oven preheated to 350° F (175° C). The turkey is fully cooked when the juices run clear and the legs move easily. To be fully cooked, the internal temperature must be 180° F (82° C).

# Turkey Ham

The dark meat of any fowl can be processed in the same way that fresh ham or pork loin is processed. After it is cured and smoked, the taste and appearance will be similar to cured ham.

Thighs are the best part of the turkey to use as raw material. The drumsticks can be used, but the numerous tendons make them troublesome. For chicken, either the thighs or the drumsticks can be processed into a ham-like product.

No matter what kind of fowl is being used, I recommend removing the skin from the drumsticks and thighs. The bones can be optionally left in place or removed before processing. However, if you do use turkey drumsticks, it is best to leave them whole with the bone and tendons intact. Removal of the bones and tendons in turkey drumsticks is difficult.

It is very easy to remove the bone from either a turkey or chicken thigh. First, lay the thigh skin-side down on a cutting board. Locate the bone with your fingers, and make a long slit through the flesh that is on top of the bone. Stroke along the bone with the tip of the knife. The flesh will gradually "peel" away from the bone. Remove the skin. The same technique can be used to remove the bone from a chicken drumstick.

### PREPARING THE MEAT

Prepare the poultry as indicated above. Rinse in cold water and drain. Put the meat on paper towels with newspaper underneath to absorb the water on the bottom surface. Blot the top surface with paper towels.

### CURING

The thickest piece of meat dictates the curing time for the batch. Six days are required if the thickest piece is 1 inch (2.5 cm) thick. Three days are required if the thickest piece is ½ inch (1.25 cm) thick.

## CURE MIX FOR 2¼ POUNDS (1 KILOGRAM) OF FOWL

1 Tbsp. (15 ml) salt
1 Tbsp. (15 ml) sugar
1 tsp. (5 ml) onion powder
½ tsp. (2.5 ml) Prague Powder #1
½ tsp. (2.5 ml) white pepper

Total: 8 tsp. = 2 Tbsp. + 2 tsp. (40 ml).

### CURE MIX MEASURING CHART
8 tsp. = 2 Tbsp. + 2 tsp. (40 ml) per 2¼ lbs. (1 kg) of fowl
4 tsp. = 1 Tbsp. + 1 tsp. (20 ml) per 1 lb. (500 g) of fowl
2 tsp. (10 ml) per ½ lb. (250 g) of fowl
1 tsp. (5 ml) per ¼ lb. (125 g) of fowl

1. Weigh the dressed poultry, and place it in a curing container. Prepare, calculate, and measure the required amount of curing mixture.
2. Rub the curing mixture on all surfaces of the meat. Cover and refrigerate.
3. Overhaul after about 12 hours. (Rub the surfaces again and restack.) Overhaul daily until the curing time has elapsed.
4. When the cure is finished, rinse each piece of meat very well in cool water. Drain. Return the meat to the curing container, but place layers of paper towels and newspapers between the layers of meat.

## SMOKING THE BIRD HAM

The instructions below are for cold smoking, followed by cooking in a steamer. However, this product may be water smoked, or it may be smoked in a portable electric smoker and then steamed.

1. Dry in front of an electric fan, or dry in a smoker (with no smoke) at less than 140° F (60° C). It is dry when your finger slides easily on the surface.
2. Smoke at less than 85° F (30° C), if possible, for three to six hours. Raise the temperature to 145° F (63° C). Continue to smoke for two or three more hours until the product has a reddish brown surface.
3. Wrap each piece in plastic food wrap. Stick the probe of an electronic thermometer into the thickest piece, and steam the meat until the internal temperature is 180° F (82° C).
4. Unwrap the pieces, and drain them in a colander. Cool at room temperature for two hours, then refrigerate overnight with no cover.

# Turkey Bacon

Commercially produced turkey bacon is, in my opinion, an amazing meat-processing accomplishment. It is impossible for us to duplicate the bacon-like layering of the dark turkey meat and the white turkey meat. Nevertheless, we can make a product that can be rightfully called turkey bacon—and it will be just as healthy.

Remove the bone and skin from turkey thighs (as described for turkey ham). Process these thighs in the same way that pork bellies are processed into bacon. Use a maple syrup cure, brown sugar cure, or honey cure. The "bacon" will be very lean, and it will be red, even after slicing and frying.

# Turkey Pastrami

The dark meat of the turkey must be used for turkey pastrami. The nitrite in the cure will fix the red color of the dark turkey meat in the same way that it fixes the red color of beef when beef is cured to make pastrami. The thighs are much easier to use than the drumsticks. Remove the skin from the thighs. The bones may be left in, or they may be cut out. If you want to remove the bones, see the instructions for turkey ham. Use the pastrami cure, and process this turkey meat in the same way as beef pastrami. However, turkey pastrami must be cooked until the internal temperature is 180° F (82° C).

# Turkey Jerky

I would like to take credit for inventing turkey jerky, but I can't. You may have never heard of it, but it has been around for a long time. Jerky is also made from duck, chicken, goose, ostrich, and emu. Dark meats make the best jerky.

Skinned thighs of the turkey are the best material for making turkey jerky. The technique for removing the bone is explained in turkey ham. Slice the flesh with the grain, or butterfly the meat. It should be not more than ¼ inch (6 mm) thick. Use the same processing procedure that is used for jerky in chapter 9, except the last two to four hours of drying should be at 185° F (85° C) instead of 175° F (80° C). You may use the same seasoning formulas that are used for beef jerky. Below, however, is a very good marinade for seasoning turkey jerky.

### SEASONING FOR 2¼ POUNDS (1 KILOGRAM) OF SLICED TURKEY

1 Tbsp. (15 ml) salt
1 Tbsp. (15 ml) honey
2 tsp. (10 ml) black pepper
½ tsp. (2.5 ml) Prague Powder #1 (optional)
½ tsp. (2.5 ml) MSG (optional)
½ tsp. (2.5 ml) hickory smoke flavor (optional)
½ tsp. (2.5 ml) cayenne
½ tsp. (2.5 ml) onion powder
½ tsp. (2.5 ml) poultry seasoning
3 Tbsp. (45 ml) soy sauce
¾ cup (180 ml) white cranberry-apple juice,
    or white cranberry-peach juice
2 cups (480 ml) cold water

# Peking Duck

Peking-style smoked duck is an excellent example of a world-famous main course that is made even tastier by smoking. It is a personal favorite of mine. Connoisseurs say that the best part of Peking duck is the flavorful skin. The instructions below simplify the complicated traditional Chinese method of preparation: You *need not* blow air between the skin and the flesh with a slender bamboo pipe, for example!

Directions for this product suggest cold/warm/hot smoking in a homemade smoker, followed by cooking in a kitchen oven. However, the duck can be smoked and cooked in a manufactured water smoker. It can also be smoked in a portable electric smoker, followed by cooking in an oven.

Caution is advised when using a homemade smoker or a portable electric smoker: Make sure that the drip pan does not fill with melted fat and overflow.

### THE DUCK

A duckling weighing between 4½ and 5 pounds (2 and 2.3 kg) is ideal. High-quality ducklings of this size—usually frozen—are sold year-round at a reasonable price; just make sure the duck has not been pumped with broth or a salt solution. However, if using a pumped duck is unavoidable, reduce the salt in the marinade from 1 tablespoon (15 ml) to 1 teaspoon (5 ml).

When processed for market, the ducklings are about seven to eight weeks old. Ducklings raised and marketed in the United States are normally the Long Island strain, which is directly descended from the yellowish white Pekin duck of China. (Pekin is often, but understandably, misspelled: Peking. *Peking duck* is the name of a Chinese main dish; *Pekin duck* is the name of a strain of duck.) The Pekin strain of duck is noted for being large and for having a thick layer of fat under its skin. Ducks have a high bone-to-meat ratio, so a 5-pound (2.3 kg) duck will not feed as many people as a 5-pound chicken. As the main course, a duck this size will serve two people. As a side dish, it may serve four to five.

### DAY 1, MORNING—Preparing and Seasoning the Duck

1. If the duck is frozen, thaw it in a plastic bag submerged in cold water for a few hours. (Refrigerator thawing requires about two days.) Refrigerate the heart, gizzard, and neck to make a special duck soup. (The recipe for this soup appears at the end of this section.)
2. Remove pinfeathers with a pair of common tweezers or fish-boning tweezers. Remove the excess fat and skin from around the neck and the rear end of the bird, but leave adequate skin to prevent the flesh from drying during smoking and roasting. To allow free passage of smoke through the body cavity, remove the stump of the neck that is attached to the backbone; cut deeply where the stump is attached to the backbone, then cut across the back of the stump, and twist it out—channel-lock pliers make this easier. Rinse the duck well.
3. Prepare about 3 quarts (3 liters) of boiling water in a large teakettle. With the duck placed in a colander in a sink, pour boiling water on it until the skin turns whitish and has a slightly puffy texture. Blot inside and out with paper towels. Pierce the duck deeply, especially the breast and thighs. Refrigerate the bird while you prepare the seasoning.

### SEASONING

¼ cup (60 ml) sherry, or *shao hsing* wine
1 Tbsp. (15 ml) salt
1 Tbsp. (15 ml) soy sauce
1 Tbsp. (15 ml) honey (clear)
1 Tbsp. (15 ml) sesame seed oil
2 tsp. (10 ml) ginger powder
1½ tsp. (7.5 ml) black pepper

1. Blend the seasoning ingredients. Place the duck in the curing container. Rub the duck inside and out with the seasoning mixture. Rather than using a basting brush, it is faster to pour some of this liquid in the palm of your hand, and rub it on.
2. Leave the duck in the curing container, breast down. Do not cover the curing container or wrap the bird while it is being cured. Refrigerate.

## DAY 1, EVENING

Overhaul the duck. (Rub with the seasoning that is in the bottom of the container.) Turn the breast up.

## DAY 2, MORNING

Overhaul the duck. Turn the breast down.

## DAY 2, EVENING

1. Rinse the duck briefly, inside and out, in cool water. Use paper towels to pat dry.
2. Stuff the body cavity with a cloth or with crumpled newspaper that has been wrapped with paper towels.
3. Place the bird on a paper towel with newspaper underneath and refrigerate, uncovered, overnight.

## DAY 3, MORNING—SMOKING THE DUCK

1. Truss the wings: Lock the wing tips in place by twisting them behind the shoulder joints. On the backside, use butcher's twine to secure the upper part of the wings.
2. Truss the legs: Tie together securely with butcher's twine. Use a sturdy metal S hook to hang this string on a hanging rod, or pass a hanging rod under the string; this will allow the bird to be hung vertically—with the tail pointed up. If the whole bird is hung vertically in the smoke chamber, the smoke can easily flow through the body cavity. Rather than hanging the duck, it can be mounted on a chicken rack. Hanging vertically or mounting on a steel chicken rack also allows melted fat to fall freely from the body cavity into a drip tray. (If you must place the duck horizontally on a smoking rack, use great care when moving the duck; spilling the hot grease that has accumulated in the body cavity could cause a fire or an injury.)

**3.** Dry the bird in the smoker for about one hour at 140º F (60º C). Drying should continue until the skin no longer feels clammy. However, there may be a little melted fat on the skin. Do not use smoke during this drying time.

**4.** Smoke at the lowest possible temperature for about three hours and then smoke at about 145º F (63º C) for three hours. Smoking is complete when the bird has taken on an attractive brownish coloration. Decrease or increase these smoking times to suit your taste.

### DAY 3, AFTERNOON OR EVENING—Cooking the Duck

**1.** Preheat the kitchen oven to 350º F (175º C). Place the duck on an elevated wire rack in a pan that is at least 1 inch (2.5 cm) deep. *Note:* Placement on an elevated wire rack within a pan is important. The high oven temperature will cause a large amount of grease to collect in the bottom of the pan; if the duck is not on an elevated rack, the back of the duck will be submerged in melted fat.

**2.** Cover the bird with a loose aluminum-foil tent, and roast it until the internal temperature is between 160º and 180º F (71º and 82º C). This will require about one and a half to two hours. Experts on the preparation of Peking duck usually cook the bird until the internal temperature is 160º F (71º C). Some food safety experts say that the internal temperature should be 180º F (82º C). I compromise at 170º F (77º C).

### GLAZE

> 2 Tbsp. (30 ml) honey
> 2 Tbsp. (30 ml) soy sauce

Remove the foil, and apply glaze to the duck with a basting brush. Raise the oven temperature to 485º F (250º C), and roast 10 or 15 minutes more without the foil tent. The skin will become a medium or dark brown color. Let the duck cool for about 15 minutes, carve it, and arrange the slices on a platter.

Don't throw away the bones! Save them to make tasty soup, as the Chinese do. This soup is very easy to make, and the procedure will be explained shortly.

### SAUCE BLEND

> ¼ cup (60 ml) *hoisin* sauce (see appendix 1)
> 1 tsp. (5 ml) sesame seed oil

1 Tbsp. (15 ml) water
2 tsp. (10 ml) sugar

Straight *hoisin* sauce is dark brown and has a tangy, hot taste. This sauce blend (above) has a milder taste than straight *hoisin* sauce. Spread a little sauce blend on the sliced duck before eating. You may garnish the meat with minced or julienne-cut green onions.

The Chinese spread this *hoisin*-based sauce on Mandarin pancakes, and then put sliced duck and julienne-cut green onions on top. The pancake is folded over the sliced duck and green onions. Then this taco-like preparation is eaten with the fingers. The Mandarin pancake is very similar to the Mexican flour tortilla. Substitute ready-made Mexican flour tortillas if you want to eat the duck Chinese style. Tortillas should be toasted on both sides in a hot, ungreased skillet. The toasting is complete when brown spots appear.

### DUCK SOUP

It takes only a few minutes of work to make a very delicious and unique soup using the bones left after carving the Peking duck.

### INGREDIENTS FOR DUCK SOUP

duck bones (bones remaining after the Peking duck is carved)
1 each: duck heart, gizzard, and neck
1½ quarts (1½ liters) water
4 green onions, roughly chopped
1 Tbsp. (15 ml) sherry, or *shao hsing* wine(optional)
¼ tsp. (1.25 ml) ginger powder (optional)
5 bouillon cubes, chicken flavor
1 cup (240 ml) very thinly sliced celery

1. Put all the ingredients except the celery in a pot, and simmer for about one hour.
2. Strain the soup into another pan. If there is froth or scum on the surface, skim it off. Save the heart, gizzard, and neck to use as a snack—or mince this meat and add it to the strained broth. Discard the bones and the green onions.
3. Add the celery to the broth and simmer for a few minutes until it is barely tender. Serve.

# Delightful Duck

A Japanese friend of mine—a retired radio announcer—enjoys duck hunting every year. One year he gave me about 10 duck breasts; he requested that I smoke them and share them with him. I was aware that smoked duck breasts are considered a delicacy in many European countries, but I could not find any information about the processing method. I decided to use the modern dry cure method and make the cure rather spicy so that it would cover any wild taste. The result was absolutely fantastic! The breasts were very tender, and they were perfectly seasoned. Because Prague Powder #1 was used, the naturally dark meat was an unbelievable maroon color. The product titillated the eyes as well as the taste buds. Needless to say, he brought duck breasts to me every year after that. Just before my family and I left Japan, I taught my duck hunter friend how to cure and smoke duck breasts.

Here in the United States, I use the same cure on whole domesticated ducks. The result is almost the same as for the wild duck breasts. I believe that you, too, will find this product delightful. The following instructions are for a whole duck, but the curing formula may be used on breasts as well. Simply weigh all of the breasts at one time, and apply the appropriate amount of cure to the meat.

It is best to use ducks that have not been pumped with a salt solution. However, if you must use a pumped duck, reduce the salt in the cure from 1 tablespoon (15 ml) to 1 teaspoon (5 ml) per 2¼ pounds (1 kg) of duck.

The process for making this product is similar to the process for Peking duck. The main differences are that the duck is not scalded with hot water, and a spicy modern dry cure is applied instead of the Chinese seasonings. Consequently, only the curing process will be described. For smoking and cooking, please use the instructions given for Peking duck.

## CURE AND SEASONING FOR 2¼ POUNDS (1 KILOGRAM) OF DUCK

> 1 Tbsp. (15 ml) salt
> 1 Tbsp. (15 ml) granulated sugar
> ½ tsp. (2.5 ml) Prague Powder #1
> 1 tsp. (5 ml) poultry seasoning—packed in the spoon
> 1 tsp. (5 ml) onion powder

½ tsp. (2.5 ml) paprika
½ tsp. (2.5 ml) rubbed sage—packed in the spoon
½ tsp. (2.5 ml) marjoram
½ tsp. (2.5 ml) thyme
½ tsp. (2.5 ml) white pepper
½ tsp. (2.5 ml) garlic powder
1 bay leaf, cut into thin strips with scissors (do not add to the
    ingredients above)

Total: 11½ tsp. (57.5 ml), excluding the bay leaf.

### CURE MIX MEASURING CHART
11½ tsp. (57.5 ml) per 2¼ lbs. (1 kg) of duck + 1 bay leaf
5¾ tsp. (28.75 ml) per 1 lb. (500 g) of duck + ½ bay leaf
3 tsp. (15 ml) per ½ lb. (250 g) of duck + ¼ bay leaf
1½ tsp. (7.5 ml) per ¼ lb. (125 g) of duck

## BULK MIX FOR 27 POUNDS (12 KILOGRAMS) OF DUCK

¾ cup (180 ml) salt
¾ cup (180 ml) granulated sugar
2 Tbsp. (30 ml) Prague Powder #1
¼ cup (60 ml) poultry seasoning—packed in the cup
¼ cup (60 ml) onion powder
2 Tbsp. (30 ml) paprika
2 Tbsp. (30 ml) rubbed sage—packed in the spoon
2 Tbsp. (30 ml) marjoram
2 Tbsp. (30 ml) thyme
2 Tbsp. (30 ml) white pepper
2 Tbsp. (30 ml) garlic powder
1 bay leaf per 2¼ lbs. (1 kg) of duck, cut into thin strips with scissors

## DAY 1

Wash the duck. Remove excess fat from around the neck and inside the
body cavity. Leave sufficient skin in the front and back to prevent the
flesh from being exposed. Pierce the duck well, especially the breast and
legs, and place in the curing container. Mix the cure thoroughly, and
apply it to the bird—inside and outside. Sprinkle on the bay leaf, and
rub the duck again. Place the lid on the curing container. Cure in the
refrigerator for six days. Overhaul several times during this period,
preferably once a day.

**DAY 6**

Rinse the duck very well with cool water. Blot it with paper towels. Stuff the inside with crumpled newspaper that has been wrapped in paper towels. Wrap the whole bird with paper towels, and wrap it again with newspaper. Put a paper towel and newspaper under the duck to absorb the water. Store it in the refrigerator overnight.

**DAY 7**

Follow the smoking and cooking directions for Peking duck. If the bird will be placed horizontally on a rack, take care not to spill melted fat from the body cavity. Neither a glaze nor a sauce is used on this product.

# Golden Goose—Marinated, No Nitrite

There was a time when roast goose was the traditional Christmas dinner. However, the National Turkey Growers' Association has convinced many Americans that turkey is suitable for both Thanksgiving and Christmas. In many parts of Europe, roast goose remains the traditional Christmas dinner, and a few families here in the United States still maintain the tradition of roast goose for dinner on December 25. If you like nostalgic things, try golden goose for your next Yuletide dinner.

Most Americans have never tasted goose. For turkey, the taste can be described by using the trite expression, "It tastes like chicken." Not so for goose; the taste is probably more comparable to beef.

The marinade for this product is entirely my own creation. When testing the formula and altering the various ingredients, I first used chicken legs for testing because they are much cheaper than goose. You might consider doing the same thing when you create a marinade: Test the formula by using chicken, and then tweak it to match your taste before using it on meat that is more expensive.

### DAY 1, MORNING—Preparing the Goose

1. Begin with a thawed or fresh goose weighing from 8 to 10 pounds (3.6 to 4.5 kg). (Young birds of this size are actually called goslings.) Check the skin for pinfeathers, and remove excess fat from around the neck and inside the body cavity. Fish-boning tweezers or common tweezers work well for removing the pinfeathers. Rinse well.
2. Put the bird in a colander in the kitchen sink, and scald the goose with about 4 to 6 quarts (4 to 6 liters) of boiling water until the skin

becomes white and puffy. Alternatively, hold the front half of the bird in a pot of boiling water for a minute and a half, and then hold the back half in boiling water for a minute and a half. It is best to practice "scalding" the goose in cold water; add or remove cold water until you have the proper amount in the pot. Next, boil the cold water that was used for practicing, and use it to scald the goose. If cold water is used to practice this method, there will be no problem due to insufficient boiling water or to boiling water overflowing the pot.

3. Pierce the goose well and deeply, especially the breast and legs. Chill the bird in the refrigerator for one day; do not cover or wrap. After the goose is chilled for a day with no cover on it, the skin will shrink and dry to some extent. When the goose is cooked, this shrunken skin will help to squeeze excess melted fat through the holes that have been pierced in the skin.

## DAY 2—Seasoning the Goose

Prepare the following marinade for a 10-pound (4.5-kg) bird, but reduce the salt by 1 teaspoon (5 ml) for a 9-pound (4 kg) bird, and by 2 teaspoons (10 ml) for an 8-pound (3.6 kg) bird. However, if the bird has been pumped by the processor, start out with 1 tablespoon of salt instead of 3 tablespoons.

## MARINADE FOR GOLDEN GOOSE

3 Tbsp. (45 ml) salt
¼ cup (60 ml) salad oil
2 cups (480 ml) chopped onions
1 cup (240 ml) prune juice
¾ cup (180 ml) sherry
⅓ cup (80 ml) honey
3 cloves garlic, minced
¼ cup (60 ml) soy sauce
2 tsp. (10 ml) cayenne
1 tsp. (5 ml) marjoram
1 tsp. (5 ml) rosemary

Blend the marinade in the curing container, and stir it until the salt and honey have dissolved. Place the goose in the container. Rub the bird, inside and out, with the seasoning mixture. Cover and refrigerate. (A large and strong plastic bag may be used instead of using a curing container.)

### DAY 3, MORNING AND EVENING

Overhaul the goose. (If it is in a plastic bag, just turn the bird over a few times.)

### DAY 4, MORNING

Overhaul the goose.

### DAY 4, EVENING

Rinse the bird briefly in cool water, inside and out. Pat dry. Crumple newspaper, wrap the crumpled newspaper with paper towels, and stuff this in the body cavity. Put the bird on a paper towel with newspaper underneath. Refrigerate overnight, uncovered.

### DAY 5, MORNING—Smoking the Goose

The instructions below are for smoking and cooking the goose in a water smoker. However, the goose can be processed in a portable electric smoker or a cold smoker and then cooked in a kitchen oven.

1. Probably the wings will have been trimmed off at the "elbows" by the processor. Use twine to secure the remaining upper part of the wings.
2. Tie the legs together with butcher's twine. It is best to mount the goose on the type of steel turkey rack illustrated earlier in this chapter. If such a rack is not available, place the bird on the smoker rack with the breast up.
3. Dry the bird in the water smoker for about 15 minutes at low heat. The skin need not be perfectly dry. Use the empty water pan to catch grease. Do not use smoke.
4. Fill the water pan with hot water. Smoke and cook the bird in the water smoker at about 250º F (121º C). This process may take eight hours or more. Much grease will accumulate in the water pan; it might be necessary to use a bulb baster from time to time to remove some. Grease will also accumulate in the body cavity if the bird has

been placed horizontally on a smoker rack. If this is the case, use extreme caution when the bird is moved—goose grease is very flammable.

5. If the goose begins to darken excessively, or if you need to hasten the cooking process, place an aluminum-foil tent on top of the bird, and move it to an oven preheated to 350° F (175° C). Grease will continue to flow from the skin, so be sure to put the goose on an elevated rack in a deep baking pan. The bird is fully cooked when the juices run clear and the legs move easily. The internal temperature should be 180° F (82° C) when fully cooked. Let the cooked goose set about 20 minutes before carving it.

# CHAPTER 11

# Fish and Other Aquatic Creatures

## About Finfish

### FISH FOR SMOKING

It is generally agreed that oily fish are best for smoking. Salmon tends to be oily. However, there are variations in the oil content depending on the species of salmon. On the average, the chinook (king) salmon and the Atlantic salmon have the highest oil content. Sockeye ranks next, followed by the coho (silver) salmon, the pink salmon, and the chum (also called keta, dog, or silverbright) salmon. Because the chum salmon has the lowest oil content of all of the species, it is the least popular for smoking. Nevertheless, it will make a better product than many other kinds of fish.

The Atlantic salmon is actually a large saltwater trout. Freshwater trout, or steelhead (a species of rainbow trout that migrates to the sea), can be substituted for salmon. Actually, ichthyologists classify both salmon and trout as members of the same *salmonid* family.

Nowadays, farmed Atlantic salmon, chinook, and steelhead are common. These farmed fish are excellent for smoking, but the flesh of farmed fish is not as firm as the flesh of those caught wild.

Many other kinds of fish are excellent for smoking. Sturgeon and tuna, for example, are favorites of many fish smokers.

Small fish should not be overlooked. There are species of small fish besides trout that are very good when smoked: smelt, sardines, catfish, herring, and horse mackerel, for example. Don't let a scarcity of salmon, trout, tuna, or sturgeon stop you. Try any kind of fish available. If it tastes good, who cares?

The required smoking time increases with the thickness of the fillet. This is another point worth considering when selecting a fish to smoke. If the fillet is thick, it might not be possible to complete the smoking process in one

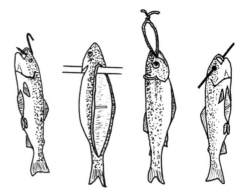

**Good ways to hang small fish. Use a toothpick to keep the body cavity open.**

day—this is important to many people. Fillets that have a thickness of ½ to ¾ inch (1.3 to 2 cm) are easy to smoke in a day if you get up early.

Use very fresh fish, or quick-frozen fresh fish. Using stale fish will produce an inferior product, and the fish might spoil during processing. Considerable effort is required to process smoked fish; using fish that is less than fresh will invite failure.

## CARING FOR FRESH FISH

A freshly caught fish will retain its freshness longer if it is properly and promptly dressed and chilled.

1. If the fish is not dead, stun it by giving it a sharp blow on the top of the head.
2. Wash the fish thoroughly. If it is very slimy, apply a solution of 1 part vinegar to 3 parts water. Wait a few minutes until the slime turns a milky color, and then wash it off with a scouring brush. Repeat, if necessary.
3. Scale the fish with a fish scaler, the dull edge of a knife, or even with the edge of a spoon.
4. If the head is to be left attached, the gills should be removed. (The gills harbor millions of bacteria. Removal of the gills also facilitates bleeding, which is desirable.)
5. Slit the belly open all the way to the vent, and remove the internal organs. (The internal organs contain countless bacteria and digestive enzymes, both of which spoil the flesh. After the fish dies, the digestive enzymes continue to work by starting to digest the stomach, the internal organs, and the flesh.)

6. The kidney lies inside the body cavity on the underside of the backbone (attached to the top of the rib cage arch). Fish have only one kidney, and it looks like a dark streak of coagulated blood. Remove all traces of the kidney; it is a source of flavor-destroying enzymes. A stiff toothbrush that is used with a stream of water is very effective for this.

7. Chill the fish to reduce the activity of any remaining bacteria and enzymes. You may pack it in crushed ice that can drain as it melts, or refrigerate it at between 34° and 39° F (1.2° and 3.8° C). Process the fish soon.

## JUDGING THE FRESHNESS OF FISH

Judging the freshness of a whole, unfrozen fish is not difficult. The signs of freshness—or spoilage—are easy to detect, so you can readily determine the freshness of a fish even if you have no knowledge about when it was caught or the care it has received.

Look at the general appearance of the fish first. The skin should be moist and glossy. The eyes should be life-like; they should be bright and bulging. A fish with dull, sunken eyes is less than fresh. The vent (anal opening) will usually be pink. A yellowish, brownish, or grayish vent usually means that deterioration of the internal organs is well advanced.

Next, press the flesh of the fish with your index finger. If it feels firm, and it springs back rather quickly without leaving a dent, the fish is fresh. This means that enzymes that cause spoilage have not yet caused the flesh to become mushy. If the fish has had its head removed, and if it has been eviscerated and tightly wrapped in plastic, this finger-pressure test may be the only test possible.

Finally, put your nose to work. It is natural for fish to smell a little fishy, but the odor should not be offensive in any way. A saltwater fish should smell a little like the ocean, and a freshwater fish will probably smell a little like the river or lake from which it came. An unpleasant odor around the gills or belly is a sure sign of spoilage. If a bad odor is present and you lift the gill covers, you will probably observe that the bright red gills have become light pink or gray, and the mucus on the gills is yellowish rather than clear.

If a fish passes all of these tests, you may be assured that it is fresh. It is of little importance whether it was caught two hours ago or two days ago.

### JUDGING THE QUALITY OF FROZEN FISH

Commercial fish-processing plants freeze fish very quickly in efficient, extremely low-temperature freezers. This process greatly helps to preserve fresh flavor.

Freshly caught fish are certainly the most desirable. Nevertheless, the commercially processed, flash-frozen fish are flavorful and high quality, and they are usually sold at a reasonable price. The widespread availability of such fish allows someone living in the middle of the United States to purchase and process seafood; someone living in Nebraska, for example, can enjoy home-smoked salmon or ocean shellfish.

A few pointers might be helpful in selecting and using high-quality frozen finfish and other seafood products:

🔥 Select packages that are frozen solid; that is, select directly from a frozen food display case. If the packages are misshapen or show any other evidence of being thawed and refrozen, reject them.

🔥 The packaging should be undamaged and airtight. A package containing fish having the white, dry-looking spots known as *freezer burn* should be rejected.

🔥 Excessive ice crystals inside the package are evidence of dehydration. Avoid such products.

To thaw, put the sealed package in a deep pan that is full of cold tap water, and weight the package so that it will stay below the surface. Better yet, if there are pieces that were individually flash-frozen, put each piece in its own sealed plastic bag, and thaw in the same way. Thawing in plastic bags that are immersed in water is much more efficient than thawing in the refrigerator. The thermal conductivity of water is much greater than that of air in the refrigerator, so thawing is much faster. Because it is thawed faster, the fish will be a little fresher if the water-thawing method is used. Never thaw fish at room temperature. It may not spoil, but the quality will suffer.

### FILLETED FISH

Small fish are usually smoked in the round, but larger fish are processed faster and better if they are split open. The curing, drying, and smoking will be much more efficient and predictable if large fish are split. Filleting is the usual way to split fish.

Usually, the large fish fillets that are sold at common retail outlets have been expertly cut in a fish-processing facility by professionals before they reach the store. If it is a large, fresh fish that is being sold in the round at a seafood market, the fishmonger will be happy to fillet it for you—and he or she will do an excellent job. However, in a common supermarket there are great differences in the fish-filleting skills of the employees. If I buy a whole fish in such a store, I take it home in the round and fillet it myself. The risk of getting a poorly filleted fish at a common supermarket is too great to do otherwise.

*Hint:* If you have your fish filleted by a retailer, tell the clerk or fishmonger that you want the bones, too. Even if the fish was skillfully filleted, there will be a lot of meat remaining on the bones. Sprinkle the bones with salt and pepper, and then steam them for 10 to 15 minutes. The steamed meat remaining on the bones will make a delicious meal or an excellent salad topping.

Many people would have you believe that there is only one correct way to fillet a fish: their way. The truth is that there is no *correct* way to fillet a fish. The way a fish is filleted depends on the expert doing it, the species and size of the fish, and even the filleting customs in various countries. Furthermore, there is no worldwide agreement on the best kind of knife for filleting.

Recently, I bought a Japanese book on the subject of culinary knife techniques. In that book, there are drawings on how to dress and fillet about 20 kinds of fish, and each explanation differs according to the species! The specified filleting knife was the thick, bevel-sharpened Japanese filleting knife illustrated in chapter 4, page 83.

Since most of us are not making a living by dressing fish, all we need to learn is how to cut reasonably attractive fillets in an efficient manner. This is an acquired skill, but the average person can acquire it readily. If you have never filleted fish, follow the instructions below—more or less—and, in a short time, you will be cutting professional-looking fillets. I suggest, by the way, that you use a U.S. style of filleting knife or a boning knife. Using the strange-looking Japanese filleting knife will most certainly bring on ridicule and howls of laughter from those

**Making a diagonal cut to the backbone.**

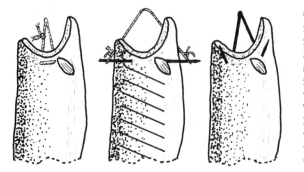

**Good methods for hanging a fillet —a string, a skewer, or a special V hook is inserted below the lug bone. The center fillet has slits cut through the skin to facilitate uniform curing.**

observing you (unless those people happen to be Japanese). Another consideration is that the instructions given below are not appropriate for a knife with a wide, thick blade.

🐟 Wash, scale, and eviscerate the fishes to be filleted, then wash them quickly again.

🐟 Make a diagonal cut just behind the lug bone and pectoral fin, as shown in the photograph. Cut down to—but not through—the backbone. (Leaving the head attached provides something to hold during the filleting operation, but some people cut the head off first because they say it gets in the way.) However, if you are going to hang the fillets in the smoke chamber rather than place them on racks, the lug bone should remain attached to give support to the fillet.

🐟 Make a slit along the top of the back, parallel to the dorsal fin. Start from the thick part of the fish, and slit the skin all the way to the tail. Use a long filleting knife, and do the same thing again, this time cutting close to the backbone and more deeply so that the side of the blade of the knife rubs on the backbone. The tip of the knife should bounce on the rib cage bones. (Some people prefer to cut through the rib bones at this time—instead of bouncing the knife tip on them.)

🐟 After the point of the knife bounces off the last rib, push the knife through the fish so that it exits the belly. Push the knife toward the tail with a slight seesaw movement, let-

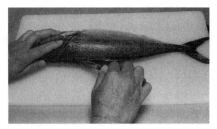

**Slitting the topside with a small, sharp knife.**

ting the side of the blade rub on the tail portion of the backbone.

♪ Lift the tail of the fillet. Reverse the direction of the blade, and cut through the rib bones to free the entire fillet. (Instead of cutting through the rib bones, some people prefer to lift the fillet and carefully trim the fillet from those bones. I cannot recommend this tedious method.)

♪ Turn the fish over, and fillet the other side in the same way.

♪ Slice out the rib bones, and pull out the small bones that often lie just above the centerline of the fillet. (Bone tweezers are shown and discussed in chapter 4, page 81.) Rinse the fillet quickly, and blot it with absorbent paper.

Filleting the tail portion.

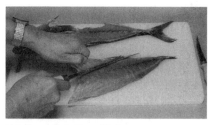
Slicing out the rib bones.

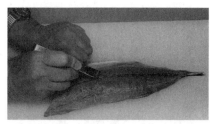
Pulling the remaining bones with bone tweezers (the extracted bones have been stacked on the fillet, directly in front of my right hand).

# Kippered (Hot Smoked) Salmon— Modern Dry Cure

The word *salmon* is used in the processing instructions that follow, but the same process may be used for many other kinds of medium to large fish. Salmon processed by this method is called smoked salmon on the west coast of Canada and in most regions of the United States. In Europe, however, the term *smoked salmon* refers to the raw, cold-smoked type that is famous in places such as Scotland and Ireland. The primary distinction between kippered and barbecued salmon is that the kippered kind is cooked with lower and more carefully controlled heat. Furthermore, kippered salmon is cured rather than simply seasoned.

## THE FISH

Thin fillets can be processed faster than thick fillets, but don't hesitate to use thick fillets if that is all that is available. If the whole fillets are too long to be processed easily, they can be cut into pieces of a more manageable size. In any case, the skin should never be removed from the fish when it is being processed. Removal of the skin will make the fish much more difficult to handle, and the appearance will suffer. Use very fresh fish or fish that has been fast-frozen.

The flesh of white-meat fish or other fish with low oil content—such as chum salmon—should be oiled. The appropriate time to oil such fish is indicated in Day 3.

Prepare the fillets, rinse them quickly, and blot dry. Refrigerate the fish while you prepare the cure.

You might notice that the cure, below, is almost the same as that used for bacon. The main difference is that the color-fixing agent, Prague Powder #1, has been omitted because it is not required for kippered fish. I experimented with various seasonings in the cure, including the much-touted dill weed, for example. However, to my taste, the following simple curing formula is the best; it enhances the salmon flavor—it does not mask it.

## CURE MIX FOR 2¼ POUNDS (1 KILOGRAM) OF SALMON

1 Tbsp. (15 ml) salt
1 Tbsp. (15 ml) brown sugar—packed in the spoon
½ tsp. (2.5 ml) white pepper
½ tsp. (2.5 ml) garlic powder
½ tsp. (2.5 ml) onion powder

Total: 7½ tsp. (37.5 ml).

### CURE MIX MEASURING CHART

7½ tsp. (37.5 ml) per 2¼ lbs. (1 kg) of salmon
3¾ tsp.(18.75 ml) per 1 lb. (500 g) of salmon
2 tsp. (10 ml) per ½ lb. (250 g) of salmon
1 tsp. (5 ml) per ¼ lb. (125 g) of salmon

## BULK MIX FOR 27 POUNDS (12 KILOGRAMS) OF SALMON)

¾ cup (180 ml) salt
¾ cup (180 ml) brown sugar—packed in the cup
2 Tbsp. (30 ml) white pepper

2 Tbsp. (30 ml) garlic powder

2 Tbsp. (30 ml) onion powder

## DAY 1

If the fish fillet is more than ¾ inch (2 cm) thick, it is best to make parallel slits in the skin, about 1½ inches (3 to 4 cm) apart, on the front half of the fish where the fillet is thickest (see drawing on page 216). A very sharp knife will do, but a razor blade or a box cutter is best. Make the slits just deep enough to cut slightly below the skin.

If slits were made in the skin, rub some cure into them. Apply the rest of the cure to the fleshy side of the fish—apply the cure a little more heavily wherever the fillet is thick. Refrigerate for 24 hours. Overhaul two or three times during this period (rub the surface of the salmon gently to redistribute the cure).

## DAY 2

Rinse off the cure *quickly* in cool water, and wrap each piece in a paper towel, then in newspaper. (When rinsing off the cure, try to keep the rinsing time to a minimum to prevent the flesh from becoming waterlogged.) Refrigerate overnight.

## DAY 3

1. Dry the fish in front of a fan, skin-side down, for about an hour. Prepare the smoker for additional drying at 100° F (40° C).
2. Oil the *skin side* of the salmon with salad oil; this oil helps to prevent the skin from sticking to the smoking rack.
3. Place the fish on the smoking racks with the skin side down. Dry at 100° F (40° C) in the smoke chamber (with no smoke) until the surface of the fish becomes dry and smooth to the touch. This drying will require about two hours for a thin salmon fillet and up to about four hours for thick salmon.
4. Cold smoke at the lowest temperature possible for about three hours. Then, *over a two-hour period*, gradually step the temperature up to 175° F (80° C) to temper the flesh. Continue to smoke. (Tempering is the technique of raising the heat gradually in order to condition the flesh to heat. Tempering will reduce the amount of water-soluble protein that tends to rise to the surface of the fillet when the fish is cooking. This yellowish white dissolved protein solution—sometimes called *curd*—is not very attractive, but it is

harmless, tasty, and very nutritious.) *Note:* If fish with low oil content (chum salmon, pink salmon, or fish with white meat, for example) are being tempered, they should be oiled on all surfaces before the tempering begins; olive oil, peanut oil, and salad oil are all suitable.

5. Continue to smoke at 175° F (80° C) for two hours. Don't go higher than 175° F (80° C); if this temperature is surpassed, the texture of the flesh might change to that of overcooked fish. After this two-hour smoking period, you may wish to try to remove the curd with a basting brush and a paper towel. Of course, removing the curd is purely to improve the appearance, so this step is optional. If the fillets are thin, they should be done after 30 to 45 minutes of additional smoking. Thicker fillets will require more time. An experienced food smoker can judge doneness by appearance, feel, and smell. It will look cooked, feel firm, and will not have a "raw smell." The tail of the fillet will probably be curved upward slightly. Furthermore, when the fish is done, it will flake. This flaking test is the most common test to determine if fish is fully cooked. If the fish is thick enough to measure the internal temperature with a probe, that temperature should be 140° F (60° C).

6. Let the salmon cool at room temperature for about one hour. Refrigerate the fish, uncovered, overnight. The next morning, the fish may be wrapped in plastic food wrap or be put in plastic bags.

# Kippered (Hot Smoked) Fish— Brine Cure

The process described in the previous section uses the modern dry cure method. That method is almost foolproof, and I highly recommend it if you are going to smoke a few fillets or pieces. However, if you intend to smoke many fillets or pieces of fish, or if you are going to smoke many small fish, the brine cure method might be easier—but the result would be less predictable. This is because the length of time that the fish is left in the brine is difficult to judge unless you are experienced in brine curing.

The strength of the brine is the first thing to consider. The thickness of the flesh is another important consideration when estimating the brining time. Whether the fish is filleted or whether you are dealing with small fish in the round is another factor. Oily fish absorb salt more slowly than fish with little oil in the flesh. Finally, your personal taste is important; some people want more salt than others do.

Below is a basic brine formula together with a chart that will help to estimate the amount of time a fillet of a certain thickness should be left in the brine. Below that chart is another chart which suggests brining times for small, whole fish in the round (cleaned, but with the heads still attached). With these charts and a little luck, the product might come out exactly right the first time. It is more likely, however, that the product will be acceptable, but a little more or a little less salt flavor would be better. Make records of exactly what you did and the results. Record in detail all of the following: the strength of the brine, the species of fish, the thickness of the fillet or the size of the whole fish, the time left in the brine, and any other variable that could affect the absorption of salt.

## BASIC BRINE CURE FOR KIPPERED FISH
## (ABOUT 80 PERCENT BRINE)

4 quarts water + 1½ cups brown sugar + 3½ cups salt (35 oz.)
*or*
4 liters water + 370 ml brown sugar + 930 ml salt (1,090 g)

## SEASONING FOR BRINE CURE

1 Tbsp. (15 ml) onion powder
1 Tbsp. (15 ml) garlic powder
1 Tbsp. (15 ml) white pepper

Measure the three seasonings into a small saucepan, and add enough water to make a thin paste. Boil the mixture for a few seconds, and then chill it in the refrigerator. Add to the brine, and chill the brine.

### SUGGESTED BRINE CURING TIMES FOR FISH FILLETS
Put all of the fish in at one time, then begin taking out the thinner ones when the appropriate time has elapsed.

| Thickness | Time |
| --- | --- |
| ⅜ inch (10 mm) | 7 minutes |
| ½ inch (13 mm) | 15 minutes |
| ¾ inch (19 mm) | 35 minutes |
| 1 inch (25 mm) | 45 minutes |
| 1¼ inches (32 mm) | 1 hour |

**SUGGESTED BRINE CURING TIMES FOR SMALL, WHOLE FISH**

| | |
|---|---|
| With the skin not slit (heads attached) | 45 minutes |
| With the skin slit every ¾ inch (19 mm) (heads attached) | 30 minutes |

After the brining is finished, drain the fillets or the small whole fish. Do not rinse. Next, follow the smoking instructions beginning with Day 3 in the previous section. Those instructions are for fillets, but the smoking process is essentially the same for small fish in the round.

# Scotch-Style Smoked Salmon

For many people in the Western world, the only true smoked salmon is the type most commonly known as *Scotch smoked salmon* (similar styles of smoked salmon are produced in Ireland and in the Scandinavian countries). Without a doubt, it is gourmet fare, and it is an acquired taste. People who like it will come back for more; those who are repelled by the thought of eating raw fish will not touch it.

Scotch smoked salmon is, indeed, an uncooked product—but it does not taste as raw as you might imagine. It almost melts in your mouth, and it does not have a rubbery texture that is associated with some kinds of raw fish. Nothing can be done about the fact that it is raw—Scotch smoked salmon is raw by definition. True Scotch smoked salmon is also a very salty product. However, if the basic process is used, but the salt content is reduced, I think it is fair to call it Scotch-*style* smoked salmon. Such a product is presented here: Scotch-style smoked salmon with reduced salt.

The process described below contains the basic steps used by many professionals to make rum-and-sugar-cured Scotch smoked salmon. The only significant difference is that the salt and sugar have been reduced to make a more palatable product.

Even if you do not want to eat this product, you should try to make it for someone who does like it. Making superb European-style smoked salmon is a milepost on the road to becoming an expert smoker. Be sure to make this product when the outside temperature is cold.

## REQUIRED EQUIPMENT

This is a cold smoked product, and the processing temperature is tightly controlled. A smoker capable of maintaining 85º F (30º C)—plus or minus 5º F (3º C)—is required. Normally, this means a homemade smoker with an external smoke generator. Depending on the ambient temperature and other factors, a supplementary heat source inside the smoke chamber may be required.

## THE FISH

Oily salmon will produce the best-tasting product. The Atlantic salmon, chinook (king salmon), and sockeye are the best kinds to use, but the coho (silver salmon) will also work well. Personally, small sockeye salmon are my favorites for smoking; the sockeye has a high oil content, and I like the bright red color of the flesh. If the salmon are small, they are easy to smoke in one day.

Traditionally, only Atlantic salmon were used to make Scotch smoked salmon. However, before farmed Atlantic salmon became plentiful, other species were used as a substitute when the wild Atlantic salmon were in short supply.

This is a raw product, so commercially frozen fish are safer to use if you are concerned about parasites—salmon occasionally harbors parasites that are harmful to humans. Commercial freezing of fish is done at temperatures low enough to kill all parasites—if there are any present. (See chapter 6, page 106.)

## THE CURING AND SMOKING PROCESS

### DAY 1

1. Scale the fish and prepare the fillets, but *do not* remove the skin. Trim off the fat that lies along the edge of the belly flap and along the edge of the back (this fat tends to become rancid quickly).
2. After all of these operations are finished, select a fillet of average thickness, weigh it, and mark it by inserting a toothpick, for example. Record this "green weight." Knowing the green weight of this fillet will be useful during the smoking process. (This is explained in When Is It Done? near the end of this section.)
3. Rinse all the fillets very briefly. Wrap the pieces individually in paper towels. Next, wrap each of these pieces with about three layers of newspaper. This wrapping will draw out an amazing amount of moisture. Chill the fish in a refrigerator.

### DAY 2, MORNING

1. If the fish fillet is more than ¾ inch (2 cm) thick, it is best to make parallel slits in the skin, about 1½ inches (3 to 4 cm) apart, on the

front half of the fish where the fillet is thickest. A good tool for this is a box cutter or a razor blade. Make the slits just deep enough to penetrate the skin. (These slits help to ensure that the cure will migrate to all parts of the flesh.)

2. Weigh one fillet, and measure 2 teaspoons (10 ml) of salt for each pound (450 g). Set that fillet aside together with the measured salt. Weigh the next fillet, and measure the salt for that fillet. Continue until the required salt has been measured for each fillet. Two teaspoons (10 ml) of salt per pound (450 g) will result in a mild and pleasant salt taste. For a saltier, more traditional taste, use 3 or 4 teaspoons (15 or 20 ml) of salt per pound (450 g).

3. If you have cut slits in the skin, rub a little of the measured salt in the slits. The remaining salt for each fillet is *gently patted* on the *flesh side* of the fillet (not the skin side), sprinkling liberally on the thick areas and sparingly on the thin areas. If your smoker is too small to accommodate the length of the fillets, you might wish to cut the fillets in half at this point. (If you do cut the fillets, make sure to get some salt on the flesh that was exposed by the cut.) Refrigerate, *uncovered*, in a suitable curing container. Rub the surface of the fillets gently every few hours and restack; this helps to ensure equal distribution of the salt. (Refrigerating the fish without a cover on the curing container will result in some desirable moisture loss.)

## DAY 3, MORNING

By now, the salt will have penetrated the flesh. Rinse each piece *very briefly* to remove excess salt on the surface. Wrap again in paper towels and about three layers of newspaper. Return the fish to the refrigerator. (The process of salt equalization will begin.)

## DAY 3, NIGHT

Remove the wrapping, and gently rub all surfaces of the fish with a liberal amount of cooking oil or salad oil. Olive oil or peanut oil is commonly used, but any cooking oil you have on hand will do very nicely. Again, refrigerate, but without covering or wrapping.

## DAY 4, MORNING

1. Pour rum on a very small cloth (a cloth about half the size of your palm) until it is dripping wet. (I use white rum, but dark is accept-

able.) Use this rum-soaked cloth to wipe the oil off all surfaces of the fish. Rub gently! Use lots of rum. Don't worry about either you or the salmon getting drunk. The salmon could not care less at this point, and when the smoking is finished, there won't be enough alcohol left to intoxicate a gnat.

2. For every pound (450 g) of fish, you need to sprinkle on 2 teaspoons (10 ml) of brown sugar (packed in the spoon). This is assuming that you applied 2 teaspoons (10 ml) of salt per pound (450 g) on Day 2, morning. If you applied 3 teaspoons (15 ml) of salt on Day 2, morning, then you should now apply 3 teaspoons (15 ml) of brown sugar per pound (450 g) of fish. You may have to weigh each piece again to determine how much brown sugar is to be applied to each fillet or hunk. Pat the brown sugar on the fish. Refrigerate with no cover.

## DAY 4, NIGHT

Wet a cloth with water, and gently wipe all surfaces of the salmon to remove excess sugar. Blot well with a paper towel or cloth. Again, rub cooking oil on the surfaces. Refrigerate with no cover.

## DAY 5, MORNING

Get up early so you can get full enjoyment from your day of smoking— and so you will have enough time to get the doggone fish finished!

1. Again, wipe the surfaces with a rum-soaked cloth. Place the fish, skin-side down, on a smoking rack, and dry in the smoker at 85° F (30° C) with *no smoke*. It is a good idea to blot the fish every 30 minutes or so during the drying process. The drying time required will vary with the following conditions: the humidity of the outside air; the velocity of the draft; the moisture content and thickness of the fish; and the drying temperature used. However, about two hours of drying will probably be adequate for fillets that are ½ to ¾ inch (1.3 to 2 cm) thick. Drying at a temperature less than 85° F (30° C) will require more time. Drying at a higher temperature than this will dry the fish faster, but the drying is likely to be uneven, cracks in the flesh might appear, and too much oil will be brought to the surface.

2. The fish is sufficiently dry when the surface looks shiny and no longer feels clammy. (This shiny, somewhat hard surface is called the *pellicle* in smoking jargon.) Some oil may have risen to the surface, but this presents no problem. (Learn to distinguish between

the feel of oil and the feel of water. When rubbed between the fore-finger and the thumb, the oil will feel—well—oily.)

3. When the surface is dry, begin cold smoking at the same tempera-ture. Try to keep the smoke chamber close to this ideal temperature of 85° F (30° C). If the temperature varies plus or minus 5° F (3° C), it presents no problem. However, if the temperature is significantly below the ideal, color development and moisture loss will be retard-ed, and you might not be able to finish the smoking in one day. Also, the increased smoking time required to properly color and dry the fish may give it too much of a smoky flavor.

4. If the smoking temperature is significantly higher than the ideal, you might see the same cracking problems and uneven drying problems mentioned a few paragraphs above. Warm-heat smoking can also cause excessive coloration. However, there is one situation when heat higher than 85° F (30° C) is advisable—when the flesh of the fish does not have enough gloss. In this case, the flesh can be given an eye-pleasing sheen by raising the temperature to about 100° F (38° C) *very briefly* (10 to 20 minutes). This will bring a little more oil to the surface and produce an attractive gloss.

## WHEN IS IT DONE?

Continue smoking until the fish takes on an attractive reddish brown hue and the flesh feels firm. This will require at least seven to ten hours for a fillet that was from ½ to ¾ inch (1.3 to 2 cm) thick in the beginning. Thicker fillets will require proportionately more time.

Another good indication of doneness is a weight loss of about 17 to 19 percent compared with the green weight (the original weight). If you intend to use this guide to determine doneness, you must record the green weight of a typical fillet just before the salting process is begun. This was suggested in the instructions for Day 1, so you may have already marked this fillet with a toothpick and recorded the weight. If this fillet is quite like all the other fillets, you may assume that the smok-ing is finished for all the fish when this typical piece has lost 17 to 19 per-cent of its weight. Pieces that vary significantly in thickness from the "typical" piece will have to be judged individually.

Sometimes, for an unforeseen reason, you might not be able to fin-ish the smoking in one day. Maybe the fish is quite thick, or maybe you got up too late. Not to worry! Refrigerate the fish, and continue processing it the next day, or at least the day after that. If you can't smoke again until three or more days have passed, you had better freeze the fish right away. The quality may suffer slightly, but it will still be delicious.

When the smoking is finished, put the salmon in the refrigerator immediately, *uncovered*, overnight. The next morning, wrap it in plastic food wrap, or put it in plastic bags. Wrapping or bagging the fish when it is warm will cause moisture condensation on the inside of the packaging material, and this will, in turn, cause a faster rate of spoilage. Chilling the fish in the refrigerator for a day or so also helps to make the fish more firm and easier to slice.

Decide how much will be consumed in the next two or three days. Freeze the rest immediately. If you wait two days before you freeze it, the shelf life will be two days shorter when you thaw it.

## HOW TO PREPARE SCOTCH SMOKED SALMON FOR EATING

Use a sharp knife to remove the skin from the portion of the fish you wish to slice. Then, starting at the front end of the fillet, turn the knife to about a 45° angle, and cut slices across the fish about ⅛ inch (3 mm) thick—or less. Arrange these slices attractively on small, individual serving plates. (White plates with a blue or green pattern make a very attractive color contrast.) Toppings that have been prepared in advance are sprinkled on the slices of salmon by each person according to his or her taste:

> fresh lemon wedges (for lemon juice)
> hard-boiled egg, grated
> thin slices of a mild onion
> minced green onion, or chives
> freshly ground black pepper
> capers

Bite-sized pieces of some variety of whole-grain bread are usually provided to clear the palate. Some epicures prefer to spread unsalted butter, or cream cheese, on whole wheat, rye, or pumpernickel bread, and top this with peppered salmon. This is similar to the Danish-style open-faced sandwich, and it is the traditional way to eat smoked salmon in Great Britain. My wife likes to eat it with just a few drops of lemon juice. I like to eat it with capers and a little freshly ground black pepper, preferably washed down with German white wine.

# Smelt—Modern Dry Cure

Smelt are native to both the northern Pacific and northern Atlantic oceans. There are several species, but *rainbow smelt* is the common variety in Atlantic waters. Atlantic rainbow smelt were transplanted to Lake Michigan in 1912, and they gradually spread to the other Great Lakes. The *eulachon* and *whitebait* are the common species in the Pacific waters. The eulachon is also called *candlefish* because Pacific Northwest Indians would dry these fish, stick a wick in the oily flesh, and use them as candles. If smelt are not available in your area, fresh sardines or any other species of small, oily fish may be substituted.

The word *smelt* is the usual name given to these fishes in both British and American English. However, both the Americans and the British sometimes call them *sparling*.

Smelt are widely used as a food fish in the Northern Hemisphere, and they are often smoked. The average length is 4 to 7 inches (10 to 17 cm). They normally have a dark, greenish back that gradually changes to mottled sides and then to a bright silver belly. The flesh is fine grain, oily, and mild flavored.

Smelt spawn like salmon. They leave the ocean or the Great Lakes, enter rivers, and search out suitable gravel beds on which to lay and fertilize their eggs. When they are making their run up the rivers to spawn, people will line the banks of the river with long-handled dip nets. This is exactly the way that I obtain my smelt every spring.

### DAY 1, MORNING—PREPARING THE SMELT

Smelt may be cleaned with a small knife, but small, pointed scissors are better.

1. Snip off the head just to the rear of the pectoral fins.
2. Clip out the pelvic fins (located on the belly) by making a V-shaped cut.
3. Insert the point of the scissors in the vent, and cut to the front of the fish to open the belly.
4. Use your thumb to expel the entrails by pushing them toward the vent.
5. Use your thumbnail, or a toothbrush, to remove the kidney. (The kidney is attached to the backbone, and it looks like clotted blood.)
6. Rinse the fish thoroughly, and place it in a colander to drain.
7. After all the fishes have been dressed, return them to the refrigerator.

### DAY 1, MORNING—BEGIN THE CURE

Most people brine smelt before smoking them. However, the curing method described below will result in a more consistent flavoring from batch to batch, and the quantity of seasoning ingredients will be much less than is required for a brine cure. The only negative point is that more curing time is required than for a brine cure.

The technique described below is actually the same technique—modern dry cure—that was previously described for curing bacon, pastrami, and other products. However, because of the use of a liberal amount of wine as a seasoning ingredient, the appearance is that of a marinade rather than a dry cure.

Please keep in mind that this technique can be used for any kind of fish—just change the ingredients to suit your taste. If the species of fish you cure does not contain very much natural oil in the flesh, be sure to use about ½ cup of salad oil in the cure mixture.

### CURE MIX FOR 2¼ POUNDS (1 KILOGRAM) OF DRESSED SMELT

    2 tsp. (10 ml) salt
    1 Tbsp. (15 ml) brown sugar—packed in the spoon
    1 Tbsp. (15 ml) soy sauce
    ¼ cup (60 ml) white wine
    2 tsp. (10 ml) chili powder
    1 tsp. (5 ml) paprika
    1 tsp. (5 ml) onion powder
    1 tsp. (5 ml) finely ground black pepper
    ½ tsp. (2.5 ml) red pepper, or cayenne

1. Weigh the total amount of dressed fish.
2. Select a curing container with a volume about twice that of the fish to be cured.
3. Measure all the ingredients directly into that container. Stir the ingredients until they are dissolved. The amount of the curing ingredients is relative to the total weight of the cleaned fish. Therefore, if the weight of the fish is about 3¼ to 3½ pounds (about 1.5 kg), for example, you need to multiply all ingredients by 1.5.
4. Add the fish to the curing mixture, and stir them for about one minute. Refrigerate.

### DAY 1, AFTERNOON AND EVENING—Overhauling

1. Overhaul about once an hour until bedtime. Overhauling is accomplished by stirring well for a minute or so—or by turning the container upside down several times.
2. Let the fish cure overnight without additional overhauling.

### DAY 2, MORNING

1. Remove the smelt from the curing container, and place them in a colander to drain. Wash the curing container; it will be needed again.
2. Rinse each fish for about three seconds under running water, and drain in a colander.
3. Put the smelt in the curing container, placing the fish between layers of paper towels and newspapers. Refrigerate for at least one hour while you prepare the smoker.
4. Remove the smelt from the curing container, and air-dry them in front of a fan. Alternatively, air-dry in the smoker at 100º F (40º C) with no smoke. The fish should be dry to the touch after about an hour.

### DAY 2, OPTION 1—Smoking the Smelt in a Portable Electric Smoker

If you are using a small, portable electric smoker, smoke the fish until they become golden brown, there is noticeable moisture loss, and the flesh flakes when it is teased with a fork. Smoking in a portable electric smoker will probably require five to seven hours.

### DAY 2, OPTION 2—Cold and Hot Smoking

If you are using a cold smoker with auxiliary heat available:
1. Cold smoke at the lowest possible temperature for two or three hours.
2. Gradually raise the temperature to 175º F (80º C). Continue to smoke at this temperature for about two or three more hours until the smelt are golden brown and there has been noticeable dehydration. (If the temperature goes too high for a long time, the flesh may become mushy and overcooked.)

# Italian Shrimp—Marinated

A few years ago, I was browsing through an Italian cookbook. I wanted to find an interesting marinade for meat or fish, and I found one. I tried it, modified it slightly, and the result became a favorite of my family and friends.

According to that cookbook, street vendors in Italian coastal towns use this marinade for shrimp. They cook the marinated shrimp before your eyes and serve them to you piping hot. Not only is the marinade excellent for shrimp, but it works very well on white-meat fish and scallops as well. You will note that the marinade contains olive oil, which complements seafood that is lacking in oil. The unforgettable feature of this product will be the superb aroma while it is being water smoked. You might find that the aroma is good enough not only to make you drool, but also good enough to make your eyes cross if you are anywhere near the smoker.

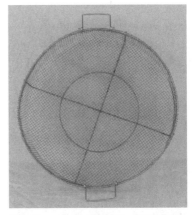

**A wire-mesh smoking basket.**

To smoke the shrimp, you will need a wire-mesh smoking rack or a flat-bottomed smoking basket. Of course, the mesh needs to be fine enough to prevent the shrimp from falling through the holes. The mesh should be made of stainless-steel wire, or steel wire plated with a suitable metal such as nickel.

Shrimp cook very fast, so the taste will not be very smoky. If you want to enhance the smoke flavor, you may add ½ to 1 teaspoon (2.5 to 5 ml) of liquid smoke to the marinade.

### SHRIMP—2¼ POUNDS (1 KILOGRAM)

Raw shrimp must be used. Medium- to large-sized shrimp work best. The expensive colossal size will offer no advantage. Peel the shrimp, leaving the tail fins attached. Devein the shrimp if you wish—I don't. Rinse with cold water and drain. Place the shrimp on a paper towel; blot them to remove excess water. Refrigerate while you prepare the marinade.

**MARINADE FOR 2¼ POUNDS (1 KILOGRAM) OF SHRIMP**

½ cup (120 ml) olive oil
¼ cup (60 ml) lemon juice
2 Tbsp. (30 ml) minced onion
2 Tbsp. (30 ml) tomato catsup
1 Tbsp. (15 ml) oregano powder
1½ tsp. (7.5 ml) salt
1 tsp. (5 ml) minced or grated garlic
½ tsp. (2.5 ml) finely ground white pepper
4 drops hot sauce

1. In a curing container large enough to hold the shrimp, combine all of the marinade ingredients. Mix well.
2. Add the shrimp, and marinate in the refrigerator throughout the day and overnight. Stir from time to time.
3. Smoke in a water smoker at about 200º F (93º C). After about 30 minutes, taste a shrimp for doneness. If the shrimp are overcooked, they will become rubbery.

# San Francisco Rockfish— Water Smoked

This marinade formula is excellent for any of the species of rockfish, or for any of the various species of fish commonly known as red snapper. The oil in the marinade combined with the humid water smoking will counteract the excessive dryness that would result if the white-meat fish were kippered like salmon.

If you desire a smokier flavor, dry the surface of the fish, and cold smoke it for about two hours before water smoking it.

### THE FISH

Clean, scale, and fillet the fish—do not remove the skin. Rinse the fillets, and drain them in a colander. Wrap each fillet in a paper towel, and then in newspaper. Refrigerate the fish for an hour or so to allow the excess water to be absorbed.

### MARINADE FOR 2¼ POUNDS (1 KILOGRAM) OF FILLETS

½ cup (120 ml) olive oil, or salad oil
¼ cup (60 ml) orange juice

¼ cup (60 ml) minced onion
4 cloves garlic, minced
2 tsp. (10 ml) salt
1 tsp. (5 ml) paprika
1 tsp. (5 ml) rubbed dried basil
½ tsp. (2.5 ml) marjoram
½ tsp. (2.5 ml) thyme
½ tsp. (2.5 ml) cayenne

### SMOKING THE FILLETS

1. Marinate the fillets for at least three hours in the refrigerator. Overhaul from time to time. Marinating overnight is much better.
2. Drain the fillets, but reserve the marinade. Do not rinse. Place the fish on smoking racks with the skin side down.
3. Water smoke the fillets at 200° F (93° C) or less. Baste the fish with the marinade after smoking for about 45 minutes. When the fish are being basted, it is a good idea to change the position of each fillet—this will help to prevent sticking.
4. When the flesh becomes opaque and flakes easily when teased with a fork, it is done. The cooking time will probably be between two and three hours—it depends on the thickness of the fish. The smoking process is much easier if the fillets are thick enough to accept the probe of an electronic cooking thermometer. The fillets are done when the internal temperature is 140° F (60° C).

# Kippered Catfish

Catfish farming is one of the great success stories of aquaculture. Prior to the late 1960s, the only way to get catfish was to catch them in the wild. Farmed catfish were not seen in the grocery store. Now they are offered year-round in all the major supermarkets.

The species of catfish called *channel catfish* is farmed. The channel cat is generally considered the best tasting of all the species. Every year, tons of channel catfish are marketed in retail stores and served in restaurants, particularly in the South.

Excellent quality control is the main reason for the success of catfish farming. For example, catfish are bottom feeders by nature, but farmed catfish are fed exclusively on high-protein food that floats atop the water; the diet of the fish is thereby carefully controlled. These floating food pellets are made of a nutritious blend of soybeans, corn, rice, wheat, vitamins, and minerals. Fish from each pond are taste-tested before harvest. The packers process the fish in state-of-the-art plants, using the finest equipment and flash-freezers.

The oil content of catfish is about the same as that of coho (silver) salmon. This high oil content makes them ideal for kippering. Considering this, it is unbelievable that there is no well-established custom of smoking catfish. It is delicious.

Catfish can be cured in the same way as kippered salmon, but there is a special cure suggested below; this cure uses seasonings that go particularly well with catfish.

Catfish are always skinned before cooking or processing, and they will likely be skinned and filleted when you buy them at the supermarket. Because there is no skin to protect the flesh and hold it together, a special smoking technique is required.

### PREPARING THE FISH

Rinse and drain the skinned catfish fillets. Wrap each piece in a paper towel and newspaper. Refrigerate the fish while you prepare the curing mix.

### CURE MIX FOR 2¼ POUNDS (1 KILOGRAM) OF CATFISH FILLETS

2 tsp. (10 ml) salt
1 Tbsp. (15 ml) sugar
½ tsp. (2.5 ml) white pepper
½ tsp. (2.5 ml) onion powder
¼ tsp. (1.25 ml) garlic powder
¼ tsp. (1.25 ml) cayenne
¼ tsp. (1.25 ml) rosemary powder
¼ tsp. (1.25 ml) basil powder

Total: 7 tsp.

### CURE MIX MEASURING CHART
7 tsp. (35 ml) per 2¼ lbs. (1 kg) of catfish
3½ tsp. (17.5 ml) per 1 lb. (500 g) of catfish
1¾ tsp. (8.75 ml) per ½ lb. (250 g) of catfish
1 tsp. (5 ml) per ¼ lb. (100 g) of catfish

### BULK MIX FOR 27 POUNDS (12 KILOGRAMS) OF CATFISH

½ cup (120 ml) salt
¾ cup (180 ml) sugar
2 Tbsp. (30 ml) white pepper
2 Tbsp. (30 ml) onion powder
1 Tbsp. (15 ml) garlic powder
1 Tbsp. (15 ml) cayenne
1 Tbsp. (15 ml) rosemary powder
1 Tbsp. (15 ml) basil powder

## DAY 1

Sprinkle the cure on both sides of the fillets, and rub the flesh to distribute the cure evenly. Stack the fish in a curing container, and refrigerate it for 24 hours. Overhaul the fillets several times during this period.

## DAY 2, EVENING

Rinse the cure off each fillet *quickly* in cool water. Lay the fillets in a food container with paper towels and newspaper between each layer. Cover, and refrigerate overnight.

## DAY 3, MORNING

1. Place the fillets on paper towels, and dry them in front of a fan for about an hour. Prepare the smoker for additional drying at 100° F (40° C).
2. Dry at 100° F (40° C) in the smoke chamber (with no smoke) until the glossy, smooth pellicle is formed. Turn the fillets over every 30 minutes so that both sides will dry. The drying time will require at least an hour.
3. Cold smoke the fish for about three hours.
4. Transfer each fillet to a small sheet of *parchment paper* that has been cut to the approximate size of the fillet and perforated with many holes. Place the fillets on the smoker racks with the parchment paper underneath. (Because the catfish have been skinned, parchment paper is required so that the fillets can be handled without breaking them when they are being hot smoked. Parchment paper can be purchased in any large grocery store; it will usually be displayed near the aluminum foil. Parchment paper is most often

used for baking cookies, and the like. This special culinary paper is coated with a substance that helps to prevent sticking.)

5. Next, *over a one-hour period*, temper the flesh by stepping up the temperature a little at a time until it reaches 175° F (80° C). Continue to smoke at 175° F (80° C) until the catfish is fully cooked; this may require several hours. The fish is fully cooked when the internal temperature is 140° F (60° C), or when the flesh is opaque and flakes easily when teased with a fork. If an electronic meat thermometer with a probe and a cable is used, the hot smoking process will be easier.

# Hangchow Scallops

When Marco Polo was exploring China in 1280, he mentioned seeing scallops being sold in the marketplace in Hangchow, China. In the past century, equipment was developed to harvest deepwater scallops economically and in large quantities. This fact resulted in scallops reaching the popularity that they enjoy today.

**A scallop shell.**

The scallop, like the oyster, is a bivalve mollusk. However, unlike the oyster that attaches itself to a bed, the scallop moves about by "swimming." The shells snapping together accomplish the swimming action; the water that is forced out of the shells propels the scallop. To accomplish this forceful shell closing, an oversized muscle called the "eye" has evolved. This sweet-flavored muscle is the only part of the scallop that is eaten by Americans, but Europeans and Asians eat the entire shucked scallop.

Many varieties of bivalve mollusks are commonly known as scallops. In the supermarkets, the most common are the very small and tender scallops that are called *bay scallops*, and the larger and less tender *sea scallops* or *ocean scallops*. Scallops cannot be sold live because they must be able to move around in an ocean environment to survive.

The color of fresh scallops may range from a pink hue to light beige. Scallops should not be stored in water; if the scallops are pure white, it may be due to that fact that they were plumped in water. They should smell clean and fresh and have a gloss. Refrigerate immediately, and use within one day, if possible. Flash-frozen scallops are a good alternative to fresh scallops.

Because of their low oil content, scallops are best processed by using a marinade containing oil and by smoking in a water smoker.

Either bay scallops or sea scallops may be used for the following product. However, if sea scallops are used, they will be more tasty and easier to cook if they are cut into quarters before marinating.

Rinse, drain, and blot the scallops. Refrigerate while preparing the marinade.

### MARINADE FOR 2¼ POUNDS (1 KILOGRAM) OF SCALLOPS

⅓ cup (80 ml) peanut oil, olive oil, or salad oil
2 Tbsp. (30 ml) soy sauce
1 Tbsp. (15 ml) sesame oil
2 tsp. (10 ml) *hoisin* sauce (see appendix 1)
1½ tsp. (7.5 ml) salt
½ tsp. (2.5 ml) onion powder
¼ tsp. (1.25 ml) ginger powder
⅛ tsp. (0.625 ml) garlic powder

### DAY 1

Combine all of the marinade ingredients in a plastic or glass container. Mix well, add the scallops, and marinate. Stir them from time to time. Store the scallops in the refrigerator overnight.

### DAY 2

Drain the scallops, but do not rinse. Discard the marinade. Smoke in a water smoker at 200° F (93° C). Because the scallops are small, they must be smoked in a wire-mesh smoking basket or on a wire-mesh screen that has been plated with a nontoxic and acid-resistant metal. Test for doneness after about 45 minutes. They are done when the raw, translucent appearance turns opaque. If the scallops are overcooked, they will become tough and rubbery. Of course, the bay scallops will cook faster than the large, whole sea scallops.

# Salmon Caviar

Connoisseurs of caviar are essentially unanimous in saying that sturgeon caviar, especially beluga sturgeon caviar, is the finest. Many of the same connoisseurs say that salmon caviar is the best substitute for sturgeon caviar.

Americans are usually not excited by the thought of eating raw salmon eggs. They may know that salmon eggs are used as bait to catch trout and steelhead, but they may not be aware that salmon eggs are eminently edible, and are considered a delicacy in countries such as Japan and Russia. For these reasons, most salmon roe obtained by sportfishing in North America is thrown in the garbage, fed to seagulls or cats, or used as fish bait. What a shame! Most people who muster the courage to try red caviar find that they like it. When you eat the eggs, they burst open in your mouth and shower your taste buds with the delicious flavor. They are superb on crackers. Try mixing them with scrambled eggs, or try them as a garnish for deviled eggs.

Salmon caviar is not a smoked product, but I believe that many readers of this book would like to know how to prepare it.

Red caviar is very easy to make if the instructions given below are followed. The technique of using warm water to remove the eggs from the sac works like magic! My wife discovered this technique in a fish cookery book written in Japanese. All the instructions written in English that I have seen have said that the best way to remove the eggs is to rub the slit sac on a wire-mesh screen having about 3/8-inch (10 mm) holes. The wire-screen technique is very laborious, is inefficient, and results in damage to many eggs. I do not recommend it. The Japanese warm water technique explained below is much faster and easier.

*Note:* Salmon eggs used to prepare caviar must be *fresh.*

1. Slit the egg sacs in several places so that the eggs will be able to exit the sacs freely.
2. Put one egg sac in a large pan of water that has been heated to 113° F (45° C). (Water heated to this temperature will not cook the eggs, but it weakens and dissolves the thread-like membrane attached to each one.) Shake the sac vigorously; the eggs will tumble out. It is so easy!
3. Use a wire-mesh strainer to dip the eggs out of the warm water. Place the eggs in ice water immediately. Stir frequently. The ice water should have numerous cubes of ice floating in it so that the cold temperature will be maintained. After the eggs are very cold, drain them for a few minutes and refrigerate. Heat a fresh batch of water to 113° F (45° C), and do the next sac of eggs. Proceed to processing Option 1 or Option 2 after all the eggs have been removed from the sacs, iced, drained, and chilled.

### OPTION 1, JAPANESE FISHING-VILLAGE-STYLE CURE

The caviar will keep for months at normal refrigerator temperature if it is processed with this Japanese cure.

### JAPANESE CURE FOR 1 QUART (1 LITER) OF SALMON EGGS

½ cup (120 ml) saké (Japanese rice wine)
½ cup (120 ml) soy sauce
ice water to cover

Mix the saké and soy sauce in a deep plastic or glass container that is large enough to hold the eggs. Put the eggs in the cure and stir well. If necessary, add enough ice water to barely cover the roe. Stir again. Refrigerate.

Whenever you wish to serve the caviar, place the desired amount in a wire strainer and rinse thoroughly in cold water. Drain the eggs for about one minute, and then put them on a paper towel with newspaper underneath for a few more minutes. Place the eggs in a dish and serve.

### OPTION 2, TRADITIONAL BRINE CURE

Eggs processed with this brine cure will keep for several months in a refrigerator kept between 34° and 36° F (2° and 3° C).

### BRINE FOR 1 QUART (1 LITER) OF SALMON EGGS

2 quarts of chilled water + 2 cups of noniodized salt
*or*
2 liters of chilled water + 500 ml of noniodized salt

Place the eggs in the brine, and stir them occasionally for 15 to 20 minutes. When the eggs begin to look cloudy, remove them from the brine. Drain them in the refrigerator for several hours, and then place them in a container with a tight-fitting lid. If oil from broken eggs collects at the bottom of the container, turn the container upside down once a week; this will cause the eggs to be bathed in that oil.

# Salmon Jerky

Fish jerky may be made from almost any kind of fish, but the Indians of Canada, Alaska, and the Pacific Northwest made salmon jerky famous, so it is the most common fish jerky. The white settlers of these regions often called this Indian-made salmon jerky *squaw candy*.

The Native Americans prefer to use chum salmon (keta salmon) as the raw material because it has the lowest oil content. When the oil content is low, jerky will keep longer before becoming rancid. However, this factor is not critical if the jerky is kept tightly wrapped and refrigerated. In fact, if good taste rather than long shelf life is the goal, use salmon with high oil content as the raw material.

Salmon has higher water content than beef, so salmon jerky will shrink more than beef jerky. Another consideration is that salmon jerky is more fragile than beef jerky, so it has to be handled more carefully when it is being dried.

Salmon jerky is usually processed by making numerous deep cuts across the fillet; these cuts are made through the flesh and all the way to the skin. When the fillet begins to dry, a gap will open where the cut was made. The opening of numerous gaps will increase the drying area and allow the flesh to dry faster. Nevertheless, if this method is used, over 24 hours of drying time is required to make salmon jerky.

However, if the skin is removed from the fillet and the salmon flesh is sliced thinly, salmon jerky can be made in one day. The use of parchment paper and oil prevents the skinned salmon from sticking to the wire mesh, and this helps to overcome the fragility problem encountered when jerky is made from skinned salmon.

To prepare the raw material, remove the skin from the fillet, and slice the flesh. It may be sliced across the fillet or cut into hunks and then sliced from head to tail—the direction of the cuts is not critical. But no matter how it is sliced, the slices should be about ¼ inch (7 mm) thick. The fillet is easier to slice if it is partially frozen.

## SEASONING FOR 2¼ POUNDS (1 KILOGRAM) OF SLICED SALMON

2½ tsp. (12.5 ml) salt
1 Tbsp. (15 ml) brown sugar—packed in the spoon
1 tsp. (5 ml) white pepper
½ tsp. (2.5 ml) garlic powder
½ tsp. (2.5 ml) onion powder
1 cup (240 ml) water

1. Prepare and chill the seasoning mixture. Add the sliced salmon, place in the refrigerator, and stir from time to time. Refrigerate overnight.
2. The next morning, drain the cured salmon slices, and rinse each

piece in cold water for about three seconds. Drain the slices again in a colander.

3. Place the slices between sheets of paper towel and newspaper for *15 minutes. Important note:* If this time is exceeded, the salmon slices may stick to the paper towels, and removal of the salmon slices from the paper towel will be very difficult.

4. Remove the slices from the paper, place them in a large bowl, and pour on about ¼ cup of salad oil. Stir until each slice of salmon is well coated with oil. *Important note:* Coating the raw salmon slices with oil is important; without a coating of oil, they will stick to the parchment paper.

5. Lay the slices of oiled salmon on parchment paper that has been placed on a wire-mesh smoking rack or in a smoking basket. (Parchment paper is explained in the instructions for kippered catfish. See page 235.)

6. Dry the slices at 160° F (71° C) for about 30 minutes, and then *carefully* turn each slice over using a spatula. In this initial drying period, the slices of salmon are very easy to tear, but they become less delicate as the drying progresses. Continue to turn the slices over every 30 to 45 minutes until the surfaces of the slices are dry enough to prevent sticking to the wire mesh. This will require four to five hours. Remove and discard the parchment paper when the slices are so dry that they will not stick to the wire mesh.

7. Maintain the same temperature, and smoke the salmon slices for two to four hours.

8. If necessary, raise temperature to 175° F (80° C), and continue drying until done. When the salmon jerky is done, it will be about half the thickness of the raw salmon, and it will have lost about half of its weight. Let the jerky cool to room temperature, then freeze or refrigerate it.

# Japanese Fish Sausage (*Kamaboko*)

Nowadays, it is easy to buy the Japanese-style fish sausage known as *kamaboko* if you look for it in a large Asian food store. Smoking *kamaboko* is very easy, and people who like fish usually enjoy this product. However, most of the people who will read this book will have never heard of *kamaboko*, so an introduction to the product is in order.

First, I must explain that *kamaboko* is not put into casings, as is most American and European sausage. It is mounded on a little wood-

en board that is about 2 inches wide and 6 inches long (5 x 15 cm). The purchased product has a texture resembling firm bologna, and the little board underneath serves as a disposable cutting board. It is fully cooked and ready to eat when purchased. The most common color is white inside with pink food color on the outside surface.

**Smoked Japanese fish sausage (smoked kamaboko). The original product was pure white, but it has become golden after smoking.**

However, the solid white type is best for smoking because it takes on a beautiful golden hue when it is smoked.

### TO SMOKE *KAMABOKO* (DON'T CUT IT OFF THE BOARD)

1. Dry the *kamaboko* in the smoker with no smoke at about 120º F (49º C) until the surface is dry to the touch. This will require about one to one and a half hours.
2. Use a smoke filter (see the explanation about the smoke filter in the section on how to smoke cheese, chapter 13). Smoke at about 115º F (46º C) for two and a half hours. If there are several layers of *kamaboko* on racks, reverse the layering order so that the bottom rack is transferred to the top, and so forth. Smoke for another two and a half hours, or stop smoking when the white *kamaboko* becomes a golden color. Chill, slice, and serve.

## Smoked Imitation Crabmeat

Imitation crabmeat, like *kamaboko* in the previous section, is a kind of fish sausage. It, too, is fully cooked and ready to eat when purchased. Imitation crabmeat is made of ground fish having white flesh that is seasoned with juice extracted from crabs. It is then processed to resemble crabmeat. It may be smoked in the same way as *kamaboko*.

## Smoked Clams

The variety of clams available depends, to some extent, on where you live. Small Manila clams and steamer clams are widely available in supermarkets in this part of the United States, so I usually use these clams. Steamer clams are also known as soft-shell clams, and there are several species. In the procedure below, please understand *clams* to mean these Manila or soft-shell clams. Nevertheless, the procedure may be adapted to any species of clam, or any species of frozen clam meats.

## PREPARING THE CLAMS

1. All clams contain sand. To get rid of most of the sand, wash the outside of the clams thoroughly, and then soak the clams for two or three hours in cold water that contains ⅓ cup (80 ml) of salt per gallon (4 liters) of water. Discard any clams that float or have broken shells. Also, discard any clams that have open shells, or shells that do not close when touched.
2. Steam the clams until the shells open. Remove the meat from the shells, and place it in a colander. If you are using frozen clam meats, rinse the meats well in cold water, and then steam them for about 30 minutes. In either case, rinse the steamed meats thoroughly in cold water; change the rinse water several times, and continue rinsing until there is no sand in the bottom of the rinse pan. Chill the clam meat while preparing the seasoning.

## SEASONING FOR 2¼ POUNDS (1 KILOGRAM) OF CLAM MEAT

1 Tbsp. (15 ml) salt
1 Tbsp. (15 ml) brown sugar—packed in the spoon
1 tsp. (5 ml) white pepper
1 cup (240 ml) water

1. Prepare the seasoning mixture. Add the steamed clam meat, and refrigerate it for the remainder of the day and overnight. Stir the meats from time to time during the curing period.
2. The next morning, drain the cured clam meat in a colander, and rinse briefly.
3. Place the meat in wire-mesh smoking baskets.
4. Dry the meat at 140º F (60º C) for one hour, or until the surface no longer feels damp. Do not use smoke. Agitate the meats occasionally while drying to ensure that all surfaces become dry.
5. Discontinue using auxiliary heat, and cold smoke for one to two hours. The smoking is finished when the clam meat takes on an attractive golden-brown coloration.

At this point, the clam meats are ready to eat, but they will taste better if they are refrigerated overnight to allow the flavor to mellow. Many people like to apply olive oil while the meats are still warm. The following paragraph describes this oiling technique. If the meats are to be oiled, they should be oiled at room temperature immediately after smoking.

To oil the clam meats, place them in a glass or plastic container with a tight-fitting lid. Add enough olive oil to coat the clams when the container is shaken, rolled, or turned upside down. About ¼ cup of olive oil is usually adequate. Continue to agitate the container every few minutes for about one hour, until the meats have absorbed most of the oil. Refrigerate.

# Smoked Oysters

Fresh oysters in the shell, or shucked oysters in a jar, may be used for this product. However, in either case, small oysters produce a better result than medium or large.

If you are starting with fresh oysters in the shell, the best way to proceed is to place them in a steamer and steam until the shells open. Discard any whose shells do not open. The oyster meats will now be firm, and they can be plucked from the shell easily.

If you have purchased oysters that have been shucked, they should be simmered in slowly boiling water. First, drain the oysters, place them in a wire-mesh strainer, and put them in boiling water until the gills curl. This will require four or five minutes for small oysters—more time for larger ones. The oysters will now be firm and plump.

After applying one of the heat treatments described above, remove excess water by placing the oysters on a paper towel with newspaper underneath. Refrigerate them while you prepare the seasoning. The seasoning below is adequate for one 10-ounce (280 g) jar of shucked oysters; increase the volume of the seasoning to match the weight of oyster meats you will process.

### SEASONING FOR ONE 10-OUNCE (280-GRAM) JAR OF OYSTERS

2 Tbsp. (30 ml) hot water
2 tsp. (10 ml) brown sugar—packed in the spoon
¾ tsp. (3.75 ml) salt
¼ tsp. (1.25 ml) finely ground pepper
⅛ tsp. (0.625 ml) thyme
⅛ tsp. (0.625 ml) marjoram

1. Mix the seasoning in a small food container that is large enough to hold the oysters. Stir the seasoning until the salt and sugar are dissolved. Chill the mixture thoroughly in the refrigerator.

2. Add the oysters to the chilled seasoning and stir. Refrigerate, stirring from time to time. Refrigerate overnight.

3. Remove the oysters from the seasoning the next morning. Discard the seasoning. Rinse the oysters well, and place them on a paper towel with a newspaper underneath. Allow the oysters to drain for about 15 minutes, then place them on wire mesh that has been sprayed with no-stick cooking spray.

4. Dry the oysters in a smoke chamber at 140º F (60º C) until they are thoroughly dry on the surface. This will require about one and a half hours. While they are drying, they should be turned over every 30 minutes to prevent sticking and to encourage even drying. The drying will shrink the oysters to some extent, and the color will darken slightly.

5. Cold smoke the oysters for 30 minutes at the lowest temperature possible. While continuing to smoke, raise the temperature to about 150º F (66º C), and maintain that temperature until the gills have dried. This will require about 30 minutes at the elevated temperature. The total smoking time should not exceed one hour; smoking oysters too long can cause a sooty taste.

6. Use olive oil to oil the oysters as described in the directions for smoked clams. Refrigerating the oysters overnight will allow the smoke flavor to mellow, greatly improving the taste. Continue to refrigerate the oysters until they are consumed.

# Smoked Octopus

Octopus is commonly eaten in many countries of the world, but the United States is not one of them. However, because of the recent increase in Asian restaurants here, more Americans have had the opportunity to eat octopus—and many of them have discovered that they like it. Nevertheless, few Americans would entertain the idea of preparing octopus in their home. For the adventuresome souls among us, a tasty and unusual way to prepare octopus is presented below. In my opinion, if this product is made using the recommended baby octopus, it makes a very tasty, attractive, and unusual gift.

There are many species of octopuses (or *octopi*, if you prefer the Latin-based plural), and there are many different sizes. I prefer dwarf octopuses; when they are raw and stretched to full length, they measure about 6 or 7 inches. However, even at this small size, they are adults. Nevertheless, they are more often called *baby* octopuses. Well-stocked fish markets and large supermarkets often offer fresh baby octopuses. If you go to an Asian grocery store, you will likely find frozen baby octopuses that have been eviscerated, washed, and flash-frozen.

Larger octopuses may be used, but the larger the octopus, the tougher the skin. The skin will be tender on an octopus weighing less than about 4 pounds (1.8 kg). However, if the octopus is considerably larger than that—25 pounds (11 kg), for example—it would be best to remove the tough skin after the meat is steamed. Steaming will tenderize the flesh of any size of octopus, so size is of little concern when tenderness is being considered.

## PREPARING THE OCTOPUS(ES)

If the creatures have not been eviscerated, you will need to cut out the beak, the anus, the yellowish pouch and attached membranes, and the ink sac. If it is a large octopus, the eyes should be removed. Scissors usually work well for these operations. Take care that the ink sac is not punctured. Rinse thoroughly.

## SEASONING FOR 2¼ POUNDS (1 KILOGRAM) OF OCTOPUS

    1 Tbsp. (15 ml) salt
    1 Tbsp. (15 ml) brown sugar—packed in the spoon
    1 tsp. (5 ml) white pepper
    ½ tsp. (2.5 ml) garlic powder
    ½ tsp. (2.5 ml) onion powder
    1 cup (240 ml) water

1. Prepare the seasoning mixture, and add the raw octopuses. Place in the refrigerator and stir from time to time. Refrigerate overnight.
2. Drain the cured octopuses the next morning. Rinse them well.
3. Steam the octopuses until the flesh can be easily pierced with a sharp, pointed object such as a fork, skewer, or sausage pricker. Steaming for 30 minutes is adequate for baby octopuses. You will notice that the skin has become pinkish brown. If you are using baby octopuses, the legs will have curled upward, toward the head.
4. Baby octopuses should be left whole, but a large octopus should be cut into pieces. If you are using a large octopus, first determine if the

skin is so tough that it needs to be removed. Remove the skin, if necessary, and then slice across the legs to make pieces about ½ inch (13 mm) thick. The head should be cut into pieces of a similar size.

5. Lay the steamed octopuses on wire mesh or in wire-mesh smoking baskets.

6. Dry the octopuses at 140° F (60° C) for one to two hours, or until the surface of the creatures no longer feels clammy. Do not use smoke.

7. Discontinue using auxiliary heat. Smoke at the lowest possible temperature for about two hours.

The octopuses are now ready to eat, but it would be better to refrigerate them overnight to allow the flavor to mellow. Many people, including myself, like to apply olive oil while they are still warm. If you wish to oil the smoked octopuses, see the oiling instructions previously given for smoked clams.

# CHAPTER 12

# Sausage

When I was learning how to make sausage many years ago, I discovered an interesting fact: The United States produces and consumes more sausage than any other country in the world. This helps to explain why Americans have such a great interest in sausage making.

Another thing that I discovered is that some of the books on sausage making do not cover the *smoking* of sausage, though they may cover other aspects of sausage making quite well. Furthermore, even if a book explains the smoking of sausage, it might not give clear information regarding the danger of contracting botulism by eating smoked sausages that were improperly cured. In the books that do discuss the curing of sausage, they often specify the old-fashioned potassium nitrate (saltpeter) curing agent instead of the modern, safer curing powders such as Prague Powder #1, Modern Cure, and Insta Cure #1. Consequently, for these various reasons, I felt that a chapter on sausage making should be included in this book. Such a chapter is required to explain how to safely cure and smoke sausage.

In order to cover these important subjects, we must begin with the fundamentals of sausage making. First, the basic tools and supplies will be explained. Next, I will describe the basic categories of sausages, and give you instructions on how to make several kinds of sausages in each of these categories.

By following the instructions in this chapter, you will be able to make some very serious, tasty, and wholesome sausages. If this sparks your interest in sausage making, please consult specialized books on the subject. You will find hundreds of recipes, including recipes for categories of sausages such as fermented sausages and dry cured sausages that are not covered in this book.

Before starting, let us explore the meaning of the word *sausage*. Sausage is usually defined as chopped or minced meat that is blended with salt and other seasonings. (The word *sausage* is related to *salsicius*, a Latin word that means "seasoned with salt.") Sausage may also contain color fixers such as sodium nitrite or, in some cases, a blend of sodium nitrite and sodium nitrate. (Potassium nitrate—commonly known as saltpeter—was used in the past, and it is still used in some amateur sausage recipes.)

The meat can be the flesh of any animal, fowl, or fish. Some sausages may contain dairy products or even grains or vegetables such as rice or potatoes. The possible combinations are unlimited. Commercial processors use preservatives as well, and they use chemicals that help to stabilize the color. If homemade sausages are handled properly, such additives are not needed.

# Equipment and Supplies

Some of the equipment and supplies you have assembled for food smoking can be used for sausage making. Most of the special equipment and supplies you will need are listed below. A good place to purchase many of these things is at a shop that specializes in butcher and sausage-making supplies. All of these items may be found on the Internet, as well. See appendix 5 for additional help in locating them.

### MEAT

Meat is not a special supply item, but it is certainly the most important.

No matter what kind of meat you are using for sausage, it should be fresh. Ground meat will spoil faster than solid, so it is best to start with fresh solid meat to ensure a wholesome product.

Traditionally, sausage containing 25 percent fat and 75 percent lean has been considered the perfect ratio, but many people who make their own sausage prefer a healthier, leaner sausage.

**Preparing meat for the grinder—large cubes of meat for coarse sausage and small cubes for finely ground sausage.**

Pork is the most commonly used meat for making sausage, and an economical cut that is variously called Boston butt, shoulder butt, or pork butt is most often used. Besides being economical, it is a very convenient cut to use because it contains about the perfect ratio of lean to fat. Any cut of pork can be used, so use the most economical. In this chapter, I will use the expression *pork butt*, but please understand this to refer to any cut of pork that contains about 25 percent fat—or whatever amount you prefer. If you are going to mix pork fat with some kind of lean meat, hard pork fat is the best kind of fat to use because it has a high melting point. Use a type of hard fat known as *fatback* whenever available.

If beef is used to make sausage, any cut may be used, but I will use the term *beef chuck* in this chapter. Beef chuck is economical, and it usually contains about the right amount of fat.

If wild game meat is used, it is best to trim and discard all the fat from the meat; very few people like the taste of wild game fat. To replace it, use enough pork fat—hard pork fat, if available—to bring the percentage of fat to the desired level.

## MEAT CHOPPERS (MEAT GRINDERS OR MEAT MINCERS)

Meat choppers are also called meat grinders or meat mincers. All these terms refer to the same kind of hand-operated or electrically powered machine. I will use the terms interchangeably in this book.

Initially, ground meats that can be bought at a food market can be used to make sausage. Eventually, however, you will need a meat chopper to process meats to suit your taste; for example, ground pork sold in grocery stores usually contains too much fat to make quality sausage. An old-fashioned (hand-operated) meat chopper made of tin-dipped cast iron will do the job very well. Either the size 8 or the slightly larger size 10 is adequate for home use. These meat choppers clamp on a table, a countertop, or on the breadboard that is built into most kitchen cabinets. If you buy a meat chopper that attaches to the countertop by suction cups, you will probably be disappointed; suction cups are inadequate to hold the machine in place. An electric meat chopper does the job a little faster, but it is not at all necessary unless you intend to make large quantities of sausage frequently.

All meat choppers operate in the same way: Pieces of meat are put into the hopper, and a worm gear forces the meat into the holes in the plate. A four-bladed knife lies flat against the back of the plate, and it rotates to cut off the meat that has been forced into the holes. If the grinder is not chopping the meat properly, or chopping it too slowly, this may be due to the plate collar not being screwed down tightly, or due to something preventing the knife from lying flat against the plate.

**A meat grinder with four plate sizes, a wooden stomper, a rubber clamp pad, and a homemade wrench for removing the plate collar.**

The size of the holes in each plate determines the coarseness of the chopped meat. You should have three plates with the following hole sizes: 3/16 inch (4.8 mm), 1/4 inch (6.4 mm), and 3/8 inch (9.5 mm). Additional plates with holes smaller or larger than these are useful, but not required.

## SAUSAGE-STUFFING TUBES AND SAUSAGE STUFFERS

**Grinding meat.**

A sausage-stuffing tube is also called a *funnel*, a *stuffing cone*, or a *horn*. If large-diameter synthetic casings are used, a common funnel with a large mouth will do. Special stuffing tubes are required if you are going to use natural hog casings, sheep casings, or collagen casings. Some of these are designed to be handheld; they have the shape of a funnel, so the word *funnel* is most appropriate for them. However, handheld sausage funnels for hog, sheep, and small collagen casings are time consuming to use, and they are becoming increasingly harder to obtain.

**A large-mouth, hand-held stuffing funnel and a synthetic casing.**

Some tubes are designed to be attached to a meat grinder. Most electric and some hand-operated meat grinders come with one or more sizes of stuffing tubes. These sausage-stuffing tubes will do the job, but two people are required to stuff the sausages. One person must keep the hopper full of the sausage mixture and try to keep it packed firmly to reduce the number of air bubbles; the other tends the casing as it is being stuffed. Because two people are required, and because air bubbles in the sausages are more likely, using a stuffing tube that attaches to a meat grinder is not recommended.

I recommend the three-pound cast-iron sausage stuffer. It is called a three-pound stuffer because the manufacturers claim that it will hold three pounds of ground meat—it won't, but that does not cause a problem. Such a stuffer is efficient, is reasonably priced, and can be operated easily by one person. In most cases, these stuffers are sold with an assortment of three diameters of stuffing tubes: ⅝ inch (16 mm), ¾ inch (19 mm), and 1 inch (25 mm). They will allow the stuffing of any size of sausage casing.

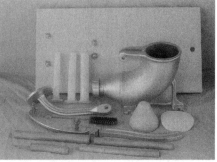

The feet of these cast-iron sausage stuffers have notches so that the stuffer can be mounted on a platform with bolts. Sausage stuffing is much easier if the stuffer is mounted on a board similar to the one in the photo. The board in the photo is 10 by 20 inches (25.5 x 51 cm), and it was cut from ¾-inch (2 cm) plywood.

**A disassembled sausage stuffer with the components and accessories listed below.**

ᐧ Left front: A homemade sausage pricker.

ᐧ Front: Three homemade tube plungers (for pushing meat out of the tube at the end of a sausage-stuffing session).

ᐧ Handle for the sausage stuffer.

ᐧ Small bottle brush (for cleaning the stuffer tubes).

ᐧ A homemade cone made of water putty. This is used for pushing out the meat that will remain in the tapered front section of the stuffer when the stuffing session is nearing completion.

꘎ A homemade disk-shaped gasket made of dense, white foam rubber. This helps to prevent "backflow" around the pressure plate.

꘎ Three diameters of sausage-stuffing tubes.

꘎ Stuffer mounting platform. The feet of the stuffer can be attached to this board with four bolts.

The diameter of the pressure plate is a little less than internal diameter of the elbow-macaroni-shaped ground-meat hopper. The smaller diameter is necessary so the pressure plate can pass through the curved hopper cavity without binding. This smaller diameter of the pressure plate creates a minor problem, however: When the lever is pushed down, most of the sausage will flow out of the tube and into the casing as it should, but some will flow back around the edges of the pressure plate.

This backflow problem can be minimized or eliminated if a homemade gasket is employed. Cut a circular gasket from dense foam rubber; the diameter should be a little larger than the internal diameter of the hopper cavity. Wrap this gasket in plastic food wrap (to keep it clean), and place it between the sausage mixture and the pressure plate. The gasket will prevent almost all of the backflow.

Another minor problem with these stuffers is that the pressure plate will not push out all of the sausage. This is because the pressure plate will stop near the front of the stuffer at the point where the stuffer's nose begins to taper toward the stuffing tube. About ⅓ pound (165 g) of sausage will remain in this conical cavity. However, most of the sausage that remains in the nose can be pushed out with a homemade cone such as the one shown in the photo on page 253.

To make this cone, a plastic funnel that had about the same degree of taper as the conical cavity was used as a mold. The bottom of the funnel was plugged with clay, and then a powder compound called *water putty* was mixed with water and poured into the funnel. (Durham's is a popular brand of water putty.) After the water putty hardened into a cone, it was removed from the funnel, dried for about one week, and then painted with about four coats of clear polyurethane varnish. Such a cone made with water putty will be about as heavy and durable as oak. Water putty can be purchased at any hardware store, and the directions for use are on the package.

Wrap the cone in plastic food wrap before it is used; this helps to keep it clean, and it helps to prevent it from becoming jammed inside the stuffer cavity.

Two sheets of newspaper crumpled into a ball and placed in a plastic bag will perform the same function as a cone, and it will work almost as well.

## SAUSAGE MOLDS AND CASINGS

Generic bulk sausage that is purchased in a grocery store is usually sold in a Styrofoam tray. However, a nationally known brand of bulk breakfast sausage is usually sold in a plastic ground-meat tube. This raw sausage can be sliced into patties by cutting through the tube at approximately 3/8-inch (10 mm) intervals.

Similar ground-meat tubes (also called *bags*) can be purchased wherever sausage casings are sold, but making patties using a mold is a cheaper and better option. A metal ground-meat mold that will make one patty at a time can be purchased, but the homemade patty mold shown in the photograph on page 257 is better—it will make four patties at a time. The mold was cut from ⅜ inch (1 cm) plywood, and the diameter of each hole is about 2½ inches (6.3 cm). Because it is coated with polyurethane varnish, it will withstand washing in hot, soapy water for a lifetime. In fact, it will certainly last long enough for me to pass it along to my grandchildren. It is very easy to use.

For stuffed sausage, the most commonly used casings are hog casings, sheep casings, collagen casings, and synthetic fibrous casings. When Rome ruled most of the Western world, the Romans used chicken neck skin as sausage casings.

Hog casings are made from carefully cleaned small intestines, and they are normally sold in four sizes that range from about 1 inch (25 mm) to 1¾ inches (45 mm). They are, of course, edible. In this introduction to sausage making, the smallest size is suggested; it varies from about 1 to 1¼ inches (25 to 30 mm). For home use, it is best to purchase casings that have been packed in salt; such casings can be preserved for years under refrigeration. The casings are prepared for use by rinsing them very well with water, inside and out. After rinsing, they should be soaked in fresh water in the refrigerator overnight. This removes the remaining traces of salt and leaves the casings more tender, more slippery, and easier to use. Always rinse a little more casing than you think you will need. If some is left over, it can be resalted with noniodized salt and preserved.

Sometimes casings that are packed in salt are not available, and the casings offered are those that are packed in brine. These casings, also, are acceptable, and they will keep for years in the freezer if handled

properly. If you buy such casings, I suggest that you divide
the casings into about six parts,
and place each part in a small
plastic bag. Add some of the
brine and a little noniodized salt
to each bag; freeze all of the
bags except the one you are cur-
rently using.

**Hog casings being rinsed.**

Natural sheep casings are
smaller and more tender than
hog casings. They are also about twice as expensive. Sheep casings
packed in salt or brine are available, and they are used in the same way
as hog casings. Sheep casings will not be used in this introduction to
sausage making.

Collagen is a gelatin that is extracted from the bones, connective tis-
sues, and hides of cattle. This gelatin is used to manufacture *collagen
casings*. The casings are edible, and they are made in various sizes. The
wall thickness varies with the intended use of the casing. For example,
casings used for smoked sausage need to be strong, so they will have
thicker walls. Some of these casings require refrigeration, but others do
not. Because these casings are uniform, and because their use requires
less labor than natural casings, they are widely used by commercial
processors despite their slightly higher price. We will not use these casings for the products in this chapter, but keep them in mind—you may
wish to use them in the future.

Synthetic fibrous casings are very useful for large-diameter snack
sausages or lunchmeat sausages. These casings are not edible, but
they are very strong, and they will not tear while they are being stuffed.
Fibrous casings are available in diameters ranging from 1½ inches (38
mm) to over 4¾ inches (120 mm). If fibrous casings are used, it is best
for the beginner to use casings not more than about 2½ inches (63
mm) in diameter and not more than 12 inches (30 cm) long. This size
is easier to process, and the cooking time will be faster than for larger
diameters. We will use this size for products in this chapter. To make
them supple, synthetic fibrous casings are soaked in water for about
20 or 30 minutes before use.

Finally, you may make casings of muslin. Such casings may be used
in place of synthetic fibrous casings. Tear—do not cut—a strip of muslin

8 inches (13 cm) wide and about 12 inches (30 cm) long. (To the extent possible, the material should be torn rather than cut; tearing reduces the amount of cloth fibers that will get into the sausage.) Fold the strip in half, and sew it along the side and around one end. This will produce a casing with a diameter of about 2¼ inches (5.7 cm). If the material is new, it is best to launder it before it is used. This will remove any fabric conditioners that are present. Turn this closed-end tube inside out, wet it with vinegar, and stuff it with sausage. (The vinegar prevents the cloth from bonding to the sausage.)

**Sausage casing made of muslin.**

## HOW TO USE A HOMEMADE SAUSAGE MOLD

1. Tear off about 18 inches (45 cm) of plastic food wrap, and spread it on the countertop. Place the homemade sausage mold in the middle of the food wrap.
2. Place an egg-sized ball of bulk sausage in the middle of each of the four mold holes.
3. Slap the top of each ball of bulk sausage repeatedly with the palm of your hand until the sausage fills the mold. Add or remove a small amount of sausage, if necessary.

**Making patties by using a homemade sausage mold.**

4. Lift one edge of the mold, and gently push the patties out of each of the mold holes. Let the patties fall back down on the food wrap.
5. Remove the mold completely, and fold over the edges of the plastic food wrap—left, right, top, and bottom—to make an airtight package for the four patties. Place the package on a flat surface in the freezer.

**Sausage patties wrapped in plastic wrap, ready for freezing.**

## HOG-RING PLIERS AND HOG RINGS

Hog rings may be used to close both the bottom and the top of fibrous casings, but they are most often used to close the top. They are easier and faster to use than twine, and they look professional. The spring-loaded pliers are easier to use, but they cost more than common hog-ring pliers. For 2½-inch-diameter (63 mm) casings, use the ⅜-inch (10 mm) hog rings. (If you wish to purchase these special hog rings and hog ring pliers, see appendix 5.)

**Synthetic casing closed with a hog ring (left) and with twine (right).**

If the casings are not closed on the bottom, common twine may be used to close them. However, a great deal of pressure is put on the bottom closure when the sausage is being stuffed. Consequently, if it is tied with twine, the very strong *butterfly tie*, shown in the photo, should be used. The top portion of the photograph demonstrates how to close the end of a synthetic casing in three steps:

1. Cut a length of twine—about 5 inches (13 cm).
2. Tie the end of the casing with a common square knot.
3. Bring the ends of the twine around the bottom of the casing, and tie another square knot in such a way that the ends of the casing flare (butterfly) to the left and right.

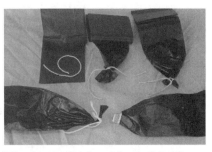

**The butterfly knot is tied in three steps at the top of the photo. At the bottom left, the end of the synthetic casing has been tied by the manufacturer. At the bottom right, a Clark clamp has been used.**

Some casings are tied on the bottom with nylon twine by the manufacturer; such casings are easiest to use. (See the bottom left of the photo above.)

Also, an aluminum cap-like device called a Clark clamp can be used to close the end of a synthetic casing. First, the end of the casing is folded several times until it is small enough to fit inside the Clark clamp.

Next, this folded end of the casing is inserted into the clamp, and the clamp is secured by squeezing it with pliers. (See the photograph.) Clark clamps can be purchased wherever sausage-making supplies are sold.

## POWDERED SKIM MILK

Professional sausage makers and some advanced amateurs often use a product called *soy protein concentrate*. This helps to bind the sausage, retains the moisture, and makes the sausage plump. Powdered skim milk will do the same thing, and it is much easier to obtain. For 2½ pounds (1,150 g) of raw material, add to the seasonings ½ cup (120 ml) of powdered skim milk and ¼ cup (60 ml) of chilled water. Mix the powdered skim milk and water with the seasonings until the powdered milk has dissolved and the mixture is uniform. Add the ground meat and mix well.

## CORN SYRUP

Some sausages taste better with a sweetener. Sugar can be used, but corn syrup will provide the same sweetening effect, and it will function as a binder as well. Professional sausage makers use powdered corn syrup solids, but this product is difficult to obtain, and it tends to cake and become as hard as a brick over time. Liquid corn syrup, however, can be found in any grocery store where pancake syrup is sold. There are two types, light and dark; light is recommended for sausage making. It is perfectly colorless like water.

# Bulk Sausage

Three formulations for bulk sausage are given in this chapter, but you can easily find hundreds of bulk sausage recipes in books, in magazines, and on the Internet. For example, my favorite formula for breakfast sausage is presented in this chapter, but I have seen numerous formulations for American-style breakfast sausage in various books. None of the formulations is the same as mine, and most of them are different from one another. Obviously, it would be very easy to write a book restricted to the subject of bulk sausage alone.

All of the following bulk sausage formulations contain powdered skim milk, which in turn contains lactose (milk sugar). Because any kind of sugar makes sausage brown very fast, patties should be cooked over *medium-low heat* and turned frequently. The sausage patties are done when they become reddish brown on both sides.

# Warren's Country-Style Bulk Breakfast Sausage

Below is my favorite formula for American-style bulk breakfast sausage. The use of poultry seasoning makes this unusual.

### THE MEAT

Prepare 2½ lbs. (1,150 g) ground pork that contains about 20 percent fat. Mince the pork with a ¼-inch (6.4 mm) or ³⁄₁₆-inch (4.8 mm) plate.

### THE SEASONING

2 tsp. (10 ml) salt
1 tsp. (5 ml) poultry seasoning—packed in the spoon
1 tsp. (5 ml) rubbed sage—packed in the spoon
½ tsp. (2.5 ml) oregano, or marjoram
½ tsp. (2.5 ml) black pepper
½ tsp. (2.5 ml) red pepper
¼ cup (60 ml) water
½ cup (120 ml) powdered skim milk

1. Grind the meat and refrigerate it. Mix the seasoning, powdered skim milk, and water in a large mixing bowl.
2. Blend the meat and the seasoning well. Shape the mixture into ³⁄₈-inch-thick (10 mm) patties, and wrap them in plastic food wrap. Refrigerate the sausage that will be eaten within the next two days, and freeze the remainder.

# Polish Kielbasa— Bulk-Style Fresh Sausage

Kielbasa is a traditional Polish sausage. There are many varieties; each region of Poland has a different way of seasoning it. Most varieties are made with coarsely chopped pork.

This sausage may be frozen for two months, but if it is left unfrozen in the refrigerator for a few days, an unusual phenomenon takes place: When the sausage is cooked, the center remains pink, even though it is fully cooked. I believe that the garlic in the seasoning formula is responsible for this color fixing. All agricultural products contain nitrate compounds, and the nitrate in the garlic could slowly degrade to nitrite while it is in the refrigerator. This could cause the color fixing. To avoid this problem, thaw the sausage overnight and use it the next day. Better yet, thaw it in a microwave oven, and then fry it right away.

### THE MEAT

Mince 2½ lbs. (1,150 g) pork butt with a ¼-inch (6.4 mm) plate.

### THE SEASONING

2½ tsp. (12.5 ml) salt
½ tsp. (2.5 ml) granulated sugar
½ tsp. (2.5 ml) marjoram
½ tsp. (2.5 ml) garlic powder
½ tsp. (2.5 ml) black pepper
⅓ cup (80 ml) water
½ cup (120 ml) powdered skim milk

1. Mix the seasonings in a large mixing bowl.
2. Blend the meat and the seasonings well. Shape the mixture into patties that are about ⅜ inch (10 mm) thick, and wrap them in plastic food wrap. Freeze all patties that will not be eaten within one day.

# Scandinavian-Style Sausage—Bulk-Style Fresh Sausage

The use of potatoes or potato flour is traditional in some of the sausages made in Sweden, Norway, and Denmark. Certain elements of several Scandinavian sausages were combined to formulate the sausage below. This simple sausage is certain to be appreciated by meat-and-potatoes people.

### THE MEAT

Mince the following meats with a ³⁄₁₆-inch (4.8 mm) plate:

2 lbs. (910 g) pork butt
½ lb. (225 g) beef chuck

### THE SEASONING

2 Tbsp. (30 ml) granulated onion, or onion powder
1½ tsp. (7.25 ml) salt

¼ tsp. (1.25 ml) white pepper

¼ tsp. (1.25 ml) allspice

¼ tsp. (1.25 ml) granulated sugar

½ tsp. (2.5 ml) chicken bouillon powder,
    or chicken consommé powder

½ cup (120 ml) water

½ cup (120 ml) powdered skim milk

1 cup boiled and mashed potatoes, unseasoned, chilled

1. Blend all the seasoning ingredients except the mashed potatoes, then add the potatoes and blend again.
2. Blend the meat with the seasoning-and-potato mixture. Shape the blend into patties about ⅜ inch (10 mm) thick, and wrap them in plastic food wrap. This sausage is very perishable; freeze all patties that will not be eaten within one day.

# Stuffed Fresh Sausage

In the world of sausage making, some expressions have a special meaning. The expression *fresh sausage* is one case in point. Fresh sausage means sausage that does not contain nitrites or nitrates. The opposite of fresh sausage is *cured sausage*. Sausage makers tend to use the word *cured* whenever nitrates or nitrites have been used. However, food smokers (not sausage makers) will often use the word *cured* even if only dry salt or common brine has been used. It is confusing, but we can't change the way people use the English language. We have to live with it.

The bulk sausages described above are, therefore, kinds of fresh sausages. If it is stuffed in casings, it is still called fresh sausage, but some people prefer to call it *stuffed fresh sausage*. Below, we will learn how to make several kinds of stuffed fresh sausage.

### STUFFING NATURAL CASINGS

Stuffing natural sausage casings is easy to do, but a few pointers should make the learning process go a little faster:

🔥 Attach the proper size stuffing tube to the stuffer. Use a ¾-inch (20 mm) tube for hog casings, and a ½- or ⅝-inch (13 or 16 mm) tube for sheep casings. The main idea is that the casing should fit loosely on the tube, but not too loosely.

❧ Filling the stuffer *half full* with the seasoned sausage mixture will allow the pressure plate handle to provide greater leverage. Pack the mixture in the stuffer a little at a time, using your fist to remove the air pockets.

❧ Wet the entire length of the stuffing tube with water, and slide the wet casing onto the tube. Bunch the casing on the tube so that it looks something like a com-

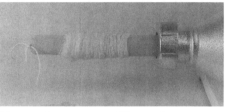

**Hog casing on a stuffing tube.**

pressed accordion (see photo). Initially, the end of the casing should be at the end of the stuffing tube.

❧ Press down the lever handle on the stuffer so that a small amount of sausage begins to emerge from the tube. Slide about 1½ inches (4 cm) of casing off the end of the tube. Force all of the air out of the end of the casing, and tie a knot in it. Alternatively, close the end of the casing by using twine—I find that twine is faster, easier, and wastes less casing.

❧ If you are right-handed, you will probably be most comfortable if you operate the stuffer handle with your right hand. With the thumb and fingers of your left hand, slide the casing off the

**Hog casing being stuffed—the rope is coiled on a plate to make the best use of limited counter space.**

end of the tube as the sausage is being forced out. Keep your left hand cupped under the tube and toward the front; part of the palm should support the sausage casing as it is being filled. As you can see, your left hand will be very busy.

❧ When the sausage mixture is forced into the casing, the goal is for the stuffed casing to be uniform and rather firm—but not so firm that the casing ruptures when you are twisting the sausage to form links. If an air bubble appears in the casing at any time, prick it right away with a sausage pricker or a large needle.

♭ Links can be made any length. Start from either end of the rope. To make 5-inch (13 cm) links, grab the sausage 5 inches from the end of the rope with one hand and 10 inches (26 cm) from the end of the rope with the other. Pinch the rope

**A sausage rope being twisted into links.**

in these two places with your thumbs and index fingers, and then twist the link that lies between your hands four or five revolutions clockwise. Pinch the rope again in two places that are located 5 and 10 inches (13 and 26 cm), respectively, from the last twist. Twirl this new link counterclockwise. Continue making links until the other end of the rope is reached. It is best to use some kind of gauge to make sure that the links are the same size; something like a measuring stick, two pieces of masking tape stuck on the counter, or two marks on a sheet of paper will work well.

## STEAMING SAUSAGE LINKS

When I make stuffed fresh sausage, I usually steam the sausages immediately after stuffing them. I often steam cured sausage, as well. If sausages are fully cooked by steaming—fresh sausages or cured sausages—the sausages are sterilized, the shelf life is longer, and they need only to be heated prior to serving; you might call them brown-and-serve sausages.

Professional sausage makers consider the sausage to be fully cooked when the internal temperature is between 152º F and 155º F (66.6º and 68.3º C). I

**Preparing to steam links.**

steam them until the internal temperature is 160º F (71.1º C). However, if the sausage contains fowl, I steam until the internal temperature is 165° F (74° C). Instructions in this chapter often suggest steaming fresh sausages immediately after stuffing, but they may be refrigerated raw instead.

Of course, steamed sausages may be eaten immediately, but one of my favorite methods of preparing either raw sausages or sausages that have been steamed is to fry them in a covered skillet at medium-low heat until they have a brown stripe on both sides.

# English Bangers— Stuffed Fresh Sausage

This sausage is stuffed in hog casings, and it is very popular in the United Kingdom. A special feature of this sausage is the use of bread crumbs as one of the main ingredients. The bread crumbs retain moisture, and a significant amount of steam is generated in the sausage when it is cooked. The pressure generated by the steam is often enough to make the sausages rupture or explode; they are called bangers for this reason.

You may use the prepared, unseasoned bread crumbs available in all grocery stores in the United States or the coarse Japanese-style bread crumbs available in Asian food stores (known as *panko*); you can also make your own by raking dried bread with the tines of a fork. Depending on the kind and amount of bread crumbs you use, you may have to adjust the moisture content of the stuffing mixture.

You will note that powdered skim milk is not used in this formula. It is not required because the bread crumbs function to retain moisture and plump the sausage links. Pork broth is often used in bangers. However, I find that chicken consommé powder mixed with water is more convenient, and tastes just as good.

### THE CASINGS

Prepare 7 feet (210 cm) of hog casings. Rinse the casings, and soak them in water overnight. Rinse again before using.

### THE MEAT

Mince 2½ lbs. (1,150 g) pork butt with a ¼-inch (6.4 mm) plate. Chill the meat while preparing the seasoning.

## OTHER INGREDIENTS AND SEASONING

1½ tsp. (7.5 ml) chicken consommé powder
1 tsp. (5 ml) salt
½ tsp. (2.5 ml) finely ground black pepper
½ tsp. (2.5 ml) sage—packed in the spoon
¼ tsp. (1.25 ml) ginger powder
¼ tsp. (1.25 ml) mace
¾ cup (180 ml) dry bread crumbs, *not* packed in the cup
½ cup (120 ml) cold water

1. Mix the seasonings and other ingredients well in a large mixing bowl, and then blend in the meat until the whole mixture is uniform.
2. Stuff the sausage. Make 5-inch (13 cm) links.
3. Steam the links until the internal temperature is 160º F (71.1º C).
4. Refrigerate the amount of sausage that will be used within one day. Freeze the remaining links.

# Carl's Italian Sausage— Stuffed Fresh Sausage

A friend of Italian ancestry helped me tailor this sausage so that it closely matched the flavor of the sausage that he ate so often as a child. Carl Preciso was raised on a farm near the Columbia River in northern Oregon, and his grandfather, a farmer who was born in northern Italy, raised hogs on this farm. Whenever a hog was butchered, Grandpa made sausage of the type presented below.

The following is the mild version that is popular in northern Italy; it is also called sweet Italian sausage. To make the hot type, add more cayenne and, if you like, more paprika.

This sausage is traditionally stuffed into hog casings, but it can also be processed as bulk sausage and made into patties or used as a pizza topping.

## THE CASINGS

Prepare 7 feet (210 cm) of hog casings. Rinse the casings, and soak them in water overnight. Rinse the casings again before using.

**THE MEAT**

Mince 2½ lbs. (1,150 g) pork butt with a ¼-inch (6.4 mm) plate. Chill the meat while preparing the seasoning.

**OTHER INGREDIENTS AND SEASONING**

2¼ tsp. (11.25 ml) salt
2 tsp. (10 ml) coarsely ground black pepper
2 tsp. (10 ml) coriander
2 tsp. (10 ml) cracked anise seeds
2 tsp. (10 ml) cracked or powdered fennel seeds
1 tsp. (5 ml) garlic powder
1½ tsp. (7.5 ml) paprika
¼ tsp. (1.25 ml) cayenne
¾ tsp. (3.75 ml) thyme powder
⅛ tsp. (0.6 ml) bay leaf powder
¼ cup (60 ml) lemon juice
3 Tbsp. (45 ml) light corn syrup
½ cup (120 ml) powdered skim milk
¼ cup (60 ml) cold water

1. Mix the seasonings and other ingredients well in a large mixing bowl, and then blend the seasonings with the meat.
2. Stuff the sausage, and make 5-inch (13 cm) links.
3. Steam the links until the internal temperature is 160º F (71º C). Alternatively, do not steam the links, and proceed to the next step.
4. Refrigerate the number of steamed or raw links that will be used within one day. Freeze the remaining links.

Sometimes Italian sausage is browned in a frying pan, then a little red wine is added; the sausage is covered and steamed in the wine until fully cooked. This is one of Carl's favorite methods of preparation.

# Bockwurst—Stuffed Fresh Sausage

To me, this light-colored sausage is elegant and delicate. In Germany, however, bockwurst is considered a two-fisted beer drinker's sausage. It is commonly eaten while drinking a strong, dark beer called bock beer—hence the name *bockwurst*. In some parts of the United States, bockwurst is also known as *white sausage* because of its light color. The

formula is complex, but the numerous and unusual ingredients com-
plement each other very well. It is one of my favorite sausages, and I
make it several times during the spring when wild chives appear in my
backyard.

## THE CASINGS

Prepare 7 feet (210 cm) of hog casings. Rinse the casings, and soak them
in water overnight. Rinse the casings again before using.

## THE MEAT

Grind the following meats with a ⅜-inch (9.5 mm) or smaller plate. Chill
the meat while preparing the seasoning.

   1¾ lbs. (800 g) fatty pork butt
   ¾ lb. (350 g) chicken breast, or veal (veal is traditional)

## OTHER INGREDIENTS AND SEASONING

   ¼ cup (60 ml) fresh milk
   2 tsp. (10 ml) salt
   ¾ tsp. (3.75 ml) finely ground white pepper
   1 Tbsp. (15 ml) onion powder
   ¼ tsp. (1.25 ml) ground celery seeds
   1 tsp. (5 ml) chopped dehydrated parsley
   ¼ tsp. (1.25 ml) mace
   1 Tbsp. (15 ml) lemon juice
   1 Tbsp. (15 ml) light corn syrup
   ¼ cup minced green onions, or chives
   2 eggs
   ½ cup (120 ml) powdered skim milk

1. Except for the meat, mix the seasonings and other ingredients well
   in a large mixing bowl. Add the ground meat, and knead the mixture
   at least three minutes until it is uniform.
2. Stuff the sausage, and make the rope into 5-inch (13 cm) links.
3. Steam the links until the internal temperature is 160° F (71° C)—or
   to 165° F (74° C) if you used chicken breast. Spray the sausage with
   cold water. Refrigerate, uncovered, until chilled. Package the
   sausage in plastic bags, and freeze the portion that will not be consumed within two days. Bockwurst is traditionally eaten with mild
   mustard.

# Onion Sausage— Stuffed Fresh Sausage

It is difficult to believe that a sausage so simple is so tasty. If freshly minced onion is used, use ¼ cup (60 ml), and reduce the ice water in the formula to 3 tablespoons (45 ml).

### THE CASINGS

Prepare 7 feet (210 cm) of hog casings. Rinse the casings, and soak them in water overnight. Rinse them again before stuffing.

### THE MEAT

Use 2½ lbs. (1,150 g) pork butt. Separate the lean meat from the fat. Grind the lean meat with a ¼-inch (6.4 mm) plate, and grind the fat with a ³⁄₁₆-inch (4.8 mm) plate.

### OTHER INGREDIENTS AND SEASONING

1 Tbsp. (15 ml) minced dehydrated onion
⅓ cup (80 ml) ice water
2½ tsp. (12.5 ml) salt
2 tsp. (10 ml) light corn syrup
¾ tsp. (3.75 ml) ground black pepper
¾ tsp. (3.75 ml) marjoram
½ cup (120 ml) powdered skim milk

1. Mix all the ingredients except the meat in a large mixing bowl. Add the meat, and knead until the sausage is uniform.
2. Stuff the sausage, and make 6-inch (15 cm) links.
3. Steam the links until the internal temperature is 160° F (71° C). Spray the sausages with cold water. Refrigerate, uncovered, until chilled. Package the stuffed sausages in plastic bags. Freeze those that will not be eaten within two days.

# Boudin-Style Sausage— Stuffed Fresh Sausage

Several distinctly different Cajun sausages use the word *boudin* in the name. The original recipe for this sausage called for pork liver in addition to pork. However, my brother omitted the pork liver and made some other changes in the method of preparation. The result is a product that is often eaten by both his family and mine. It is certainly the most unusual sausage I have ever made. In addition to meat, it contains vegetables and rice. It is truly a meal in one.

## THE CASINGS

Prepare 10 feet (300 cm) of hog casings. Rinse the casings, and soak them in water overnight. Rinse again the next morning.

## THE MEAT

Prepare 2½ lbs. (1,150 g) minced pork butt. Use a ¼-inch (6.4 mm) plate.

## OTHER INGREDIENTS AND SEASONING

6 cups (1,500 ml) cooked rice, medium grain preferred, cooled
¾ cup (180 ml) finely chopped onions
¾ cup (180 ml) finely chopped parsley
¾ cup (180 ml) chopped green onions
⅓ cup (80 ml) finely chopped green bell pepper
⅓ cup (80 ml) finely chopped celery
4 tsp. (20 ml) salt
1 tsp. (5 ml) minced garlic
1 tsp. (5 ml) black pepper
½ tsp. (2.5 ml) cayenne

1. Except for the meat, mix the seasonings and all other ingredients in a large plastic or stainless-steel container. Next, add the meat and mix again.
2. Stuff the sausage. Make 6-inch (15 cm) links. Put the sausage links in plastic bags, expelling as much air as possible. Freeze or refrigerate immediately; this sausage is very perishable.
3. To cook, steam the thawed sausage until it is plump, firm, and fully cooked. If you wish, you may use a baby-dial or electronic thermometer to measure the internal temperature, which must be 160ºF (71ºC), minimum.

# Cured Sausage and Smoked Sausage

As mentioned previously, cured sausage is fresh sausage with the addition of Prague Powder #1 or some other brand of curing agent that contains sodium nitrite or a blend of sodium nitrite and sodium nitrate. (In this book, curing powder that contains 6.25 percent sodium nitrite is used exclusively.) The addition of a very small amount of a curing agent makes three big differences:

🜍 If the meat in the sausage is a red meat such as beef, pork, or dark bird meat, the sausage will be pink or red after it is cooked.

🜍 In addition to the attractive color, the use of the curing compound will impart a different and appealing taste.

🜍 If the sausage is to be smoked, it can be smoked safely, without fear of botulism.

The addition of Prague Powder #1 to achieve color fixing and to cause a taste change is clearly a matter of personal preference. However, smoking sausage without the proper use of a curing compound is akin to playing Russian roulette. The temperature and time involved in smoking, together with the potentially oxygen-free condition at the center of the sausage, makes botulin formation possible. Just ½ teaspoon (2.5 ml) of Prague Powder #1 per 2½ pounds (1,150 g) of meat will positively prevent botulism. How much sodium nitrite is in that much Prague Powder #1? Well, Prague Powder #1 is composed of 16 parts salt to 1 part sodium nitrite. So, divide ½ teaspoon (or 2.5 ml) by 16. Life insurance is provided by about ¹⁄₃₂ teaspoon (0.156 ml) of sodium nitrite. Life insurance will never get cheaper than that.

Cured and stuffed sausage is often allowed to set in the refrigerator overnight before it is cooked or smoked. This is especially true for coarsely ground sausage. This resting time in the refrigerator allows the curing powder to penetrate the individual bits of meat thoroughly. However, if all of the meat is finely ground, penetration is very fast, and a resting time in the refrigerator of an hour or so is adequate.

# Vienna Sausage— Cured, Stuffed, Not Smoked

You may have heard of Vienna sausage. If you are an American, you may have sampled the tiny Vienna sausages that are sold in a small can. Many of the ingredients in the formula below are the same as those in the canned variety, but the finished product will be different. You should not expect the same taste and texture as the canned variety, but you should expect that it will be something very good to eat. The product we will make will be the real thing: Vienna sausage as it is made in Europe. In Europe—to the best of my knowledge—they do not put the Vienna sausage in cans.

Vienna sausage is a cured sausage, but it is not normally smoked. However, it does have Prague Powder #1 in the formula, so it can be smoked, if you wish.

## THE CASINGS

Prepare 7 feet (210 cm) of hog casings. Rinse the casings, and soak them in water overnight. Rinse them again before stuffing.

## THE MEAT

> 1½ lbs. (680 g) fatty pork
> ½ lb. (225 g) lean beef
> ½ lb. (225 g) lean veal (traditional), or chicken (either white or dark meat)

Mince the meats with a ³⁄₁₆-inch (4.8 mm) or smaller plate. It would be best to mince the meats two times; mincing twice provides a finely textured sausage. Chill the meat between each grinding. Blend the pork, beef, and veal (or chicken) and refrigerate.

## OTHER INGREDIENTS AND SEASONING

> 4 tsp. (20 ml) finely minced onions
> 1 Tbsp. (15 ml) flour
> 2 tsp. (10 ml) salt
> 1 tsp. (5 ml) coriander
> ¾ tsp. (3.75 ml) paprika
> ¾ tsp. (3.75 ml) sugar
> ½ tsp. (2.5 ml) Prague Powder #1
> ¼ tsp. (1.25 ml) cayenne
> ⅛ tsp. (0.6 ml) mace powder
> ¼ cup (60 ml) cold water
> ½ cup (120 ml) powdered skim milk

1. Mix the seasonings and other ingredients well in a large mixing bowl, then add the meat and blend well.
2. Stuff the sausage.

3. To ensure migration of the curing agent and seasonings, let the sausage rest at least one hour in the refrigerator.

4. Steam the links until the internal temperature reaches 160° F (71° C). However, if chicken was used in place of veal, steam to an internal temperature of 165° F (74° C). Spray with cold water. Refrigerate, uncovered, until chilled. Package the sausages in plastic bags, and freeze the portion that will not be consumed within two days.

# Old-Fashioned Frankfurters— Cured, Stuffed, and Smoked

The commercially produced frankfurter (aka wiener, frank, hot dog, or frankforter) that we know today is prepared with emulsified meat. This permits the processors to use meats that we would normally not use: beef tripe, pork snouts, chicken skin, and so forth. Of course, these meats are considered fit for human consumption, but many people do not want to eat scrap parts.

It is easy for us to use higher-quality meats, but troublesome for us to emulsify the meat even if we use the best-quality food processor. To be sure, the original frankfurter made in Frankfort, Germany, was not made with emulsified meat; meat emulsifiers did not exist at that time. It is with this fact in mind that the words *old-fashioned* are used to name this product, which is much closer to the original frankfurters than to the kind sold in grocery stores today.

### THE CASINGS

Prepare 7 feet (210 cm) of hog casing; rinse thoroughly. Soak in water, in the refrigerator, overnight. Rinse again before using.

### THE MEAT

Grind 1½ lbs. (680 g) pork butt and 1 lb. (450 g) beef chuck with a 3/16-inch (4.8 mm) plate—or use a plate with smaller holes, if available. If the meat is ground twice, it will become a little finer the second time. Chill the meat thoroughly.

### THE SEASONING

2 tsp. (10 ml) salt
½ tsp. (2.5 ml) Prague Powder #1

1½ tsp. (7.5 ml) ground coriander
1 tsp. (5 ml) onion powder
1 tsp. (5 ml) finely ground black pepper
½ tsp. (2.5 ml) ground mustard seeds
¼ tsp. (1.25 ml) garlic powder
¼ tsp. (1.25 ml) marjoram
¼ tsp. (1.25 ml) mace
1 large egg, well beaten
⅓ cup (80 ml) water
½ cup (120 ml) powdered skim milk

1. Mix the seasonings, water, and skim milk in a large stainless-steel mixing bowl until they are thoroughly blended and the powdered milk has dissolved.
2. Add the meat and mix well.
3. Stuff the sausage in hog casings, and twist the sausage rope into links.
4. Refrigerate at least one hour—overnight is better.
5. Continue processing by using one of the three options described below. (Frankfurters are traditionally smoked.)

## OPTION 1—STEAMING THE FRANKFURTERS—NO SMOKE

Steam the links until the internal temperature reaches 160° F (71° C). Eat immediately, or refrigerate uncovered. After the sausage is chilled, package it in plastic bags. Freeze the links that will not be consumed within two days.

## OPTION 2—HOT SMOKED

If you wish to hot smoke the frankfurters, hang the raw links in a 130° F (55° C) smoker until the outside is dry to the touch (this will require at least 30 minutes). Make sure that the damper is fully open. Raise the temperature gradually to 165° F (75° C). Close the damper most of the way in order to reduce the airflow and, thereby, reduce dehydration. Hot smoke at this temperature until the internal temperature is 160° F (71° C). Remove the links from the smoker, and spray them with cold water until the internal temperature is below 110° F (43° C). Hang at room temperature for about 30 minutes. Refrigerate overnight before eating; this allows the smoke flavor to mellow.

**Ready to smoke—links spiraled on a plastic water pipe that covers the steel support rod.**

### OPTION 3—SMOKING AND STEAM COOKING

Steam cooking will result in less shrinkage than cooking in the smoker. Follow the directions for hot smoking (above), but remove the links from the smoker when the internal temperature is about 135º F (57º C). Steam the sausage until the internal temperature is 160º F (71º C). Spray with cold water, hang at room temperature for about 30 minutes, and refrigerate.

# Polish Kielbasa— Cured, Stuffed, and Smoked

The Polish kielbasa presented below differs a little from the bulk sausage kielbasa described earlier in this chapter. The seasoning is the same, but ½ teaspoon (2.5 ml) of Prague Powder #1 will be added. This curing powder will cause the kielbasa to become pink when it is cooked, and it will impart a little different flavor. Most importantly, because Prague Powder #1 is used, the sausage can be smoked and eaten without risk of botulism.

### THE CASINGS

Prepare 7 feet (210 cm) of hog casing; rinse, and then soak in water, in the refrigerator, overnight. Rinse again before stuffing the casing.

### THE MEAT

Grind 2½ lbs. (1,150 g) pork butt with a ¼-inch (6.4 mm) plate.

### THE SEASONING

  2½ tsp. (12.5 ml) salt
  ½ tsp. (2.5 ml) Prague Powder #1
  ½ tsp. (2.5 ml) granulated sugar
  ½ tsp. (2.5 ml) marjoram
  ½ tsp. (2.5 ml) garlic powder
  ½ tsp. (2.5 ml) black pepper
  ⅓ cup (80 ml) water
  ½ cup (120 ml) powdered skim milk

1. Mix the seasonings, water, and skim milk in a large stainless-steel mixing bowl until they are thoroughly blended and the powdered milk has dissolved.
2. Add the meat and mix well.
3. Stuff the sausage in hog casings, and twist the sausage rope into links. Alternatively, tie the rope into four rings. Each ring will have a circumference a little greater than 1½ feet (45 cm).

### COOKING AND SMOKING

Continue processing the sausage by following Option 1, 2, or 3 for making old-fashioned frankfurters.

**Sausage rings—used for kielbasa and ring bologna.**

# German Bologna—
# Cured, Stuffed, and Smoked

The commercially produced bologna luncheon meat that is sold here in the United States is, in my opinion, almost inedible. However, this home-made bologna is delicious. The taste, texture, and appearance are completely different from what is offered in supermarkets. Furthermore, we can be sure that this product does not contain any mystery meat such as pig snouts or cow navels.

## THE CASINGS

Soak fibrous casings in water for 30 minutes prior to using. If you are using 2½-inch-diameter (6.4 cm) casings that are about 12 inches (30 cm) long, two of them will be required.

## THE MEAT

Grind 1½ lbs. (680 g) beef chuck and 1 lb. (450 g) pork butt with a ³⁄₁₆-inch (4.8 mm) plate—use a plate with smaller holes, if available. Pass the meat through the grinder twice if you want it to be finer. Chill the meat thoroughly.

## THE SEASONING

> 2 tsp. (10 ml) salt
> ½ tsp. (2.5 ml) Prague Powder #1
> 1 tsp. (5 ml) finely ground black pepper
> ½ tsp. (2.5 ml) ground mustard seeds
> ½ tsp. (2.5 ml) ground celery seeds
> ½ tsp. (2.5 ml) garlic powder
> ¼ tsp. (1.25 ml) coriander
> ¼ tsp. (1.25 ml) nutmeg
> 1 Tbsp. (15 ml) light corn syrup
> ¼ cup (60 ml) water
> ½ cup (120 ml) powdered skim milk

1. Mix the seasonings, water, and powdered milk in a large bowl until the ingredients are uniform.
2. Add the meat to the seasoning mixture. Blend it until it is uniform.
3. Stuff the sausage into fibrous casings. Insert the cable probe of an electronic thermometer in the open end of one of the sausages, and close the casing around the probe with butcher's twine.

**Preparing to steam sausage that was stuffed in synthetic casing. An electronic thermometer probe has been inserted into one of the sausages.**

**4.** Refrigerate the stuffed sausages for a minimum of one hour; overnight is better.

### SMOKING

Remove the sausage from the refrigerator, and place it in a smoker that has been heated to 150º F (65º C). Maintain this temperature with no smoke until the casing is dry to the touch. Raise the temperature to 165º F (75º C), and smoke the sausage for three to six hours.

### COOKING—OPTION 1

After smoking, wrap each sausage in plastic food wrap, and then place each sausage in a plastic bag. Cook in 165º F (75º C) water until the internal temperature is 160º F (71º C). (See Hot Water Cooking in chapter 8, page 140.)

### COOKING—OPTION 2

After smoking, wrap each sausage in plastic food wrap (optional), and then steam them until the internal temperature is 160º F (71º C).

### COOLING

As soon as the hot water cooking or steam cooking is finished, chill the sausage in cold water until the internal temperature drops below 100º F (38º C). Refrigerate overnight before using.

# Minced-Ham Lunchmeat— Cured, Smoked

Many kinds of lunchmeats are actually sausages. *Minced ham* or *pressed ham* is one such product, and it is widely sold in grocery stores. The commercial product looks very good, but the flavor offers little more than salty pork. The following product will look similar to its commercial counterparts, but it contains the flavor they lack.

### THE CASINGS

Fibrous casings about 2½ inch (6.4 cm) in diameter are used for this sausage. Two casings that are about 12 inches (30 cm) long will be required. Soak the casings in water for 30 minutes before stuffing.

## THE MEAT

Use 2½ lbs. (1,150 g) pork butt. Separate the lean meat from the fat. Mince the lean meat with a ¼-inch (6.4 mm) plate, and the fat with a ³⁄₁₆-inch (4.8 mm) plate. Combine the lean meat and the fat. Refrigerate the meat while you prepare the curing mixture.

## OTHER INGREDIENTS AND SEASONING

2 tsp. (10 ml) salt
½ tsp. (2.5 ml) Prague Powder #1
½ tsp. (2.5 ml) white pepper
½ tsp. (2.5 ml) onion powder
½ tsp. (2.5 ml) garlic powder
4 tsp. (20 ml) maple syrup, or 1 Tbsp. (15 ml) honey
¼ cup (60 ml) water
½ cup (120 ml) powdered skim milk

1. Mix the seasonings, water, and powdered milk in a large bowl until the ingredients are uniform.
2. Add the meat to the seasoning mixture and blend well.
3. Stuff the mixture into fibrous casings. Insert the cable probe of an electronic thermometer in the top of one of the sausages, and close the casing around the probe with butcher's twine.
4. Refrigerate the stuffed sausages overnight.
5. Smoke and cook the minced ham by follow the instructions given previously for German bologna.

# Salami—Cured, Stuffed, and Smoked

There are many kinds of salami. Most kinds are dry cured for many weeks, and they are neither cooked nor smoked. (In sausage maker's jargon, *dry curing* has a special meaning: to dry raw sausage under controlled temperature conditions until the sausage weight has been reduced by a certain percent.)

This product contains ingredients that are common in salamis, but the processing is more like that of bologna; it is not dry cured, and it is fully cooked.

## THE CASINGS

Soak fibrous casings in water for 30 minutes prior to using. Two casings will be required if they are 2½ inches (6.4 cm) in diameter and 12 inches (30 cm) long.

## THE MEAT

Grind 1½ lbs. (680 g) beef chuck and 1 lb. (450 g) pork butt with a ³⁄₁₆-inch (4.8 mm) plate.

## THE SEASONING

> 2 tsp. (10 ml) salt
> ½ tsp. (2.5 ml) Prague Powder #1
> 2 tsp. (10 ml) cracked black peppercorns
> 1 tsp. (5 ml) paprika
> ½ tsp. (2.5 ml) ground black pepper
> ½ tsp. (2.5 ml) onion powder
> ½ tsp. (2.5 ml) garlic powder
> ¼ tsp. (1.25 ml) nutmeg
> ¼ tsp. (1.25 ml) allspice
> ⅛ tsp. (0.625 ml) cayenne
> 2 Tbsp. (30 ml) sherry (optional, but recommended)
> 1 Tbsp. (15 ml) light corn syrup
> ¼ cup (60 ml) water
> ½ cup (120 ml) powdered skim milk

1. Mix the seasonings, water, and the powdered milk in a large bowl until the ingredients are perfectly blended.
2. Add the meat to the seasoning mixture and mix thoroughly.
3. Stuff the sausage mixture into the fibrous casings. Insert the cable probe of an electronic thermometer in the open end of one of the sausages. Close the casing around the probe with butcher's twine.
4. Refrigerate the salami overnight.

## SMOKING AND COOKING

Follow the smoking and cooking suggestions given previously for German bologna.

# Sausage Loaf (Lunchmeat Loaf)

Sausage need not be made into patties or stuffed into casings—a common bread-baking pan can be used to mold and process the sausage. The finished product will be a loaf that can be sliced into delicious and economical luncheon meat.

**A sausage loaf in a bread pan.**

# Old-Fashioned Loaf— Cured, Not Smoked

When I was young (and that was awhile ago), this product could be found in all of the large grocery stores, but I have not seen it in recent years. It was not as popular as pressed ham, for example, but it was a good lunchmeat when made with quality ingredients.

### THE MEAT

Use a ³⁄₁₆-inch (4.8 mm) plate to grind 1¾ lbs. (800 g) pork butt and ¾ lb. (350 g) beef chuck. Refrigerate.

### THE SEASONING

> ¼ cup (60 ml) ice water
> ½ cup (120 ml) powdered skim milk
> 2 Tbsp. (30 ml) light corn syrup
> 1 Tbsp. (15 ml) onion powder
> 2 tsp. (10 ml) salt
> ¾ tsp. (3.75 ml) white pepper
> ½ tsp. (2.5 ml) Prague Powder #1
> ½ tsp. (2.5 ml) ground celery seeds
> ½ tsp. (2.5 ml) ground coriander

1. Mix the seasonings, water, and the powdered milk in a large bowl until the ingredients are well blended.

2. Add the minced pork and beef to the seasoning mixture. Knead the mixture about three minutes or until it is uniform.

3. Line a loaf pan with plastic food wrap, and pack the mixture into the pan. Cover with plastic food wrap.

4. Refrigerate the sausage overnight to harden it and make it easier to handle.

5. Remove the sausage from the loaf pan by lifting the plastic wrap that was used to line the pan. Wrap the loaf with plastic food wrap, and insert the probe of an electronic thermometer into the center. (Stick the probe through the plastic wrap.) Steam the loaf until the internal temperature is 160º F (71º C).

6. Remove the plastic food wrap and refrigerate immediately, uncovered. The next morning, the loaf may be sliced and wrapped.

# Liver and Onion Loaf— Cured, Optionally Smoked

Liver is an acquired taste, but it is well liked by those who have acquired the taste. Unfortunately, liver is very high in cholesterol, so many of us have been forced to cut down. This liver and onion loaf is a reasonable compromise: The 20 percent liver content provides a liver flavor, and the cholesterol level is acceptable for most people.

The directions below are for molding this product into a loaf, and then steaming it. However, if you wish, you could stuff it into fibrous casings, smoke it, and cook it like German bologna. Alternatively, it could be stuffed into hog casings and processed like frankfurters.

**THE MEAT**

Mince the following meats with a ³⁄₁₆-inch (4.8 mm) plate:

½ lb. (225 g) beef chuck
1½ lbs. (680 g) pork butt
½ lb. (225 g) liver (any kind of liver may be used)

**OTHER INGREDIENTS AND SEASONING**

¼ cup (60 ml) ice water
½ cup (120 ml) powdered skim milk
1 small onion, about 2 inches (5 cm) in diameter, minced

2 Tbsp. (30 ml) light corn syrup
2 tsp. (10 ml) salt
1½ tsp. (7.25 ml) black pepper
½ tsp. (2.5 ml) Prague Powder #1
½ tsp. (2.5 ml) marjoram
¼ tsp. (1.25 ml) ground mustard
¼ tsp. (1.25 ml) ground nutmeg
¼ tsp. (1.25 ml) ground ginger

Process this product in the same way as old-fashioned loaf.

# Pastrami Sausage—Cured, Smoked

After successfully making several kinds of tasty luncheon meats, I realized that I had never made a luncheon meat with 100 percent beef. I have never heard of a product called *pastrami sausage*, but I thought that a beef-based product seasoned like pastrami would be very good; I was correct. The seasoning for this product is based on the seasoning for pastrami in chapter 9, page 173.

### THE CASINGS

Either a bread-loaf pan or fibrous casings can be used for this sausage. If fibrous casings are used, soak them in water for 30 minutes before stuffing. See the processing options below.

### THE MEAT

Use 2½ lbs. (1,150 g) fatty ground chuck. You could also use 2 lbs. (900 g) lean beef and ½ lb. (225 g) pork fat if you have only lean beef on hand. Mince the meat with a ³⁄₁₆-inch (4.8 mm) plate. Refrigerate.

Other options for the raw material would be venison, bear, elk, or moose. Wild game meat that has been trimmed of all fat and mixed with an equal amount of fatty pork would make an excellent product. Alternatively, rather than using 50 percent fatty pork, 75 percent well-trimmed game and 25 percent pure pork fat could be used.

### OTHER INGREDIENTS AND SEASONING

2 tsp. (10 ml) salt
2 tsp. (10 ml) light corn syrup

2 tsp. (10 ml) black peppercorns, cracked
½ tsp. (2.5 ml) Prague Powder #1
½ tsp. (2.5 ml) onion powder
½ tsp. (2.5 ml) garlic powder
¼ tsp. (1.25 ml) cayenne
¼ tsp. (1.25 ml) paprika
¼ tsp. (1.25 ml) oregano
⅛ tsp. (0.625 ml) allspice
⅛ tsp. (0.625 ml) ginger
¼ cup (60 ml) water
½ cup (120 ml) powdered skim milk

1. Mix the seasoning, water, and the powdered skim milk in a large bowl until the ingredients are uniform.
2. Add the meat to the seasoning mixture. Knead it until it is well blended.
3. If fibrous casings will be used, stuff the mixture into the casings. Insert the cable probe of an electronic thermometer in the top of one of the sausages, and close the casing around the probe with butcher's twine.
4. If the sausage will be made into a loaf, line a loaf pan with plastic food wrap, and pack the mixture into the pan. Cover with plastic food wrap. (See the sausage loaf earlier in this chapter.)
5. Refrigerate the sausage for a few hours, or overnight, to allow the curing agent to migrate to the center of each particle of meat.

Because pastrami is a smoked product, it is logical that this sausage should also be smoked. If you intend to smoke the sausage, note that different procedures are used for smoking sausage in fibrous casings and for smoking sausage that was formed in a loaf pan. If you do not intend to smoke the sausage, proceed to the instructions for cooking.

### SMOKING THE SAUSAGE IN FIBROUS CASING (OPTIONAL)

Remove the stuffed casings from the refrigerator, and place them in a smoker that has been heated to 150° F (65° C). Maintain this temperature with no smoke until the casings are dry to the touch. Raise the temperature to 165° F (75° C), and smoke for three to six hours. Cook the sausage according to the instructions below.

### SMOKING THE PASTRAMI LOAF (OPTIONAL)

Remove the loaf from the loaf pan by lifting the plastic food wrap liner. Put the loaf on a piece of parchment paper that has been perforated with many small holes. Dry the loaf in the smoker at less than 120° F (49° C). Blot the sausage with a paper towel from time to time while it is drying. Raise the temperature to about 150° F (65° C), and smoke for three to six hours. Cook the sausage according to the instructions below.

### COOKING SAUSAGE STUFFED IN FIBROUS CASING

Wrap each sausage in plastic food wrap (optional). Twist the ends of the food wrap, securing them with a wire bread-bag tie. Steam the sausages until the internal temperature is 160° F (71° C).

### COOKING A PASTRAMI LOAF

These instructions for cooking apply to either a smoked or an unsmoked loaf.

Wrap the loaf with plastic food wrap. Insert the probe of an electronic thermometer into the center; you may pierce the plastic wrap with the probe. Steam the loaf until the internal temperature is 160° F (71° C).

### COOLING

If the sausage was stuffed in casing, chill it in cold water as soon as the cooking is finished. Continue chilling until the internal temperature drops below 100° F (38° C). Refrigerate overnight before using.

If the sausage was formed into a loaf, refrigerate the loaf overnight, uncovered, as soon as the cooking is finished.

# CHAPTER 13

# Miscellaneous Smoked Foods

## Smoked Cheese

Contrary to the opinion of several others who have written on the subject of smoked foods, I think that the smoking of *natural cheese* results in a product that tastes awful at best and inedible at worst.

I have tried to smoke many of the recommended varieties of natural cheese. They were smoked with light smoke for a short time as suggested, and the result was always bad. Invariably, the cheese seemed to absorb only the bad odors in the smoke. Therefore, I suggest that if you have some good-tasting natural cheese, count your blessings, and eat it as it is. Don't smoke it! You will not likely be able to improve on the flavor resulting from 4,000 years of experience accumulated by cheese-makers.

What about the smoked cheeses sold in the grocery stores or those available by mail order? Some taste very good. If it is natural cheese being sold as smoked cheese, look at the small print where the ingredients are listed. "Natural smoke flavor" will most likely appear there. This means that the cheese was seasoned with something like liquid smoke. It was not smoked.

If the cheese was truly smoked, somewhere on the package it probably says something like "Smoked with real hickory!" In that case, if you look closely, you will most likely find that the cheese is *processed*, not natural. I have tasted many brands of smoked processed cheese, and most are excellent. They usually have a mellow natural smoke flavor, and the cheese, although it is processed, does not taste substandard in any way.

I have seen, on rare occasions, smoked cheese that appeared to be natural cheese. However, if they are using natural cheese, they most likely have a special processing technique. For example, I have heard of a company in Europe that produces excellent smoked, natural cheese by smoking the milk before it is made into cheese. Unfortunately, such technology is not available to us.

Nevertheless, the good news is that we can easily make smoked *processed cheese*, and it tastes great! But why is it that smoked processed cheese tastes so good and smoked natural cheese tastes so bad? Well, smoked natural cheese contains butterfat—a lot of butterfat, and butterfat absorbs foul odors readily. No doubt you have tasted butter that has absorbed odors from raw onions, and the like, while in the refrigerator. Natural cheese does the same thing, and it absorbs foul odors in the smoke chamber much faster than in the refrigerator.

Processed cheese is made from natural cheese that has been finely ground and blended with emulsifiers, conditioners, flavorings, and sometimes coloring and preservatives. The cheese is then melted and formed into blocks or some other shape. These additives attach themselves enthusiastically to the butterfat molecules in the cheese; consequently, the foul odor molecules in the smoke no longer have a place to attach. If there is no place for the foul odor molecules to attach, then they can't be absorbed by the cheese. This is why processed cheese will not acquire an unpleasant taste when it is smoked. (A Japanese government agricultural researcher, Ms. Munekado, kindly explained this odor absorption and odor-blocking phenomenon to me.)

In Japan, I smoked about 88 pounds (40 kg) of processed cheese every winter. It was attractively packaged, and each package weighed a little less than ½ pound (200 g). About half of the smoked cheese was given to friends and acquaintances as year-end gifts. The rest I sold to local pubs and to acquaintances who wanted to give it away to their friends. The smoked processed cheese was so well received that I could have easily sold twice as much. I mention all

**The author preparing to smoke cheese.**

of this only to encourage you to try it once, even if you are not fond of processed cheese.

To smoke processed cheese you will need the following:

**Gift-wrapped smoked cheese.**

🕯 Processed cheese. I suggest that you use *white American processed cheese*. This cheese has a light and creamy color, and will take on a very nice golden hue when smoked. The yellow American cheese may be easier to find, but the color of the finished product will not be as attractive. Large blocks, packaged in plastic, are usually available in the delicatessen of large grocery stores. If they do not have it in stock, they may be willing to order it for you. Land O'Lakes is a good brand to use; the finished product will taste exactly like the product that I made in Japan with Japanese processed cheese—I tested it.

🕯 A smoker capable of cold smoking at less than 80° F (27° C). To accomplish this, your smoker will have to have an external smoke generator, and the ambient temperature will probably have to be under 70° F (21° C).

🕯 Loosely woven cotton cloth, or the like. This prevents the cheese from being stained by the smoker rack. The material also absorbs moisture from the cheese, which is desirable. Because it is loosely woven, smoke will pass through the cloth. The best material to use is called *dress solid* and can be obtained from a fabric store. Dress solid is ideal because it is 100 percent cotton, loosely woven, and washable. (The cloth needs to be laundered after each use.) It should be cut a little larger than the smoking racks to allow for both shrinkage and hemming of the cut edges. Alternatively, several layers of cheesecloth will work. Another option would be disposable cleaning cloths; these have hundreds of tiny holes, similar to loosely woven cotton. Before using any new cloth material, rinse it well in hot water to remove any starches or conditioners.

🕯 Smoking racks on which to put the cotton material and cheese.

🕯 A smoke filter to trap the tiny specks of black soot that are produced by the smoke generator. Such a filter is not truly essential, but the light-colored cheese will be much more attractive if there are no soot specks on it. A smoke filter is nothing more than a *very fine* metal screen (or even women's nylon hose material) placed over the smoke inlet. The screen, or nylon hose material, will filter the smoke and trap the soot before it enters the chamber.

The cheese should be cut into "sticks" about 1 inch by 1 inch by 5 inches (2.5 x 2.5 x 12 cm). The measurements are not critical, but there will be better smoke aroma penetration if the thickness does not exceed about an inch. If you are going to cut the large block of cheese yourself, you should first leave it at room temperature for about eight hours. Warmed blocks of cheese can be cut easily. Failure to warm the cheese to room temperature could result in unsightly broken pieces.

Place the cotton-net material on the racks, and then place the cheese on that material. There should be spacing of about 1 inch (2.5 cm) between the sticks of cheese. Cheese placed too closely together will not color properly. Let the uncovered sticks of cheese dry overnight in a *cold* room with no fan. This slight drying will aid coloration. (The golden color of the finished product results from both the smoke and the slight drying.) Excessive drying will cause the cheese to crack.

Cold smoke the cheese for three hours at a temperature of less than 80° F (27° C), remove the racks from the smoker, and inspect each stick. If there are moisture droplets on the tops and sides of the sticks, blot them with a paper towel, and then turn over each stick of cheese.

Return the racks to the smoker. If you are using several layers of racks, be sure to layer the racks in the reverse order: The top rack should now be placed on the bottom, et cetera. (Cheese on the bottom rack will dry faster than that on top because the rising hot air becomes more humid as it collects moisture from the cheese in the lower levels.)

Cold smoke the cheese for three more hours. At the end of the smoking period, the cheese should have taken on a beautiful golden color. Remove it from the smoker. Inspect each stick of cheese, and use the point of a paring knife to brush off any soot specks that may be present. Refrigerate in plastic bags or plastic containers.

If this cheese is refrigerated in sealed plastic bags, it will keep in perfect condition for many months; as a test, I kept a stick of this smoked cheese in the refrigerator for one year, and it still tasted great. It will not mold because the imparted smoke flavoring acts as a fungicide. (Some brands of American cheese have excessive salt, and this causes white salt deposits on the surface—this is not mold. To prevent this minor problem, buy cheese with reduced salt, if it is available.) Slice thinly, and *eat at room temperature*, preferably with your favorite wine.

# Smoked Eggs

There are several methods to smoke eggs. In all cases, the eggs are hard boiled before smoking. Extremely fresh eggs do not peel easily after boiling, so make sure that the eggs are at least three days old.

Boiling eggs is certainly a simple cooking operation, but the following method minimizes the problem of cracking:

1. Put the eggs in a pan (preferably stainless steel, enamelware, or glass), and cover them with *cold* water. Discard any egg that floats.
2. Gradually bring the water to a slow boil with *medium* heat, and then turn the heat down to maintain the slow boil. Cook the eggs for 15 to 20 minutes. (If you observe the eggshells while the temperature of the water rises, you will see tiny bubbles of air escaping from the microscopic holes in the shells. If the water is heated to a boil slowly, the heated air within the eggs will have time to escape. This will reduce cracking due to high pressure in the eggs.)
3. Flood the pan with cold water to cool the eggs. (If the eggs are not cooled, the surface of the yolks will turn a greenish color.)

Several books on food smoking mention the smoking of eggs. One method suggests placing the boiled, unpeeled eggs on a smoking rack or on a wire net, and then smoking them at 70° to 90° F (21° to 32° C) for many hours until they take on a rich amber color. If your smoker will not operate at such a low temperature, keep the temperature as low as possible. Actually, the eggs will color faster at higher temperatures, but they may become too dark. If these smoked eggs are refrigerated for a day or so in a plastic bag, the smoke aroma will mellow and penetrate the eggshells to some extent.

Another method suggests sprinkling boiled and peeled eggs with seasoned salt and then cold smoking them until they have absorbed enough smoke to suit your taste.

If you try these two methods, you may conclude, as I did, that the results are not dramatic enough to warrant the effort.

Because of my disappointment with the eggs that were smoked by using the methods described above, I have tried, over the years, to develop a process to make the perfect smoked egg. This quest has led me to study the "anatomy" of eggs and conduct many experiments.

Much was learned from these experiments. In retrospect, however, a few of the many experiments were quite harebrained, and they resulted in nothing more than the destruction of perfectly good eggs!

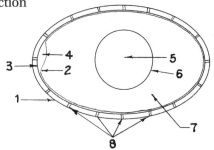

1. Shell
2. Inner shell membrane
3. Outer shell membrane
4. Air cell
5. Yolk
6. Yolk membrane
7. Albumen (the white)
8. Pores

**The anatomy of an egg (simplified).**

The process explained below is the result of the more fruitful of my experiments mentioned above. Knowledge gained from those experiments helped me develop this improved process for smoking eggs. I cannot call the product "perfect," but the smoked eggs produced by the following method are extraordinary and very good to eat. *Smoked eggs supreme* is an immeasurable improvement over either of the two simple methods of smoking eggs mentioned above.

## SMOKED EGGS SUPREME

Eggs with sturdy shells are desirable because the shells will undergo considerable stress. According to an acquaintance of mine, a veterinarian who specializes in chickens, small- or medium-sized eggs are apt to have stronger shells than large or extra-large eggs. One reason for this, he says, is that the smaller eggs are likely to come from young hens, and young hens produce stronger shells. All this assumes that the hens have been fed adequate eggshell-producing nutrients such as powdered oyster shells. But no matter what size eggs you use, try to use the same size every time so that the quality of your product will be consistent. Use white eggs. If brown eggs are used, the degree of coloration due to smoking is difficult to judge, and the degree of coloration on the outside of the egg is an indication of what is happening inside the egg.

## DAY 1, MORNING

Boil the eggs using the method previously explained. After cooling the eggs in cold water, remove them to a towel to drain and dry. Inspect each egg for cracks. If a crack is found, use the egg for some other purpose. Let them set at room temperature the rest of the day and overnight. Boiling, and then leaving the eggs at room temperature for one day and one night, will weaken the waterproof properties of the *two layers* of white, plastic-like membranes that lie just under the shell. By osmosis, these weakened membranes will allow salt to penetrate slowly into the interior of the egg. If the shell has a crack, the membranes will probably be damaged, and excessive salt will penetrate when the eggs are soaked in brine.

### DAY 2, MORNING

Use the brine table in appendix 3 to make sufficient 80 percent brine to cover the eggs. One quart (1 liter) of brine will cover about 10 to 12 eggs. Brine the eggs for 72 hours at room temperature. Use a plastic, glass, stainless-steel, or enameled container—not aluminum.

### DAY 5, MORNING

By this time, 72 hours will have elapsed, and sufficient salt will have penetrated the eggshells and the two membranes. Give them a quick rinse in fresh water, drain, and let them dry on a towel overnight, unrefrigerated.

### DAY 6, MORNING

Begin dehydrating the eggs in the smoke chamber by *slowly* bringing the temperature up to 140° F (60° C) over a 45-minute period (with no smoke). (When the entire process has been completed, the finished product will have become partially dehydrated—this is the first step in removing some of the moisture from within the eggs.) Hold at this temperature for about four hours. Then, over a period of one hour, *slowly* raise the temperature to 195° F (90° C). Look at the eggs; there may be tiny droplets of water on the shells. If there are no droplets, or only a few, begin smoking. The smoke will penetrate the microscopic holes in the shells, dissolving in the moisture escaping from those holes; the flavoring components of the smoke will pass through the weakened membranes by osmosis—similar to the way that smoke flavor passes through a sausage casing.

### SMOKING

Smoke at about 195° F (90° C). The smoking will probably require seven hours. Sample one egg after five hours of smoking, and sample another every hour after that to determine when to stop smoking. When the first egg is sampled, use this opportunity to turn all the eggs over so that coloration will be even. The smoking is finished when the albumen (the white) has become a light tan color and the total edible part of the egg has shrunk about 20 percent. The egg, including the yolk, will have a mellow, smoky taste, and it will have just the right amount of salt. Because about 20 percent of the moisture will have been lost, the bite texture will be delightfully different from a common boiled egg.

If none of the eggs has exploded or imploded, then the process control has been very good, and you are blessed with good luck. Exploded eggs result when the processing temperature has exceeded 212° F (100° C), or the temperature has been raised too rapidly. Imploded eggs result when moisture loss has been too rapid. When the moisture loss has been too rapid, the atmospheric pressure is greater than the pressure inside the egg; the shell may break inward (implode).

Cool the eggs at room temperature. After they reach room temperature, rinse off the "freckles" with cold water (but don't soak them in water). Refrigerate. (The freckles result from smoke dissolving in the salty moisture that escapes from the eggs during smoking.) The eggs will taste even better if they are allowed to set in the refrigerator for one day. Boiled eggs may be one of the least interesting of foods, but smoked eggs processed by this method are guaranteed to be an unforgettable delicacy.

# Smoked Salt

Smoked salt is one of the easiest products to make, and it has numerous uses. Keep it in the kitchen, and use it in place of regular salt anytime you think a slightly smoky flavor might improve a dish you are preparing. Sprinkle it on eggs, salads, boiled foods, or baked foods.

The best time to make smoked salt is when you are smoking some other product and there is some unused space in the smoke chamber. The smoke chamber temperature is not critical, but it is best if the smoke chamber humidity is not too high. Any type of salt can be used, but the type that contains a free-flow agent is best.

Put about ⅜ inch (about 1 cm) of salt in a shallow, nonmetallic dish that is heat resistant. A chinaware dish is ideal. (The smoke could permanently stain the dish, so don't use anything precious.) The humidity is always lowest in the lower levels of the smoke chamber, so place the dish on the lowest rack, if possible.

Stir the salt about once every hour while smoking. Stirring will allow all the salt crystals to get their share of smoke. The smoking is complete when the salt has become a uniform amber color.

## Smoked Nuts and Seeds

Spread the nuts or seeds on a fine screen. If a fine screen is not available, put them in a shallow baking pan, and stir them from time to time while they are smoking. If possible, cold smoke at below 85° F (29° C). Smoke the nuts for about 30 minutes. Sample some of the nuts to determine if they have been sufficiently smoked. If 30 minutes does not provide enough smoky flavor, increase the smoking time to an hour or hour and a half. *Note:* Nuts and seeds will easily acquire a sooty taste if the smoking time is too long.

The proper smoking time varies according to the kind of nut or seed, so it is best to sample each variety as they are being processed. Record the smoking conditions that give the best results, according to your taste.

If the nuts are unsalted and you wish to impart a salt flavor, you can easily oil and salt them—before or after smoking. First, shake them in a plastic bag together with a piece of paper towel that has been moistened with peanut oil or olive oil. This will put a light coating of oil on the nuts. Next, remove the paper towel, sprinkle the desired amount of salt on the nuts, and shake them again. Because the nuts have been oiled, the salt will adhere to the nuts much better than if they were completely dry. Use smoked salt, if it is available.

My favorite smoked nut is the cashew, but other varieties are good, too. For me, a smoking time of one hour is just right for cashew nuts.

# Spices, Herbs, and Seasonings

Comments on the applications of the various spices, herbs, and seasonings that are listed below are generally limited to their use for smoked food products and sausage. Culinary specialists, among others, distinguish between a spice and an herb. I have not necessarily maintained this distinction in the descriptions that follow.

**ALLSPICE** The name of this spice comes from the fact that it has a flavor similar to a blend of three spices: cinnamon, cloves, and nutmeg. It is most commonly used with red meats such as beef, pork, and lamb.

**ANISE SEEDS** These small seeds have a mild licorice flavor and are sometimes used in sausage. Some varieties of Italian sausage, for example, use anise seeds as an essential ingredient.

**BASIL** This essential herb for Italian cooking is also used to season lamb, poultry, fish, and shellfish. It is used occasionally for other meats such as beef, pork, and game. Basil is a member of the mint family.

**BAY LEAF** Bay leaf is very pungent. Use sparingly. It goes well with all red meats, variety meats (tongue, heart, and so forth), and especially game meats. If used in powdered form, consider a pinch (less than ⅛ teaspoon, or 0.6 ml) to be equal to one bay leaf.

**BLACK PEPPER** See Pepper.

**CAYENNE** True cayenne is extremely hot—hotter than red pepper. Quite often, unfortunately, the names and labeling of these two spices are confused. Nevertheless, both produce lots of heat, and they are used most often to flavor highly spiced meats. Neither cayenne nor red pepper is related to common black pepper.

**CELERY SEEDS** The seeds come from a plant related to the common celery that we eat as a vegetable. Use this spice sparingly in sausages and marinades. It has a bitter, celery-like flavor.

**CINNAMON** The use of cinnamon to flavor pork, lamb, and other meats is not unheard of, but you should try it cautiously. Many palates rebel at the combination of cinnamon and meat.

**CLOVES**  Use judiciously with pork, beef, or fish. Cloves are very pungent. Used in excess, cloves can be mouth numbing and overpowering.

**CORIANDER SEEDS**  The ground seeds have a mild flavor somewhere between the flavor of nuts and citrus fruit. Taste a pinch of it. If you like it, use it on any kind of meat, poultry, or fish.

**CUMIN SEEDS**  Cumin is an essential ingredient in chili powder and curry powder. It has a strong and spicy-sweet taste, and it is commonly used to season meats. The Germans use it to flavor some varieties of sausage.

**DILL**  Both dill seeds and dried dill leaves are used (the plant and leaves are sometimes called dillweed). Both have a mild, caraway-like taste. Dill is often used on fish, lamb, and fowl.

**FENNEL SEEDS**  These seeds have a mild licorice flavor, and they are sometimes used on oily fish and in sausages. They are an essential ingredient in many Italian sausage formulas.

**GARLIC**  Garlic powder is specified throughout this book, but garlic in other forms can be used in most cases. Substitute granulated garlic, minced garlic, or garlic juice.

**GINGER**  The root of this plant is used worldwide to season all varieties of meat, fish, and fowl. It has a distinctive bite and aroma. The tolerance for the aroma of this spice varies enormously. Start with a small amount and, if you like it, add a little more the next time. Fresh ginger (root)—grated, minced, or sliced thinly—can replace ginger powder in cures and marinades.

***HOISIN* SAUCE**  *Hoisin* is a dark brown sauce with a hot, tangy taste. It is commonly used in Chinese cooking. Imported brands will certainly be stocked at Asian food markets, but common supermarkets often stock Sun Luck brand of Chinese condiments, including *hoisin* sauce. Sun Luck products are made in the United States, and they are available in most areas of the country. If you are unable to buy *hoisin*, you can make it yourself. I was able to find a recipe for *hoisin* sauce on the Internet: www.recipesource.com.

**JUNIPER BERRIES**  Most of the berries harvested from this evergreen tree are used to flavor gin. They are used occasionally in fish and meat marinades. Just a few berries will impart a piney, gin-like taste.

**MACE**  Mace is the outer covering of nutmeg. The two spices have a similar taste, and both are used in some sausage varieties. The sweet, nut-like flavor can be imparted with very little mace or nutmeg. Use sparingly.

**MARJORAM** This herb is closely related to oregano, and it has a similar, but milder, taste. These herbs are in the mint family. Both are widely used to season any kind of fish, meat, or fowl.

**MINT** Lamb is sometimes seasoned with fragrant mint leaves before it is processed. There are many varieties of mint, each with a distinctive aroma.

**MSG** Monosodium glutamate is not a true seasoning; it is a flavor enhancer. It works to intensify other flavors. MSG is made from natural products, but it is considered a chemical food additive. Used in excess, it tends to produce a distinctive "MSG-intensified flavor." Many people like it; many don't. It is quite rare, but some people have an allergic reaction to this product if it is used in excess. The symptoms are dizziness, sweating, and chest pains. These symptoms are unpleasant, to be sure, but no fatalities have been reported.

**MUSTARD** Powdered mustard seeds are used in many varieties of highly seasoned smoked sausages. The flavor is similar to, but much sharper than, the prepared mustard we eat on hot dogs.

**NUTMEG** See Mace.

**ONION** Onion powder is specified throughout this book, but granulated onion, minced onion, or onion juice can be substituted in many cases.

**OREGANO** See Marjoram.

**PAPRIKA** This bright red powder is made from certain kinds of ripened red peppers. The sweet paprika widely available in the United States has a very mild taste, and it is used for red coloration as well as for its mild flavoring. Hungarian paprika is considered the most flavorful, and there are several varieties.

**PEPPER** Black pepper is the most widely used spice in the world, and it needs no introduction. White pepper is a little more aromatic than black pepper, but black pepper is more pungent. However, the flavors of the two are essentially the same. Use powdered white pepper when the black specks are not desired. Alternatively, use black pepper *powder* whenever large black specks would distract from the appearance of the product. Black pepper powder can usually be found in Asian food markets, and it will probably be cheaper than the white pepper powder sold in a common supermarket. White pepper is made from the husked berries of the pepper plant, but black pepper is made from the unhusked berries. The husk, of course, is black.

**PICKLING SPICE** This is a mixture of cinnamon, allspice, mustard seeds, coriander, bay leaves, ginger, chilies, cloves, black pepper, mace, and cardamom. The blend consists mainly of whole seeds, cracked seeds, and roughly broken dried spice leaves. It is sometimes used in marinades for meat, poultry, and fish.

**POULTRY SEASONING**   This blend of spices and herbs contains sage, thyme, black pepper, and—depending on the processor—may contain coriander, rosemary, allspice, onion powder, marjoram, celery seeds, and cayenne. It is, as the name implies, excellent on poultry, but it is also appreciated for seasoning pork.

**PRAGUE POWDER**   Prague Powder #1 is nothing more than common salt with the addition of a very small amount of sodium nitrite (6.25 percent). It is used as a curing agent and color fixer in many seasoning and curing formulas in this book. When processing smoked sausage, it is used to prevent botulism. (See Curing Powder in chapter 5, page 97, for additional information.)

**RED PEPPER**   See Cayenne.

**ROSEMARY**   The needle-like leaves of this evergreen shrub have a strong, piney scent, and they are used sparingly to flavor game, poultry, fish, and other meats.

**SAGE**   This very aromatic herb is an essential ingredient in American country-style fresh sausage. It can be used to flavor all varieties of domesticated poultry and wildfowl, in addition to pork. Overuse can impart a musty taste. Avoid using sage with fish.

**SAVORY**   This herb has a peppery taste, and it is used with sausages and fowl. Summer savory is milder than winter savory. Summer savory is the more popular of the two.

**SEASONED SALT AND SEASONING SALT**   This blend of salt, spices, herbs, and sometimes MSG will improve the flavor of almost anything that is smoked. Excellent quality commercially produced blends are available, but it is a simple task to make it. Depending on the manufacturer, this product is known as seasoned salt or seasoning salt. Confusingly, a blend of salt and one other seasoning is also known by the same two names—again, depending on the manufacturer. Examples are celery salt, garlic salt, lemon salt, and onion salt.

**THYME**   Thyme (pronounced *time*) is an herb that has very small leaves with the aroma of mint. It is widely used with fish and fowl, and it is occasionally used with pork, veal, and mutton. It is a pungent, but pleasant, herb.

**WHITE PEPPER**   See Pepper.

# Fahrenheit–Celsius Conversion Table

| F | to | C | F | to | C | F | to | C |
|---|---|---|---|---|---|---|---|---|
| -35 | = | -37.2 | 145 | = | 62.8 | 325 | = | 162.8 |
| -30 | = | -34.4 | 150 | = | 65.6 | 330 | = | 165.6 |
| -25 | = | -31.7 | 155 | = | 68.3 | 335 | = | 168.3 |
| -20 | = | -28.9 | 160 | = | 71.1 | 340 | = | 171.1 |
| -15 | = | -26.1 | 165 | = | 73.9 | 345 | = | 173.9 |
| -10 | = | -23.3 | 170 | = | 76.7 | 350 | = | 176.7 |
| -5 | = | -20.6 | 175 | = | 79.4 | 355 | = | 179.4 |
| 0 | = | -17.8 | 180 | = | 82.2 | 360 | = | 182.2 |
| 5 | = | -15.0 | 185 | – | 85.0 | 365 | = | 185.0 |
| 10 | = | -12.2 | 190 | = | 87.8 | 370 | = | 187.8 |
| 15 | = | -9.4 | 195 | = | 90.6 | 375 | = | 190.6 |
| 20 | = | -6.7 | 200 | = | 93.3 | 380 | = | 193.3 |
| 25 | = | -3.9 | 205 | = | 96.1 | 385 | = | 196.1 |
| 30 | = | -1.1 | 210 | = | 98.9 | 390 | = | 198.9 |
| 35 | = | 1.7 | 215 | = | 101.7 | 395 | = | 201.7 |
| 40 | = | 4.4 | 220 | = | 104.4 | 400 | = | 204.4 |
| 45 | = | 7.2 | 225 | = | 107.2 | 405 | = | 207.2 |
| 50 | = | 10.0 | 230 | = | 110.0 | 410 | = | 210.0 |
| 55 | = | 12.8 | 235 | = | 112.8 | 415 | = | 212.8 |
| 60 | = | 15.6 | 240 | = | 115.6 | 420 | = | 215.6 |
| 65 | = | 18.3 | 245 | = | 118.3 | 425 | = | 218.3 |
| 70 | = | 21.1 | 250 | = | 121.1 | 430 | = | 221.1 |
| 75 | = | 23.9 | 255 | = | 123.9 | 435 | = | 223.9 |
| 80 | = | 26.7 | 260 | = | 126.7 | 440 | = | 226.7 |
| 85 | = | 29.4 | 265 | = | 129.4 | 445 | = | 229.4 |
| 90 | = | 32.2 | 270 | = | 132.2 | 450 | = | 232.2 |
| 95 | = | 35.0 | 275 | = | 135.0 | 455 | = | 235.0 |
| 100 | = | 37.8 | 280 | = | 137.8 | 460 | = | 237.8 |
| 105 | = | 40.6 | 285 | = | 140.6 | 465 | = | 240.6 |
| 110 | = | 43.3 | 290 | = | 143.3 | 470 | = | 243.3 |
| 115 | = | 46.1 | 295 | = | 146.1 | 475 | = | 246.1 |
| 120 | = | 48.9 | 300 | = | 148.9 | 480 | = | 248.9 |
| 125 | = | 51.7 | 305 | = | 151.7 | 485 | = | 251.7 |
| 130 | = | 54.4 | 310 | = | 154.4 | 490 | = | 254.4 |
| 135 | = | 57.2 | 315 | = | 157.2 | 495 | = | 257.2 |
| 140 | = | 60.0 | 320 | = | 160.0 | 500 | = | 260.0 |

$$F = ((9/5)C)+32 \qquad C = (5/9)(F-32)$$

# Brine Tables

## BRINE TABLE (U.S. SYSTEM)

Ounces of salt (weight ounces) required for XX percent saturation strength

| SALINOMETER PERCENT | 1 QUART | 2 QUARTS | 3 QUARTS | 4 QUARTS |
|---|---|---|---|---|
| 10 percent | 0.9 oz | 1.8 oz. | 2.7 oz. | 3.6 oz. |
| 20 percent | 1.8 oz. | 3.6 oz. | 5.4 oz. | 7.2 oz. |
| 30 percent | 2.8 oz. | 5.6 oz. | 8.4 oz. | 11.2 oz. |
| 40 percent | 3.85 oz. | 7.7 oz. | 11.5 oz. | 15.4 oz. |
| 50 percent | 4.95 oz. | 9.9 oz. | 14.85 oz. | 19.8 oz. |
| 60 percent | 6.1 oz. | 12.2 oz. | 18.3 oz. | 24.4 oz. |
| 70 percent | 7.35 oz. | 14.7 oz. | 22.05 oz. | 29.4 oz. |
| 80 percent | 8.65 oz. | 17.3 oz. | 25.95 oz. | 34.6 oz. |
| 90 percent | 10.1 oz. | 20.2 oz. | 30.3 oz. | 40.4 oz. |
| 100 percent | 11.65 oz. | 23.3 oz. | 34.95 oz. | 46.6 oz. |

## APPROXIMATE EQUIVALENTS (Volume to Weight Ounces of Salt)

1 cup salt = 10 oz.
½ cup salt = 5 oz.
¼ cup salt = 2.5 oz.
2 Tbsp. salt = 1.25 oz.
1 Tbsp. salt = 0.625 oz.
1 tsp. salt = 0.208 oz.
½ tsp. salt = 0.104 oz.

*Note:* When measuring salt by volume, the measurements will be accurate and consistent if fine-grain salt is used.

## BRINE TABLE (METRIC SYSTEM)

Grams of salt required for XX percent saturation strength

| SALINOMETER PERCENT | 1 LITER | 2 LITERS | 3 LITERS | 4 LITERS |
|---|---|---|---|---|
| 10  percent | 28.5 g | 57 g | 85.5 g | 114 g |
| 20  percent | 57 g | 114 g | 171 g | 228 g |
| 30 percent | 88 g | 176 g | 264 g | 352 g |
| 40 percent | 121.5 g | 243 g | 364.5 g | 486 g |
| 50 percent | 155.5 g | 311 g | 466.5 g | 622 g |
| 60 percent | 192.5 g | 385 g | 577.5 g | 770 g |
| 70 percent | 231.5 g | 463 g | 694.5 g | 926 g |
| 80 percent | 272.5 g | 545 g | 817.5 g | 1,090 g |
| 90 percent | 318 g | 636 g | 954 g | 1,272 g |
| 100 percent | 367 g | 734 g | 1,101 g | 1,468 g |

## APPROXIMATE VOLUME EQUIVALENTS (Volume to Grams of Salt)

200 ml salt = 233 g
100 ml salt = 117 g
50 ml salt = 58 g
10 ml salt = 11.7 g
5 ml salt = 5.8 g

*Note:* When measuring salt by volume, measurements will be accurate and consistent if fine-grain salt is used.

# Weight and Volume Conversion Tables

Metric equivalents for U.S. weight and volume measurements are indicated all through the body of this book. The measurements are not always precisely converted, but the conversion accuracy is sufficient, I believe, to produce essentially the same product. Precise conversion would result in very awkward measurements, and it might require brain-numbing calculations. Such precision is not needed.

Imperial (UK) units of measurement are not mentioned in the body of this book for two reasons. First, Imperial units are being replaced rapidly by metric units. Second, great confusion could result because the words used for the Imperial units of measurement are often the same words used for the U.S. units, even though the actual quantity may be different. You may assume the *weight* measurements in the British system to be the same as those in the U.S. system: An Imperial pound is the same as a U.S. pound. If it is a *volume* measurement, however, you should assume that it is different from the U.S. system: An Imperial gallon, for example is not the same as a U.S. gallon. The last table in this appendix will help with conversions of the Imperial system to the metric system. Conversion to the metric system will allow conversion to the U.S. system, should that be necessary.

There are many other systems of measurement besides the American, the British, and the metric. If you need to covert something from one of these systems, try the Web site www.conversions.com. With a few clicks of the mouse and a few strokes on the keyboard, anything can be converted into your favorite measuring system.

## WEIGHT CONVERSION TABLE

|  | OUNCES | POUNDS | GRAMS | KILOGRAMS |
|---|---|---|---|---|
| 1 ounce | 1 | 1/16 | 28.35 | 0.028 |
| 1 pound | 16 | 1 | 454 | 0.454 |
| 1 gram | 0.032 | 0.002 | 1 | 0.001 |
| 1 kilogram | 0.000032 | 2.2 | 1,000 | 1 |

## VOLUME AND FLUID CONVERSIONS: U.S.–METRIC

This table does not represent precise conversions: 1 cup actually equals 236 ml, and 1 gallon equals 3,785.4 ml, for example. However, such precision is meaningless when processing food for smoking. The table presented below is quite easy to commit to memory, easy to calculate, and accuracy is sufficient.

| U.S. SYSTEM | METRIC (ML) | METRIC (LITERS) |
|---|---|---|
| ⅛ tsp. | 0.625 ml | |
| ¼ tsp. | 1.25 ml | |
| ½ tsp. | 2.5 ml | |
| ¾ tsp. | 3.75 ml | |
| 1 tsp. | 5 ml | |
| 1 Tbsp. (3 tsp.) | 15 ml | |
| 1 fluid ounce (2 Tbsp.) | 30 ml | |
| ¼ cup (4 Tbsp.) | 60 ml | |
| ½ cup (8 Tbsp.) | 120 ml | |
| ¾ cup (12 Tbsp.) | 180 ml | |
| 1 cup (16 Tbsp.) | 240 ml | 0.24 liter |
| 1 pint (2 cups) (16 fl. oz.) | 480 ml | 0.48 liter |
| 1 quart (4 cups) (32 fl. oz.) | 960 ml | 0.96 liters |
| 1 gallon (4 quarts) | 3,840 ml | 3.840 ml |

## BRITISH VOLUME MEASURING SYSTEM— METRIC CONVERSION TABLE

If you compare the metric conversions for the British system of volume measurement with those of the American system, you will note significant differences—despite the fact that the same words are used. For example, 1 U.S. quart is about 960 ml, but 1 UK quart is 1,136 ml.

Another interesting feature is that 4 UK teaspoons are equal to 1 UK tablespoon, whereas 3 U.S. teaspoons are equal to 1 U.S. tablespoon.

For food processing, the conversions indicated below are unnecessarily precise; they should be rounded off to a unit that is convenient to measure. One tablespoon, for example should be rounded off from 14.2 ml to 15 ml.

| BRITISH VOLUME MEASURING SYSTEM | MILLILITERS | LITERS |
|---|---|---|
| 1 teaspoon | 3.55 ml | |
| 1 tablespoon | 14.2 ml | |
| 1 fluid ounce | 28.4 ml | 0.028 l |
| ¼ cup | 71 ml | 0.071 l |
| ½ cup (1 gill) | 142 ml | 0.142 l |
| 1 cup (1 breakfast cup) | 284 ml | 0.284 l |
| 1 fluid pint | 568 ml | 0.568 l |
| 1 fluid quart | 1,136 ml | 1.136 l |
| 1 fluid gallon | 4,544 ml | 4.544 l |

# Equipment and Supply Resources

You should be able to obtain most of your equipment and supplies locally at such places as supermarkets, hardware stores, and home centers. For hard-to-find items, consult the yellow pages under the headings of butcher's supplies, culinary equipment and supplies, restaurant equipment and supplies, sausage making supplies, and the like. In some large cities, the local industrial suppliers are not listed in the common yellow pages; you will have to consult a commercial or an industrial telephone directory. For example, companies that sell restaurant equipment do not normally sell to the general public, so they might be listed in a special telephone directory. If your telephone company publishes such a directory, a nearby library may have a copy of it. Another option would be to request a copy from the telephone company.

Some equipment and supplies are most easily obtained by mail order, or by searching the Internet. If you are connected to the Internet, or have a friend who is, you will be able to fine many suppliers who are eager for your business. The larger, well-established firms will send a free catalog. A few suppliers are listed below, but you will find many more on the Internet.

### THE SAUSAGE MAKER, INC.—
### SAUSAGE AND SMOKING SUPPLIES AND EQUIPMENT

The Sausage Maker, Inc., is one of the largest and best-stocked suppliers. It has a very comprehensive catalog that it will send to you free of charge. Of course, the company stocks countless items that are useful for a sausage maker, but many of the items are of interest to anyone who processes food, including a food smoker.

For shipments outside the United States, you will need to contact the Customer Service Department. Telephone that department at 716-824-5814, send an e-mail to customerservice@sausagemaker.com, write a letter, or send a fax. There may be a charge for international mailing of the Sausage Maker catalog.

> The Sausage Maker, Inc.
> 1500 Clinton Street, Building 123
> Buffalo, NY 14206-3099
> 888-490-8525  Fax: 716-824-6465
> www.sausagemaker.com

## STUFFERS SUPPLY (CANADA)—
## SAUSAGE EQUIPMENT AND SUPPLIES

If you are a Canadian, or if you like doing business with Canadians, Stuffers Supply Company is a good company to contact. It offers a complete line of sausage-making equipment and supplies, and provides friendly and personalized service. If you have any questions about sausage making, staff members will do their best to get an answer for you. Even though their merchandise is primarily for sausage makers, many of the items that they offer are also used by food smokers. Many years ago, I dealt with Bill Leathem of Stuffers Supply, and he was instrumental in shipping the supplies I needed to Japan. I am sure that they will ship anywhere in the world. Payment must be made in Canadian dollars, but if you have an internationally recognized credit card, that should present no problem.

> Stuffers Supply Company
> 22958 Fraser Highway
> Langley, British Columbia V2Z 2T9
> Canada
> 604-534-7374  Fax: 604-534-3089
> bleathem@telus.net
> www.stuffers.com

## NORTHERN TOOL AND EQUIPMENT CO.—
## SAUSAGE STUFFERS, MEAT GRINDERS

This company offers only a modest amount of food-processing equipment, but the prices are very reasonable. Compare the prices for sausage stuffers and meat grinders, for example. Northern Tool offers a sausage stuffer for about $27, and a meat grinder for $15. Call the toll-free customer service phone number to get a free catalog—and be sure to mention that you need a catalog with listings for *food preparation equipment*. For international shipments, telephone or fax the International Sales Department: 800-221-1589, fax 952-895-6889.

> Northern Tool and Equipment Co.
> P.O. Box 1499
> Burnsville, MN 55337-0499
> Customer service: 800-222-5381
> www.northerntool.com

## THE WOK SHOP—ALUMINUM CHINESE STEAMER

A good place to buy an aluminum Chinese steamer is at a large Asian food store. However, if you do not live near such a store, or if you can't find what you need for some reason, try The Wok Shop. It is located in the heart of San Francisco's China Town, but sells all kinds of Asian cookware on the Internet. It offers several sizes of aluminum steamers on the Web site. The 12-inch-diameter (30 cm) size that I use sells for about $40.

If you want to search for other sites on the Internet, search for *wok steamer* (no quotation marks)—these two words are effective in pulling up various sites, and some will have what you are looking for.

The Wok Shop
718 Grant Avenue
San Francisco CA 94108
415-989-3797
www.wokshop.com

## BRINKMANN CORPORATION—SMOKING BASKETS, CHICKEN AND TURKEY RACKS

Smoker baskets are often stocked by stores that sell barbecue equipment. If they do not have smoker baskets in stock, they may be willing to order them for you. Another option would be to buy them on the Internet. If you would like to order the Brinkmann basket pictured in chapter 11 (see Italian shrimp, page 231), go to the Brinkmann Web site: www.brinkmanncorp.com.

You may wish to obtain a chicken rack or a turkey rack such as those described in chapter 10, page 183. Try to buy or order them at barbecue equipment shop. If you can't obtain them there, you might find them at a culinary supply shop. I saw such racks at a culinary supply shop, but the ones offered at the Brinkmann Web site were much cheaper.

Brinkmann offers a catalog that you can obtain by ordering it on the Web site or telephoning customer service. According to the site, Brinkmann will not ship overseas.

The Brinkmann Corporation
4215 McEwen Road
Dallas, TX 75244
Customer service: 800-527-0717
www.brinkmanncorp.com

## CAST-IRON PROPANE BURNERS

Web sites come and go, and the site that I used to buy my cast-iron propane burners no longer exists. However, if you use a good Internet search engine such as Google, you should be able to find them if you search for *"cast iron pots" burners* (use these four words with the quotation marks as indicated).

## HOG RINGS AND HOG-RING PLIERS

Hog rings and hog-ring pliers are offered by companies dealing in sausage-making supplies. They are available from The Sausage Maker, for example (see above).

## DRY-CURING COUNTRY-STYLE (SOUTHERN-STYLE) HAM

The dry curing and smoking of ham is a lengthy and difficult process, and it is beyond the scope of this book. However, good information about how to cure such ham is available if you wish to try it.

The southern part of the United States is famous for a type of hard-cured ham called country-style ham or southern-style ham. Each region of the South has a slightly different method of curing ham. The Web site indicated below will provide very detailed information about how Virginia-style ham is cured—and Virginia-style ham is considered one of the best. The curing procedure document was prepared by professors connected with the Virginia Polytechnic Institute and State University.

To get to that Web site, use Google and type in: *Dry Curing Virginia Style Ham*. When you get to the site, hyperlink to Virginia Cooperative Extension and search for document 458 223. If this does not work, go to the following site:
http://www.ext.vt.edu/pubs/foods/458-223458-223.html

You can also contact Virginia Cooperative Extension and ask for Publication 458-223, *Dry-Curing Virginia Style Ham*, as well as any or all related ham-curing publications.

> VSU, Cooperative Extension Building
> First Floor, Suite 107
> P.O. Box 9400
> Virginia State University
> Petersburg, VA 23806

Good luck!

# Cooking Chart

| **PRODUCT** | **°F (°C)** |
|---|---|
| **GROUND MEAT & MEAT MIXTURES** | |
| Turkey, chicken | 165° F (73.9° C) |
| Veal, beef, lamb, pork | 160° F (71.1° C) |
| **FRESH BEEF** | |
| Medium rare | 145° F (62.8° C) |
| Medium | 160° F (71.1° C) |
| Well done | 170° F (76.7° C) |
| **FRESH VEAL** | |
| Medium rare | 145° F (62.8° C) |
| Medium | 160° F (71.1° C) |
| Well done | 170° F (76.7° C) |
| **FRESH LAMB** | |
| Medium rare | 145° F (62.8° C) |
| Medium | 160° F (71.1° C) |
| Well done | 170° F (76.7° C) |
| **FRESH PORK** | |
| Medium | 160° F (71.1° C) |
| Well done | 170° F (76.7° C) |
| **POULTRY** | |
| Chicken, whole | 180° F (82.2° C) |
| Turkey, whole | 180° F (82.2° C) |
| Poultry breasts, roast | 170° F (76.7° C) |
| Poultry thighs, wings | 180° F (82.2° C) |
| Stuffing (cooked alone or in bird) | 165° F (73.9° C) |
| Duck, goose | 180° F (82.2° C) |
| **HAM** | |
| Fresh (raw) | 160° F (71.1° C) |
| Precooked (to reheat) | 140° F (60.0° C) |

**SEAFOOD**

Finfish—Cook until opaque and flakes easily with a fork.
Shrimp, lobster, crab—Should turn red, and flesh should become pearly opaque.
Scallops—Should turn milky white or opaque and firm.
Clams, mussels, oysters—Cook until shells open.

# About the Author

PHOTOGRAPH BY TOM ANDERSON

Warren Anderson has worked as a chemical technician, an electronic technician, a carpenter's helper, a bilingual social worker, an Asian business specialist, and an instructor of English as a foreign language. As an English instructor, Mr. Anderson taught at several Japanese universities for over twenty years. He also owned and operated a private English school in Kyushu, Japan. He speaks Japanese fluently.

Mr. Anderson is a graduate of the University of Oregon, where he studied the Japanese language and majored in East Asian Studies. He also earned a master's degree in international business at Sophia University in Tokyo, Japan.

While teaching and living in Japan, he took up food smoking as a hobby, and he has pursued that hobby earnestly since 1985. At one point, he seriously considered launching a new career in Japan as a professional food smoker. He concluded, however, that it would be a better idea for him to use his teaching skills to write a manual about food smoking. Consequently, in 1995, he began to write this book so that he could share with others the knowledge that he had accumulated.

Mr. Anderson returned to the United States in 1998, and he is presently semi-retired and living with his wife in Aloha, Oregon, a suburb of Portland.

# Index